DETROIT PUBLIC LIBRARY

3 5674 01017424 2

RELEASED BY THE
DETROIT PUBLIC LIBRARY

D1154109

THE SOUND
of OUR OWN
⋙·VOICES·⋘

Theodora Penny Martin

THE SOUND
of OUR OWN
➤·VOICES·➤

Women's Study Clubs 1860–1910

BEACON PRESS • BOSTON

R305.406 M365s

c,1 JUN 2 '89

Beacon Press
25 Beacon Street
Boston, Massachusetts 02108

Beacon Press books
are published under the auspices of
the Unitarian Universalist Association of Congregations.

© 1987 by Theodora Penny Martin
All rights reserved
Printed in the United States of America

94 93 92 91 90 89 88 87   1 2 3 4 5 6 7 8

Library of Congress Cataloging-in-Publication Data
Martin, Theodora Penny.
The sound of our own voices.

Bibliography: p.
Includes index.
1. Women—United States—Societies and clubs—
History—19th century.   2. Women—Education—United
States—History—19th century.   3. Continuing education—
United States—History—19th century.   I. Title.
HQ1904.M37   1987   305.4'06'073   87-47535
ISBN 0-8070-6710-5

≫· FOR ·≪

my mother, my sisters, and my father,

the ladies and honorary gentleman

of my club

We dreamed still more of larger possibilities; of the chance to think to the best advantage by working together; for it is a strange thing but true, when people are in earnest that, given a certain number of human souls, the result of their coalescence is not as the sum of their units, but something larger and other. It sometimes happens that, to quote our poet Browning, 'out of three sounds we frame not a fourth sound, but a star.' And that is the bottom reason why we women desired to combine.

New Century Club History as Told at
the Coming-of-Age Celebration, 1899

My mother had demonstrated that the best way to defeat the numbing ambivalence of middle age is to surprise yourself —by pulling off some cartwheel of thought or action never imagined at a younger age.

Gail Sheehy, Spirit of Survival, 1986

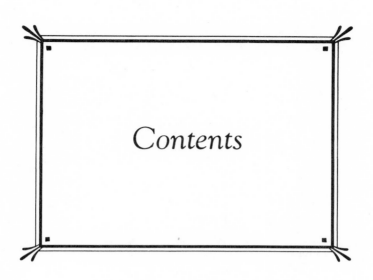

Contents

Contents

List of Illustrations

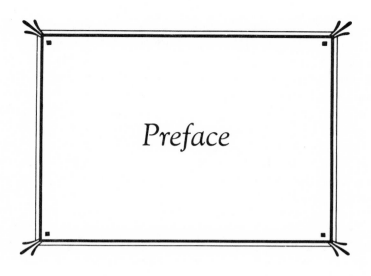

Preface

I grew up in a sorority. My sole siblings were three sisters, and that is how I learned to look at the world. As small children in my mother's tow, following my father from one army base to another during World War II, we of necessity created our own stable world at home—in our family. Despite the profusion of females, ours was not a single-gender world. Without a brother, we knew no limitations on our roles: we were Josephs as well as Marys in our Christmas plays, our passions were wildlife and baseball as well as art. Widely divergent in ages, temperaments, and interests, we were, nevertheless, close-knit and intensely loyal to one another. We were no Pollyannas; we pinched and pummeled one another, but mainly we believed in each other, supported and encouraged each other, expected great things from each other, worked with each other to accomplish them, and, above all, learned night and day from each other. What I saw in the world changed once I left my circle of sisters, but the manner of my viewing it did not. In the coeducational college I attended in the 1950s, it was the women in my single-sex dormitories who became my sisters, who helped me make the connections as we studied together, who shared and encouraged my aspirations. In the public schools in which I later taught among boys and men, it was my women colleagues who appointed themselves my mentors, who challenged and nurtured me as I would those who came after. And in my fortieth year it was still another in the widening sorority, Frances Mayfarth, by then retired president of Wheelock College, an institution devoted to the education of women teachers, who urged me to start a doctorate and who knew that I would complete it. Three women's colleges—Simmons, Radcliffe, and Wellesley—supported me materially during that graduate study and understood with immediate resonance the importance of the story I wanted intensely to tell about study clubs, the story in which women and their families and teaching and learning were inseparable. "The historian," says George F. Kennan, "does not stand entirely outside the historical evidence [s]he brings to your attention. [S]he stands in many ways inside it. [S]he is in many ways a part of it."[1] Along with my "evidence," then, I bring to this study a kinship, respect, and sisterly affection for these "unexceptional" study-club women who worked together in sorority so hard and so conscientiously, so innocently and so sincerely—and through it all so happily—to educate themselves and each other.

In narrating the story of women's study clubs in nineteenth-century America, I became involved, as always in women's stories, with the metaphor of generation. The structure of this story is one of familiar symmetry. It begins with the roots of the movement that led to the overnight burgeoning of study clubs across the land; picks up the forces that hastened their growth; examines the needs and desires that shaped their configuration; describes their day in the sun; and concludes with their transformation at the hands of those they had nurtured. The elements of the story—the setting, the characters, the action—were there, of course, when I began my study, but they lay in fragments scattered among newspaper clippings, hinted at in now-defunct ladies' magazines, alluded to in histories of "municipal housekeeping," acknowledged in feminist reconstructions, sidebarred in diaries and biographies. What was missing was the unity, the coherence, the full development of body and spirit—an artful, generative narrative to bring it all to life.

Jane Cunningham Croly's *The History of the Woman's Club Movement in America*, published in 1898, supplied the substance. The 1,200-page work is a compendium based on firsthand reports by hundreds of individual clubs, the majority with membership in the newly formed General Federation of Women's Clubs. Organized by states, the reports follow a standard format: club history, method of operation, study topics (on occasion a year's program in detail), and particular club personalities, traditions, highlights, and achievements. Croly's exhaustive history enabled me to flesh out the skeleton I had assembled from the pieces. But it was a generic product, a no-name club, filtered through the lens of one woman and based moreover on public accounts, from which, quite possibly, private activities might substantially differ. Without a more personal record, a primary source that represented a continuum over time, I knew the story could not be told.

I wrote to Frances Mayfarth, who had returned to Decatur, Illinois (where she had begun her teaching career sixty years before in a one-room schoolhouse), to live in the Anna B. Millikin Home, a retirement residence for women. Would she ask her "sisters" if they or their mothers or grandmothers had belonged to study clubs? In reply Fran enclosed a brief member-written history of the Decatur Art Class, a study club founded in 1880 and still in existence today. Vivian Barnes's history, compiled in 1976, quoted liberally from club minutes, especially before the turn of the century. In their detail and fullness, in their intelligence and style, in their purposefulness and personality, the minutes surged with vitality. And, far from fragmentary, over one hundred years of complete Art Class minutes and files lay undisturbed in cardboard boxes in the basement of the Anna B. Millikin Home, which is named for its benefactress, who had also founded the Art Class. The minutes had been brought there coincidentally but fittingly by a past president of the club when she had taken up residence in the home several years before. Once again I was dependent on a sorority to take me in and to help me learn as I asked the Art Class to share the minutes with me. With the faith and trust of sisterhood, they did, sending me the first thirty years of club minutes, and in January 1985 I was able to celebrate with them in Decatur their 105th birthday. The one thousand pages of minutes did not deconstruct the generalities I had formed from Croly's account. What they did was to reveal the variety and subtle changes beneath the surface, to illuminate the interstices, to allow the individual "ordinary" woman to bear witness, so that I could see education through her eyes and begin to understand the central role it played in who she was and who she was becoming.

For *my* education throughout the course of this book, I pay tribute to a number of teachers, both in name and in heart: to K. Patricia Cross (whose mother was a member of the Idlers Club of Normal, Illinois), to Marvin Lazerson, and to Sara Lawrence Lightfoot, all of the Harvard Graduate School of Education ("Between the idea / And the reality / Between the motion / And the act" falls my shadow); to Frances Mayfarth, who believed and made it possible; to the Decatur Art Class for their generosity and courage; to Kate Barnes for the definition of friendship; to Harold Lewis, photographer without peer; to Radcliffe College and President Matina S. Horner and Dean Philippa A. Bovet for an initial research travel grant; to the Spencer Foundation and the National Academy of Education for the fellowship which gave me the gift of time.

Theodora Penny Martin

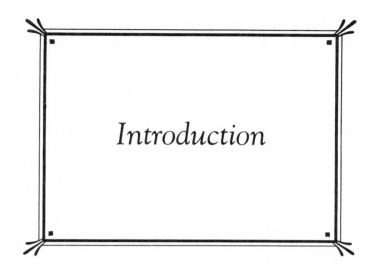

Introduction

This is a story of paradoxes. It is a chronicle of women at once unexceptional and uncommon, ordinary and extraordinary, of women who found individuality in groups, who, unschooled, defined education, women "working silently as leaven"[1] who dispelled the sounds of silence, selfless women who understood the primacy of self-education. It is the story of women's study clubs in post–Civil War America, a historical study of anonymous women whose distinctive voices call for an audience today.

Springing up apparently from nowhere, women's study clubs spread across the American scene in the late 1860s, gathering momentum and increasing in number through the early 1890s. Known by their first chronicler, Jane C. Croly, as "Light Seekers," these small local groups of middle-aged, middle-class women met in each other's homes to study art, music, history, geography, and literature. Their purpose, as the Fortnightly of Chicago proclaimed, was "to enlarge the mental horizon as well as the knowledge of our members."[2] Their focus was often revealed in their names: the Clio Club, the Shakespeare Society, the Boston History Class, the Castilian Club, the Armchair Travelers. Their mottoes seconded their motion:

"Knowledge is the treasure of which study is the key."
"Live with great minds and you will learn to think."

"And in these cities, there are not only men who pride
themselves on learning, but women also."

Until recently, women's clubs have been the preserve of *New
Yorker* cartoonist Helen Hokinson—tea and iced cakes, malaprop-
isms and vacuity their badges. With the emergence of women's history in the past fifteen years, however, women's voluntary organizations have come in for serious study. Karen Blair has looked at
women's clubs as latent feminist organizations; Anne F. Scott has
focused on their service ethic, which developed after 1900.[3] While
acknowledging the genesis of the powerful twentieth-century club
movement in post–Civil War ladies' literary societies, historians
have yet to set study clubs in the context which was avowedly
theirs—education. As a piece of the history of American education, the study-club movement calls for illumination. For the part it
played in raising the educational aspirations of women, the movement helps to explain the rapid increase in the numbers of women
entering college in the early 1900s. It illustrates clearly education's
important and often understated role as an institution which en-
compasses and nurtures both tradition and transition. It speaks to
the sociology and anthropology of education as those disciplines
ponder the relationships among class, gender, and access or the effects of dominant groups on the educational aspirations of muted
groups. Equally important, the lessons of the study-club movement
can help to inform current research on how women learn, on the
intersections between psychology and pedagogy. The study-club
movement has implications as well for adult education with its increasing tendency to formalize and institutionalize its practices. Finally, the study-club movement is a paean to the transformation
that education can effect for individuals and for society.

From the country's beginning, most Americans placed a high
value on education, but until the twentieth century, education of
women beyond secondary schooling was reserved for a "radical" few.
Although a number of ivied gates had swung open to women by the
1880s—Oberlin College, the University of Wisconsin, Vassar College, Cornell University, and Smith College among them—the
college-educated woman was still a rarity. Those "bluestockings"
who dared to persist did learn, among other things, that they had
put on the line not only their mental capacities but their physical

endurance, femininity, motives, and future as well. These few exceptional young women—fourteen were awarded B.A.'s from the University of Wisconsin in 1874 and the same number entered Smith's doors a year later[4]—were indispensable leaders, to be sure, but as Anne Scott reminds us: "to produce a major social change many ordinary people must also be involved. In the face of the strong cultural pattern [of nineteenth-century America] with its narrowly defined role for women, how could anything in the way of a following emerge?"[5]

Between 1860 and 1910 women's study clubs quietly and quite without design nurtured the "many ordinary people" into the necessary "following" as their members proved to themselves their intellectual capability and interest and to the public their continued commitment to women's "proper" role. For the daughters of these women, who had observed their mothers studying Chaucer and writing papers on Egyptian art, who had watched them enthusiastically learning to learn, college education appeared a natural and realistic option as well as a conventional aspiration. While more "radical" women challenged tradition by entering colleges and universities, "unexceptional" women, with their dread of deviance, began to educate themselves unobtrusively and for the future through their study clubs. With mastery of the "great minds" as their charge, women had necessarily to look beyond their dooryards, to think beyond the personal, and to express themselves with some scholarly semblance of ordered inquiry. Taking their work seriously and, equally important, being taken seriously by their peers, study-club members quickly modified their views of what women could achieve intellectually. In these clubs, which filled the gaps between society's formal institutions and the informal needs of individual women, members developed—along with the stirrings of intellectual independence—an awareness of and confidence in themselves and in their sex which they had not been able to accomplish alone. With new respect for themselves and for the transforming power of education, study-club women enlarged the dimensions of women's "proper sphere" to include thereafter the expectation, challenge, and opportunities of higher education.

The numbers of women in the study-club movement were not insignificant. By 1906, five thousand local organizations had joined the General Federation of Women's Clubs, and it has been estimated that they constituted only five to ten percent of the clubs in existence.[6] Almost as quickly as they had mushroomed, however, by the turn of the century most clubs had changed their focus. Having educated themselves and opened wide the doors of higher education for their daughters, exuberant club women turned from the realm of abstract thought to the arena of practical action, from education for self to education for service. Their efforts on behalf of public schooling—campaigns for kindergartens, smaller class size, safe playgrounds, and the inclusion of art and music in the curriculum—have been termed "heroic." Dubbed "municipal housekeepers," urban club members did much to improve sanitation and living conditions in the cities. They became leaders in the establishment of local and national conservation sites. These new club women moved quickly and efficiently from philosophy to philanthropy and rarely looked back.

Still, the study club, true to its original purpose of self- and mutual education, remained on the scene to become a permanent part of informal adult education. Even the Federation while urging its members to social action in 1906 paid homage to its purpose: "It was proved by the Literature Committee that the day of the study club would never pass, that as the federation movement sprung from the trained mind of true culture, so for each new inspiration we must go to the well-springs of the world's best thought."[7] Just as Jane Croly had observed that the pioneers of the study-club movement "eagerly seized the idea of clubs and shaped it according to their own conditions and needs,"[8] those who came after were also guided by organic principles. Succeeding generations of women who joined study clubs were increasingly college-educated and looked to their clubs not for validation but for further food for trained, inquiring minds, for the renewal that comes from drinking of "the well-springs of the world's best thought," and for the respectful interchange and the courage to continue that comes from a sorority of scholars.

≋·1·≋

"Our Foremothers"

Study-Club Genealogy

While some enthusiastic club women traced the roots of women's study clubs back to Periclean Athens and the home of Aspasia, where, it is said, women met weekly for "intellectual improvement,"[1] others, like Jane C. Croly, looked to women's religious orders of the Middle Ages for their clubs' forebears. Croly, founder of Sorosis, a path-breaking New York City women's club, asserted that the orders were "inspired by a love of well-doing" and were fueled by women's "desire for study, the acquisition of knowledge, and its distribution."[2] Most chroniclers, however, began their genealogical search with the first American colonists. Club women, they declared, were descendants of Anne Hutchinson. En route by ship to the Massachusetts Bay Colony, Hutchinson is reported to have gathered the women travelers together for discussion of the weekly sermons they had heard.[3] Once in Boston, Hutchinson, then in her mid-forties, opened her home twice a week to women friends for a similar purpose. Although her 1635 venture was short-lived, the meetings, as historian Anne Scott has noted, were an early paradigm of study clubs: (1) all the participants were women; (2) they were women attempting to educate themselves; (3) the leader was a woman of strong personal characteristics; (4) the content was uplifting; and (5) the purpose widened over time, in Hutchinson's case from explication of weekly sermons to critique of current theology.[4]

The criticism of Anne Hutchinson by the all-male Puritan establishment proved to be part of the pattern as well, although it was not so severe in the case of later study clubs. In addition to the charge of "troubling the peace of the commonwealth," Hutchinson was accused of "maintaining a meeting and an assembly in your house that hath been condemned by the general assembly as a thing not tolerable nor comely in the sight of God nor fitting for your sex."[5]

Certainly on American soil Hutchinson's religious gatherings appear as apropos progenitors to women's study clubs, for in the intervening two hundred years until such clubs shyly proclaimed their public existence, it was primarily the church which fostered organizations of women. Beginning as sewing circles which made salable items for the upkeep of the church or for the training of young men for the ministry, these early women's groups plied their handiwork to the accompaniment of the reading aloud and discussion of religious works.[6] By the early 1800s, stitching became subsidiary to the weekly Bible readings in the "mite" or "cent" societies. Contributing a penny a week for the purchase of Bibles or tracts, members began looking beyond their own community, and by the 1830s they were personally involved in missionary support, temperance groups, and Magdalen Societies devoted to the salvation of "fallen women."[7] Run by men or serving as auxiliaries to men's organizations, the nearly eight hundred "cent" societies in existence by 1840[8] did not encounter the criticism and opposition that assailed study clubs twenty years later. Although they met outside the home, women retained their traditional role of doing for others; church work, sanctioned by ministers who loudly proclaimed woman's proper sphere to be her home, would not make her "less domestic, less submissive, or less of a True Woman."[9] Nationally it was not until the founding of the National Woman's Suffrage Association (1869) and the Woman's Christian Temperance Union (1873) that any distinct groups of women worked along independent lines.[10]

In addition to substance, Anne Hutchinson's meetings gave geographical roots to several forerunners of women's study clubs. Boston was the site of Elizabeth P. Peabody's Historical School, a series of lectures begun in her home in 1827 and carried on at intervals for several years.[11] While the audience was mixed, organization by a woman was a novelty (as was almost every endeavor Peabody embarked on). Shortly after, Reading Parties became vogue in the Athens of America. A circle of friends meeting at home would engage a lecturer of an evening paid for by ticket sales to friends. Although most lecturers were men, at one party, sponsored by the Russell and Lowell clans, Elizabeth Peabody was invited to read and discuss anything she liked, gift enough for her without the $100 in "take."[12] Carefully avoiding the word *club* as had Peabody and the Reading Parties, Margaret Fuller in the late 1840s held Conversations on literature and culture in Elizabeth Peabody's bookshop at 13 West Street in Boston. Seated instead of standing so as not to be considered a public lecturer, a tactic also employed by Emma Willard,[13] Fuller addressed a predominantly female audience of paid series subscribers.[14]

A few miles to the north in Lowell, the City of Spindles, where Francis Lowell and Nathan Appleton had in the 1820s conceived what they hoped would be a new kind of factory system, departing as widely as possible from dehumanizing Old World models, Lucy Larcom and her mill-girl "sisters" prefigured study-club women of later generations. Coming from "oldest American stock,"[15] Larcom entered the mills in 1835 at age eleven after her father's death left behind in Beverly little but a family of eight children, the oldest eighteen. Still in its golden age, the Lowell system provided free grammar schools and organized church "social circles," night schools, and a lyceum in an effort to contribute to the intellectual and spiritual development of the mill girls and "to nourish a belief in the dignity of labor."[16] Lowell's ideal mill girl was one who could lay claim to education and social refinement and who regarded her mill work as a temporary financial expedient.[17] Reminiscing toward the end of her life on her formative Lowell experience, Larcom recalled her "sisters":

> Our composite photograph, had it been taken, would have been the representative New England girlhood of those days. We had all been fairly educated at public or private schools, and many of us were resolutely bent upon obtaining a better education. Very few among us were without some distinct plan for bettering the condition of themselves and those they loved. For the first time, our young women had come forth from their home retirement in a throng, each with her own individual

7

purpose. For twenty years or so, Lowell might have been looked upon as a rather select industrial school for young people. The girls there were just such girls as are knocking at the doors of young women's colleges today. They had come to work with their hands, but they could not hinder the workings of their minds also. Their mental activity was overflowing at every possible outlet.[18]

Some of the young mill women were teachers during the summers when girls had access to school rooms vacated by boys for summer recess. Others came to the mills only in the summer, saving their wages to support themselves during the rest of the year at schools like nearby Bradford Academy or Ipswich Seminary. Education, present and future, was a common theme, according to Larcom:

> Mount Holyoke Seminary broke upon the thoughts of many of them as a vision of hope . . . and Mary Lyon's [founder of Mount Holyoke] name was honored nowhere more than among the Lowell mill girls. Meanwhile they were improving themselves and preparing for their future in every possible way, by purchasing and reading standard books, and by attending lectures and evening classes of their own getting up, and by meeting each other for reading and conversation.[19]

The Lowell "classes" might have been called clubs a generation later (indeed, even two generations later many clubs called themselves "classes" to avoid the unfeminine connotations of the word *club*).

> A native professor had formed a class among young women connected with the mills, and we joined it. We met, six or eight of us, at the home of two of these young women—a factory boarding house—in a neat little parlor. . . . We went through Follen's German Grammar and Reader:—what a choice collection of extracts that "Reader" was! We conquered the difficult gutturals, like those in the numeral "acht und achtzig" . . . so completely that the professor told us a native would really understand us![20]

Larcom joined a botany class (which failed to awaken in her an appreciation of the Linnaean system but did instill a love of wild-flowers) and the Improvement Circle, a group of "bright girls" who met fortnightly for writing and discussion. A Larcom sister a few years older than Lucy was president of the group, and although Lucy confessed that much of the discussion was above her head, it was here she began writing "little essays," which eventually appeared in the *Operatives' Magazine.* The periodical, devoted to the literary efforts of mill operatives, was a production of weekly literary meetings in the vestry of the First Congregational Church. There Larcom was encouraged to read the essays she had written for the Improvement Circle; others followed her example, contributing original poems and sketches; the minister made critical comments, and the magazine was edited by two young teachers who had been mill girls themselves.[21] Although of dubious literary merit—a mill superintendent told Larcom that one of her published essays "has plenty of pith, but it lacks point"—the magazine pieces engendered in their authors the same sense of pride and self-respect experienced by later generations of club women on completion of a paper. Exclaimed one Lowell author, "They appeared to us as good as anybody's writings. They sounded as if written by people who had never worked at all!"[22] Despite Larcom's unquenchable curiosity and desire to learn, she would never find in Lowell the education she sought—a disciplined, structured, systematic accumulation of knowledge. That would come later at Monticello Seminary in Illinois, but her Lowell classes provided her with an environment that responded to and encouraged her intellectual efforts and aspirations, an environment of young women peers supportive of her independent self-exploration and discovery, an environment that would be replicated before too long in women's study clubs.

As with the designation of most "firsts," there is scant agreement on which study club deserves the appellation; differences in designation rest on definition of terms. Conjecture, based solely on the appearance of a title in a diary or in a public record, has unearthed some early nominees: the Woman's Literary Society of Chelsea, Connecticut, in 1800 and the Female Improvement Society of Smithfield, Rhode Island, in 1820.[23] Another plausible, but unverified, contender appears in a brief notice in the *New Harmony* (Indiana) *Gazette* in October 1825: "The regular meeting of the

Female Social Society is postponed till Monday evening 14th instant."[24] Wishful thinking or not, several club chroniclers see in the Female Social Society the hand of reformer Fanny Wright, an occasional visitor to Robert Owen's utopian community at New Harmony. Outspoken lecturer on equal rights and education for women, Wright could have been a prime mover in an organization for women, and it is not likely, given her nature, that social chit-chat, needlework, and tea would suffice for an agenda.

Although it left behind a short account, the Edgeworthalean Society of Bloomington, Indiana, organized in January 1841, appears to be the first club with extant minutes to devote itself to the intellectual improvement of women. The name of the society was a composite derived from Maria Edgeworth, popular author of *Moral Tales,* and Thalia, Muse of comedy and pastoral song. Meeting year-round once a week in the afternoon at the Monroe County Female Seminary, the group had duly elected officers, including two critics to point out the "beauties and defects" in the papers that members presented: "It is to be hoped," read the minutes, "that the embarrassment which is still consequent on our exercises may soon be done away with or exchanged for that modest freedom which is necessary to the proper criticism of all the exercises and to the right improvement of the members."[25] The application for membership in the society suggests its seriousness of purpose:

> The undersigned feeling the need of something to stimulate her mental and moral culture, and believing the means may be the concentration in a literary society or body associated expressly to impart and receive instruction, hereby offers herself for a candidate for the honor of membership in the Edgeworthalean Society. She has long meditated this step, and has hitherto been withheld by a sense of her deficiencies, and shame at exposing them to that honorable literary body; but knowing that shame often proceeds from pride, that great bar to the acquisition of knowledge, she intends laying it aside and coming forward as a simple learner to the feet of those, whose years, if measured by their attainments, would far exceed those of
>
> Your humble petitioner.[26]

With its object "cultivation and improvement of the mind," Edge-worthalean alternated the presentation of papers with discussions. Most discussion topics were of a serious nature: "Which is the most important, male or female education?" "Should women be allowed to vote?" (the answer was no). The Muse Thalia in her comic mode inspired others: "Would it not be advisable for the young ladies and gentlemen of Bloomington to have charts taken of their heads and sent on to Fowler [a noted phrenologist of the time] to see which would make suitable companions for life?"[27]

That so high-minded and apparently innocuous an enterprise should have provoked community criticism seems farfetched today, but the inaugural address of the first president depicts the Society on the defensive:

> When discussing the propriety of our present under-taking, it has been objected by many that a part, at least, of the exercises customary in such societies was too mas-culine to be proper for females and was calculated to dim the lustre of that modest reserve which is justly consid-ered the sex's best ornament.
>
> It is agreed by many that mental culture unfits a woman for the performance of those domestic employ-ments which make a part of her daily duties. That this pursuit, like everything under the sun, may be abused, perverted, cannot be denied; but surely when properly directed it has no such tendency, and I trust I do not misrepresent the sentiments of my fellow-members when I assert that we advocate it because we believe it to be eminently calculated to strengthen and perfect the sex in the discharge of all their duties, thereby rendering home the seat of happiness.[28]

As would later study clubs, the Edgeworthalean Society thus turned against its detractors the very arguments they had propounded for woman's proper sphere—the home and nothing but the home. The intensity of opposition to the Society is revealed a year later in an-other presidential inaugural: "and if our aim is still high, our object noble, and our motto TRUTH, we will advance upward and onward in spite of bitter scorn, cruel oppression, and indeed, in spite of every opposition."[29] Whether the members' resolve faltered under continued attack, whether Fowler's matchmaking removed the younger and feistier members from the meetings, or whether further club records are simply lost, the Edgeworthalean minutes end abruptly on 14 June 1844, without comment or hint of demise.

While years later Sorosis of New York and the New England Women's Club of Boston, both founded in 1868, would argue over the title Mother of Women's Clubs, the Midwest continued to introduce sprightly "spinster" clubs, which produced no progeny but nonetheless left their mark. The Minerva Society was founded in New Harmony, Indiana, in 1859 by Constance Owen Fauntleroy. A granddaughter of Robert Owen, Fauntleroy accompanied her family to Germany at age sixteen on the death of her father, studying music, drawing, painting, and languages during her several years there. Recalling the founding of Minerva on her return to New Harmony, Fauntleroy later wrote: "The Owens were literary, but the place was stifling to me, who had just returned from Europe and was accustomed to society and study. . . . With all the longings for a larger life and filled with the spirit of helpfulness which I had breathed in from the Owen Community, I said, 'Let us organize a Literary Society.'"[30] Robert Dale Owen drafted the society's constitution, with officers elected every six weeks in order that all might have executive experience. The twenty-six members, all young women, chose the name Minerva "because we wished to become wise"; their motto was "Wisdom is the crown of Glory," and their badge was a Latin cross of laurel wood set in gold.[31]

Minerva meetings were conducted along strict parliamentary lines, and absences required excuses, which were meticulously recorded in the minutes (Della Mann, engaged to Lieutenant Eugene F. Owen, was excused upon the young man's furlough from the Civil War). The programs included original compositions and poems, discussion of selected readings, debates ("Are We Made Happier by Education?" "Which Is the Greater Evil, War or Slavery?" "Do Facts or Fiction Contribute Most to Mental Enjoyment?"), and a novelette to which each member contributed a chapter. Members of the club were "cultured" young women of their day: a number were descendants of the original Owen community members, a few had attended girls' boarding schools, and several had traveled or had been educated abroad. As was often the case in later study clubs, family lines ran strong in the Minerva Society: of the twenty-six members, three were Fauntleroys; three Owens; three Manns; and two Hinckleys.[32] Although short-lived (it disbanded in 1863), the Minerva was not without influence in the study-club movement. Moving to Madison, Indiana, as the wife of James Runcie, Constance Fauntleroy founded the Brontë Club in 1864[33] and because of her subsequent involvement in club work was made an honorary president of the General Federation of Women's Clubs in 1906. Ella Dietz Clymer, a charter Minerva member and niece of Mrs. Robert Dale Owen, was among the founders of Sorosis and one of the early presidents of the General Federation of Women's Clubs. A more tangible legacy is the five-room house built in 1815 in which the Minerva Society met, now open to the public as a State of Indiana historical site.

Thirty-four years after the Minerva Society disbanded, the newly formed Elizabethan Club of Tyler, Texas, adopted as its motto "There is a future which is still our own."[34] The precept might describe as well the motivation of those eminent and obscure women, in Boston and in Bloomington, with full-fledged club constitutions and inchoate dreams who were beginning to sound the notes of women's need for association.

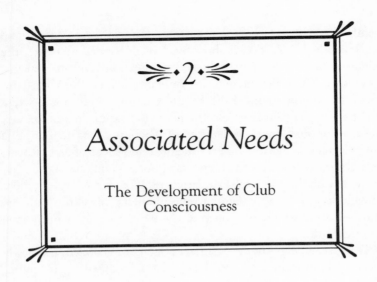

Associated Needs

The Development of Club
Consciousness

*Any association, in order to suc-
ceed, must answer some need or
object which the ordinary intercourse of society does not reach.*[1]

The four hundred women who gathered in New York City in 1873
for the First Woman's Congress of the Association for the Advancement of Woman were evidence of the "need" to which Julia Ward
Howe referred in her address to them. "How Can Women Best Associate?" she asked in the title of her speech, but women throughout
the nation had already determined the answer. Beginning immediately after the Civil War and continuing for the next twenty to
thirty years, women, at an amazing rate and often unaware that
their "sisters" were doing likewise, formed study clubs almost iden-
tical in structure, purpose, and operation. Were it not an anachro-
nism, Vida D. Scudder's observation on the rise of settlement
houses would apply as well to the burgeoning of women's study clubs:
"Strange how spiritual radios all over the world will at the appointed
moment catch the same vibrations!"[2] Although pre–Civil War
clubs attest to the presence of vibrations already in the air, full resonance was not sounded until the echoes of martial cymbals had

faded. The notes that made up the chords to which American women then responded with clubs of all kinds were numerous.

Paradoxically, perhaps, one need which impelled women to form associations came from an increasing acceptance of respect for the individual. Club woman cum historian Mary I. Wood saw it that way:

> [The club movement] is a simple phase of the whole scheme of evolution, a natural result of the readjustment necessary to the great economic and moral awakening of the late Eighteenth and Nineteenth centuries. The germ of its existence may be found as far back as that period of awakening known to history as the Renaissance, which placed the first emphasis upon the value of the individual.[3]

A historical marker more relevant for American women may have been the Revolution, fueled by the philosophy of natural rights which, in Arthur Schlesinger's words, "exalted the individual's capacity to act for himself."[4] Although "himself" was gender-specific in 1776, spillover was inevitable, and by the beginning of the nineteenth century the Revolutionary spirit brought to women, according to Jane Croly, "a change in point of view, an awareness of a basis of equality among a wide diversity of conditions and individualities."[5] The egalitarian ideology that the Revolution had substituted for the hierarchical concepts of colonial life suggested opportunities for individual self-development, a process few women had explored. In addition to the political and economic spirit of manifest destiny and upward mobility that was abroad in the public, women in their churches and revival meetings encountered a similar theological spirit: predestination was passé—it was the individual with her own free will who determined her salvation through her good works here on earth. While expressions of individuality appeared to be genetic gifts in some nineteenth-century women such as Emma Willard, Margaret Fuller, Sojourner Truth, or Charlotte Perkins Gilman, for the unexceptional woman, whose idealization as a True Woman blurred distinctive characteristics, individuality needed nurturing. For such support she turned to a circle of like-minded women— often friends, relatives, and acquaintances—who were to become her club.

Although most early women's organizations had been religious in purpose, the Civil War proved to be the hothouse which forced the organizational development of women, most especially in the North under the Union's Sanitary Commission. Organized regionally, the Commission, whose ranks were composed entirely of women, raised thirty million dollars for food, uniforms, and medical supplies for Union soldiers. It staffed army hospitals, competed with men for army contracts for the manufacture of military clothing, hired wives of volunteer soldiers to make uniforms, cared for families of drafted men, set up free "hotels" and provided meals for soldiers in transport, and guided wounded veterans back into civilian life.[6] A few women, such as Mary A. Livermore, who later became a leader in the General Federation of Women's Clubs, rose to national prominence through their Commission work, but most volunteers remained nameless at the rank-and-file local level. Anonymous though they were in the overall war effort, thousands of American women found sanction for work outside the home, discovered for the first time the satisfaction of formally organized cooperative achievement with others of their sex, developed the self-confidence that arises from success in new endeavors, and were imbued with a sense of self-respect for the part they had played in a cause of larger purpose. Ralph Waldo Emerson's observation that "the energy of the nation seems to have expended itself in the war"[7] may have applied to battle-weary men, but women participants found themselves with a new vitality and vision—unchanneled new needs—which soon found outlets in the clubs they were to form.

While the Civil War engendered a sense of solidarity in women who organized for the cause, it did not leave in its wake unity or stability for the nation at large. Of the years immediately after the war, Henry Adams wrote: "Society in America was trying, almost blindly as an earthworm, to realize and understand itself; to catch up with its own head and to twist about in search of its tail."[8] Nor did the ensuing decades give the country time to sort itself out as it was rapidly transformed from a rural republic into an urban industrial empire. "From the moment that railways were introduced," Adams continued, "life took on extravagance,"[9] and the adaptations required by the railroad alone would have been enough to upset any prewar equilibrium. The railroads demanded new "capital, banks, mines, furnaces, shops, powerhouses, technical knowledge, mechanical population, together with a steady remodelling of social and political habits, ideas, and institutions to fit the new scale and suit the new conditions."[10] While it was men who raised the capital, managed the banks, dug the mines, and tended the furnaces, women—perhaps precisely because of their inability to participate and to help direct—turned to clubs as one way of seeking "continuity and predictability in a world of endless change."[11] Before the war, the United States had been a nation of small enterprises and many self-sufficient communities, where social order was in large part still hierarchical and was determined by kinship, neighborhood, and the church; women were not the only ones who knew their place. As society became more mobile and more polyglot and as wealth became more "ostensibly egalitarian,"[12] the axes of the social grid began to shift, loosening the entire structure. With identification of individuals no longer possible by traditional categories, a new sorting process had to be established. For men, work became a sorting device—farmer, banker, doctor, manufacturer. For many women, clubs served the same purpose; they provided a visible distinction between likeminded women and others in the community. And, as the sense of community itself was eroded by the torrents of new population and tides of institutional change, the club functioned as a smaller, orderly society where traditional community values could be expressed and affirmed. Jane Croly in *The History of the Woman's Club Movement in America* recounts, from notes submitted to her by the secretary, the history of the Cedar Rapids (Iowa) Ladies' Literary Club, founded in the mid-1870s:

> Cedar Rapids is picturesquely situated midway between Chicago and Omaha, and was, in the beginning, a rendezvous for horse thieves and outlaws. These, however, were soon suppressed and the growth of the town, under a wise and strong executive, became rapid and full of promise of civic advancement. . . . At the time the Cedar Rapids Ladies' Literary Club was formed, the society of the place was in a state of transition, the old and new breaking up into cliques, social, religious, and political, that threatened to annihilate all possibilities of unity on a higher basis.
> It is not too much to say that the inspiration of the Ladies' Literary Club arrested this process of disintegra-

> tion, and concentrated the work of the most cultivated
> and thoughtful women in an effort that became the nu-
> cleus of the social growth and intellectual development
> of a town . . . as distinguished now for the high charac-
> ter of its community, as it was in the beginning for law-
> lessness.[13]

With "the old and new breaking up into cliques, social, religious,
and political" across the nation just as they had in Cedar Rapids,
white, middle-class women, firmly committed to their solid place in
the rising bourgeoisie, began to replicate in clubs the familial order
and values they had established in their homes, the one source of
their expertise and power. In a dislocated and fragmented world,
clubs were small centers of stability and status, and club meetings
were "rituals of cohesion."[14] They were a way for women to identify
with others like themselves and a way to prevent that identity from
changing. In the very process of preservation, however, club women
would find a new identity—and themselves changed.

A need for a kind of psychic order as well may also help explain
the explosion of women's clubs in the last quarter of the century.
Increasingly throughout the nineteenth century the model of society became that of the dominant, male group. Increasingly women
lived in a world apart, a predominantly female world, unable for the
most part to give public expression to any alternative model of society. By creating their own semipublic societies in clubs, women,
the muted group, were transforming "their own unconscious percep-
tions into such conscious ideas as would accord with those generated by the dominant group."[15] Such transformations, anthropolo-
gists posit, require a great deal of disciplined mental energy and may
explain the conservative nature of the muted group's world views.[16]
Small groups of women friends, meeting in their homes during the
leisure time their husbands had bought for them, discussing classical
works of art and elevated authors, little disturbed the American
male's model of the world; while within the small societies these
women created, they could comfortably, without awareness, confirm
and assert and eventually modify their own model.

Despite the needs women may have felt to develop their individual potential and to help preserve the orderly society which had
shaped them (two needs perhaps at odds), they would not have been

able to form their clubs but for the advent of a phenomenon only a few had experienced before—a marked increase in leisure time. Between 1860 and 1900 more than 676,000 patents were issued by the United States Patent Office;[17] while many inventions, such as the combine and the telegraph cable, brought the country to its feet, others allowed women to sink back onto their horsehair sofas. By the 1880s hot and cold running water began to appear in middle-class urban homes, enabling the housewife to dispense with buckets, pumps, and heavy tubs heated on stoves—the apparatus with which she had tackled the family laundry, a task that had consumed one-third of her time.[18] Factories now relieved her of bread baking, beer brewing, and soap making. Although most women today look upon home canning and preserving as time-consuming, to women of the 1880s the new process was enormously time-saving. The rise of the department store during the same period not only cut down on shopping time but also with its "ready-mades" gave women some relief from countless hours spent at the treadle sewing machine. In addition to her role as housekeeper, nineteenth-century woman functioned as nurse and guardian of the family health. While the great vaccines would not appear until the twentieth century, by the 1870s the thermometer was coming into use, Pasteur and Koch were discovering that specific microorganisms caused diseases, and hospitals were winning a grudging acceptance for care of the most seriously ill. The falling birthrate for white American women from 7.04 in 1800 to 4.24 in 1880[19] not only reduced the number of children for whom health care was necessary but also yielded women extra years free from the restraints and often debilitating effects of confinement, childbirth, and nursing. With the increase in public schools and years of mandatory attendance, woman's third major role in the home—that of educator—became far less demanding. Although it was still necessary to educate her daughter into domesticity, the responsibility for the alphabet, multiplication tables, and their accouterments was now that of someone else. Just as the demands on women's time decreased, the number of women living in the home increased: the age of marriage rose, and the proportion of women who never married (and thus remained in their parents' home or moved in with other family members, often married siblings) was highest for those born in the last four decades of the century.[20] In many states, particularly in the South and New England, adult women significantly outnumbered adult men.[21] Lessening the need for women to spend every waking hour on household work, however, gave rise to another need: what to do with new leisure time.

The coin of leisure (an image especially apt as women's leisure became an outward sign of men's prosperity) was not always an asset. The alternatives to domesticity were few. Until the 1890s recreational physical exercise for women was generally considered dangerous (and *was*, in fact, for such corseted creatures). Not until the turn of the century did public libraries appear with any regularity (their ancestors, more often than not, were the small circulating libraries established by women's clubs). Sentimental novels abounded, gossip flourished, as did decorative needlework, and women's magazines advertised patent remedies for yawning. Incentives for intellectual development and aspiration were not readily apparent. Except for teaching, employment for other than lower-class women was negligible. In 1870 of the 1,300,000 nonagricultural wage-earning women in the United States, seventy percent were domestic servants and twenty-four percent were operatives in textile, clothing, and shoe factories.[22] For two years after she graduated from Smith College in 1884, Vida Scudder lived a semineurasthenic life with her mother in Boston trying a little writing and suffering well-meaning visits from her minister; her call to teach at Wellesley College, although it involved rigorous preparation and a strenuous daily commute, revitalized her overnight. Few women, however, had such an opportunity.

And although physically life was easier for the American woman, especially if she was in the middle class, her new leisure exacted a psychological toll. Whereas previously her functions in the dairy, the storeroom, the poultry garden, the kitchen, and at the loom had had an economic value to the family, now, as the focus of money-making shifted outside the home, she found herself more a liability than an asset, and foundations for self-respect became more elusive.[23] Increasingly, positive attributes for marriage were ornamentation and sprightly conversation rather than a capacity to contribute to the vital economic well-being of the family.[24] In another ironic twist, leisure brought time for companionship, but when the free hours finally materialized, women had to seek meaningful contact outside the home: the Industrial Revolution, the common schools, the continued westward migration which attenuated kin groups all contributed to the bland and lonely life of the American housewife. With their excess time and energy, then, women by the thousands formed clubs, seeking in them the purpose, self-respect, and companionship they had previously found in their homes.

Although some bright primary colors had begun to appear on the emerging postwar portrait of the American woman, the whole canvas was suffused in the golden glow of True Womanhood, an ideology which, since the 1830s, had at once muted and intensified the vibrancy of women's growing needs for association and which strongly influenced the form and content that such association would assume. Both warning and exalting the women of his New England parish in 1841, the Reverend Mr. Stearns declaimed: "Yours it is to determine whether the beautiful order of society . . . shall continue as it has been . . . or whether society shall break up and become a chaos of disjointed and unsightly elements."[25] In his discourse the clergyman touched on several themes of what has been variously called the Cult of Domesticity, the Cult of the Home, the Cult of True Womanhood: nineteenth-century woman in her singular role as conservator of beauty, order, and morals. Until the Industrial Revolution, the place of most women *and* men was in the home. As the economy changed from subsistence to cash and men went out of the home to work, the gender division of labor became more pronounced and "came to be regarded as a divine law—not a product of social conditions."[26] As Gerda Lerner has written, " 'Woman's place is in the home' changed from a description of reality to an ideology."[27] In 1869 Orestes A. Brownson, journalist, critic, and social reformer, editorialized:

> Woman was created to be a wife and mother; that is her destiny. To that destiny all her instincts point, and for it nature has specially qualified her. Her proper sphere is home, and her proper function is care of the household, to manage a family, to take care of children, and attend to their early training. For this she is endowed with patience, endurance, passive courage, quick sensibilities, a sympathetic nature, and great executive and administrative ability. She was born to be a queen in her own household, and to make home cheerful, bright, and happy.[28]

Other factors had contributed to the development of the ideology. After 1776 the rise of democratic self-government brought with
it an emphasis on individual moral strength and responsibility. As
men went out of the home to fashion the new republic, women,
remaining behind, were charged with the task of inculcating the
piety and patriotism that the new nation demanded. Hailed as
"Republican Mothers," they found that their foremost task was to
train their sons for effective citizenship. With the fruits of their labor no longer economic but moral, women's idealization was well
on its way.

Puritan ethics, a legacy with an even longer lineage, may also
have played a part in the development of the True Woman. As men
left "the garden" to chase the dollar in the world of "the machine"
where morality was not a guiding concern, domestic morality developed as a counterbalance.[29] In William Dean Howells's 1885 novel
The Rise of Silas Lapham, the first significant fictional study of an
American businessman, it is Persis Lapham who acts as a conscience
to her husband for whom the manufacture of paint has become
"something more than a business . . . almost a passion."[30] Twenty
years after Silas bought out his partner in a legal but unethical ma-
neuver, Persis urges him to face the truth: "You crowded him out. A
man that had saved you! You had got greedy, Silas. You had made
paint your god, and you couldn't bear to let anybody else share in its
blessings. . . . Oh, if only I could get you once to acknowledge that
you did wrong about it, then I should have some hope."[31] Not even
the world of letters remained safe from sordid temptations. Inter-
viewing Silas Lapham, a young journalist, a "potential reprobate,"
admits: "If my wife wasn't good enough to keep both of us straight,
I don't know what would become of me."[32] Because women were not
directly involved in money-making, they were ideal moral guardians, and home became an unsullied retreat for men from the knock-
about, materialistic world.[33]

The economic and social instability that rumbled throughout
much of the nineteenth century contributed as well to the Cult of
Domesticity: women, unchanging, timeless, and enthroned in the
home, could uphold the temple.[34] "In a society that often felt itself
on the verge of chaos—a 'frontier' in the broadest sense of the
term—women came to represent cohesion, decency, and self-
restraint; and the Cult of the Home, over which they presided, be-

came the national religion."[35] In addition, by giving women more power in their own sphere, men, consciously or not, were taking a preventive measure against a potential outbreak of feminism.[36] By defining social problems in moral terms, efforts could be focused more on the individual than on the system.[37]

The True Woman's position was elevated, and her function was to inspire others to rise to her heights. Although her celestial nature appeared to be innate, the number of exhortations and guidelines delivered to her suggests the necessity of constant reinforcement in the face of headlong abandonment, as in the didactic observation of Le Baron R. Briggs, dean of the faculty at Harvard College and later president of Radcliffe College, in an essay entitled "To Schoolgirls at Graduation":

> There are women . . . in whose presence it is impossible to dwell on a low thought, to live on any level but the highest—who are a kind of revelation of heaven. . . . There are such women that when their friends or their husbands or children think evil or are tempted in business or in social life one hair's breadth from what is true, the thought of them shall make it harder to do wrong than to do right.[38]

The novel *Unleavened Bread*, written in 1915, chronicles the life of Selma White, a woman in whom the yeast of True Womanhood is missing. In her restless passage through the novel, she leaves behind her dead children and ruined husbands. As yet not disillusioned, Selma's first husband describes the ingredients and final product of American matrimony:

> At first blush the husband's rough and material, but he's shrewd and enterprising and vigorous—the bread winner. He's enormously proud of her, and he has reason to be, for she is a constant stimulus to higher things. Little by little, and without his knowing it, perhaps, she will smoothe and elevate him, and they will develop together, growing in intelligence and cultivation as they wax in worldly goods.[39]

Women served not only as antidotes to spiritual lapses; they were also expected to fill the cultural voids left by men too coarse and too busy to pursue the arts that would add refinement to their lives: "Our young men come into active life so early that, if our girls were not educated to something beyond mere practical duties, our material prosperity would outstrip our culture, as it often does in places where money is made too rapidly."[40]

The True Woman was both fragile and powerful. As Briggs continued in his "Schoolgirls" essay, "I find it hard to see by what right the ballot is denied to women; yet with direct political responsibility comes much that would tend to weaken or destroy the power by which they rule the world today. 'To women,' said President Eliot, 'we owe the charm and the beauty of life.'"[41] Woman's power, then, resided in her "charm and beauty," and almost "any form of social change such as suffrage was tantamount to an attack on women's virtue, if only it was correctly understood."[42] Clearly the best refuge for such a delicate being was her home.

Caught in another paradox, women were at once superior and inferior. Men might worship at their feet, but women were not men's equals. Writing in 1840, educator Catharine E. Beecher observed: "Heaven has appointed to one sex the superior and to the other the subordinate station, and this without any reference to the character or conduct of either. It is therefore as much for the dignity as it is for the interest of females, in all respects to conform to the duties of this relation."[43] Men and women now operated in two different stations, two different spheres, as a gentleman speaker at Mount Holyoke's 1876 commencement exercises reminded the graduates, who already by virtue of their higher education were pushing at the conventional spherical limits: "The sum total of general belief of the most enlightened of both sexes appears to be that there is a difference of kind in their natural endowments and that there is for each an appropriate field of development and action."[44] Woman lived in a world apart where she was a "companion, wife, mother, wielder not of public power but of private influence."[45] Indeed, so strong was the stricture on separation of public and private spheres that the yearbooks of many early women's clubs did not list the names of their members.

The two spheres were implicit in Victorian definitions of *male* and *female*: man, wrote club woman Mary Wood, is "the inventor, the explorer, the discoverer; [woman is] the conserver, preserver, and helpmeet."[46] And as these words suggest, women's cardinal virtues were piety, purity, submission, and domesticity.[47] Women were often urged to "become as little children," to enjoy the innocent here and now, and not to "trample on the flowers while longing for the stars."[48] Ambition was denied the True Woman except as she might nurture it in others, the males in her life; through their achievements, not through her own efforts and talents, was her social status defined.[49] While she might be "schooled," education's potential for transformation was not to be hers. Henry James, Sr., who worshiped his daughter Alice—and devoted his life to the education of his sons—expressed his double vision in 1853:

> The very virtue of woman, her practical sense, which leaves her indifferent to past and future alike, and keeps her the busy blessing of the present hour, disqualifies her for all didactic dignity. Learning and wisdom do not become her. Even the ten commandments seem unamiable and superfluous on her lips, so much should her own pleasure form the best outward law for man.[50]

In a journal entry in 1872, M. Carey Thomas, later president of Bryn Mawr College but then age fourteen, reported a conversation in her parents' Baltimore home between two visiting gentlemen:

> They said that they didn't see any good of a womans learning Latin or Greek it didn't make them any more entertaining to their *husbands*. A woman had plenty of other things to do sewing, cooking taking care of children dressing and flirting. "What noble elevating things for a whole life time to be occupied with." In fact they talked as if the whole end and aim of a woman's life was to get *married* and when she attained that *greatest state of earthly bliss* it was her duty to amuse her husband and to learn nothing; never to exercise the powers of her mind so that he might have the *exquisite* pleasure of knowing more than his wife. Of course they talked the usual cant of woman being too *high* too *exalted* to do anything but sit up in perfect ignorance with folded hands and let men worship at her shrine, meaning in other words like all the rest of such high faluting stuff that woman ought to be mere dolls for men to be amused with.[51]

Daughter, wife, and mother were the three rungs of ascendancy. Marriage was *the* goal for daughters. In *The President of Quex*, a novel about the early club life of American women, Hope Norton speaks for the unchosen:

> "Isn't it so, Mrs. Norton?"
> "*Miss* Norton," corrected that individual. "Hope Norton, spinster, by grace of God and cruelty of man."[52]

Motherhood was *the* goal for young brides as "the family became above all an agency for building character, for consciously and deliberately forming the child from birth to adulthood. These changes dictated not merely a new regard for children but . . . a new regard for women: if children were in some sense sacred, then motherhood was nothing short of a holy office."[53] Or, as a popular rhyme summarized:

> Don't poets know it
> Better than others?
> God can't be always everywhere: and, so
> Invented Mothers.[54]

Even at the First Woman's Congress in 1873, motherhood was a major theme. Albeit the five papers delivered on the topic were entitled "Enlightened Motherhood" and the message was "She who rocks the cradle rules the world," the concept was still sacred enough that it was afforded homage even among these most intellectual and advanced of women.

In general, women's education, both secondary and collegiate, incorporated the tenets of True Womanhood or, at the very least, couched itself in its terminology. "American women," said Charles W. Eliot, president of Harvard University, "should recognize that the most satisfying intellectual pursuits of women are those associated with marriage, childrearing, and the schooling of young children."[55] In agreement, a turn-of-the-century U.S. commissioner of education proclaimed: "Educate a man and you have educated one person; educate a mother and you have educated the whole family."[56] Academies for young ladies and early colleges for women were careful not to engender suspicion that they were tampering with the Cult of Domesticity. Some were, such as Vassar, Smith, and Bryn

Mawr colleges. Others were not, such as the Young Ladies Seminary and Collegiate Institute in Monroe City, Michigan. Its catalogue declared that few of its graduates "would fill the learned professions"; instead it hoped to turn out a young woman who would be "the presiding genius of love" in the home, where she would "give a correct and elevated literary taste to her children, and assume that influential station that she ought to possess as the companion of an educated man."[57] Writing to a friend in 1872 about his fiancée, Clover Hooper, the educated Henry Adams soft-pedaled her intellectual achievements attained at a school for girls in Cambridge run by Elizabeth Cary Agassiz:

> One of my congratulatory letters . . . describes my "fiancée" to me as "a charming blue" [stocking]. . . . She reads German—also Latin—also, I fear, a little Greek, but very little. She talks garrulously, but on the whole pretty sensibly. She is very open to instruction. We shall improve her. . . . It *is* rather droll to examine women's minds. They are a queer mixture of odds and ends, poorly mastered and utterly unconnected. But to a young man they are perhaps all the more attractive on that account.[58]

Most academies offered little beyond "accomplishments" and "the gentle science of homemaking."[59] Among those which offered more, Catharine Beecher's female seminary in Hartford described its curriculum as "the appropriate scientific and practical training for woman's distinctive profession as housekeeper, nurse of infants and the sick, educator of children, trainer of servants and minister of charities."[60] With a husband so much away from home, Beecher argued, a woman needed more than a rudimentary understanding of science and mathematics. It was the wife who would have to plan with an architect the details of ventilation, water supplies, and setting of the furnace. It was she who must know the first principles of "floriculture" for successful landscape gardening. Hers was the responsibility for family nutrition, demanding a knowledge of physiology and "animal chemistry." While her husband amassed the money, she was the regulator of family expenditures.[61] By the nineteenth century John Locke's idea that learning was significant mainly for its use in everyday life was well established in the United

States; woman's education, then, was delineated by its projected utility in her circumscribed sphere and role as a True Woman.

While the proponents of True Womanhood would have had the arms of women fixed permanently in a gesture of encirclement, there were elements outside and within the ideology itself that caused women instead to reach out, sometimes only in confusion, sometimes with purpose. Mill girl Lucy Larcom recalled her adolescence in the 1830s:

> Girls, as well as boys, must often have been conscious of their own peculiar capabilities—must have desired to cultivate and make use of their individual powers. When I was growing up, they had already been encouraged to do so. We were often told that it was our duty to develop any talent we might possess, or at least to learn how to do some one thing which the world needed.[62]

Simultaneously degraded and elevated, hailed as a saint and guilt-ridden when she sinned, given custody of the home precisely when its social, educational, and economic functions were waning, it is no wonder that the American woman reached out to others in an attempt to dispel any suggestion of deviancy and to make sense of the incoherent world she inhabited. Written at age twenty-seven when she was already the mother of five children, Julia Ward Howe's letter to her sister seethes with the frustration which years later she hoped to eliminate from the lives of other women with the founding of the New England Women's Club: "Must I sew and trot babies and sing songs and tell Mother Goose stories, and still be expected to know how to write? My fingers are becoming less and less familiar with the pen, my thoughts grow daily more insignificant and commonplace."[63]

Carried to its natural extension, the Cult of True Womanhood itself seemed to demand an enlargement of woman's activities beyond the home. If a mother were to mold her children, she must have the education to do so. If novels were to be morally improving, then women, with their moral superiority, must write them. If women were to exert a wise, virtuous influence on male legislators, they must understand politics and current events. If the poor were to be aided, it must be through organizations run by women, mater-

nal and morally matchless.[64] The maternal image alone could ex-
onerate almost any action taken under its banner: Civil War Sanitary Commission work, the medical profession, suffrage, teaching.[65]
Even at the turn of the century, Jane Addams would define settlement work, which brought young college women into city slums, as
"the great mother breast of our common humanity."[66] Nancy
Phayre, the heroine of *The President of Quex,* at the beginning of
the novel is a young True Widow whose life is ostensibly over: within
nine months she has lost mother, infant, and husband, and she
embraces her solitary grief. Members of the women's club Quex
reach out to her, and soon she is embracing the "whole world":

> Domesticity when indulged in to a marked extent,
> causes divergence from social and mental development
> [she observes]. . . . While marriage is woman's aim in
> life, and the creation of a home her uppermost thought,
> coupled with this must be development on a broad
> plane. Club-women cannot fill the role of loving wife
> and tender mother to their families only, but can be the
> loving cultivated women and tender mothers to the
> whole world.[67]

"A man's reach should exceed his grasp or what's a heaven for," wrote
Robert Browning; his advice was gender-specific. Although in
theory the True Woman might embrace the "whole world," in practice for the several decades after the Civil War her reach was defined
and confined by the limits of the prevailing ideology.[68] "A Rhyme of
True Women" appeared as late as 1892 in the yearbook of the Ladies
Literary Club of Grand Rapids, Michigan. Early verses praised the
biblical Miriam, Jael, and Judith; the final verse pledged continua-
tion of the divinely inspired legacy:

> Such noble women may we be,
> Joined heart and hand in L.L.C.
> A woman, with a lamp, shall stand
> Elect, as champion of this band
> Forevermore the type of good,
> True, earnest, helpful womanhood.[69]

The women's club, at first little more than a gathering in a
friend's or neighbor's home, was a natural extension of female bond-

ing and enabled women to reach out while remaining within the conventions of True Womanhood. The biological realities of frequent childbirth, nursing, and menopause had long drawn women into a physical and emotional supportive network,[70] and close female friendships that often lasted throughout a lifetime had the social sanction of nineteenth-century America. The prerequisites for the one career open to all women, that of finding a husband, demanded an endless round of social visiting among the mothers, daughters, sisters, and cousins of the eligibles. Young women who had gone to boarding school knew even more vividly the value of a close circle of friends.[71] But female intimacy and bonding, always limited in scope by time and difficulties in transportation, led to the creation of a separate female culture, not to connection with the outside world; women's clubs were a first inchoate step in that direction, serving the function long noted by sociologists of "integrating a minority group into the larger society" and creating "new roles and relationships, reinforcing new values and behavior patterns."[72] Clubs, as voluntary organizations often do, served as interstitial social mechanisms for women, filling the gaps between major institutions of society and easing the strains imposed on women by the system.[73] Shut out by social convention from participation in public life, women used clubs as a means of adaptation to the role society had set for them.

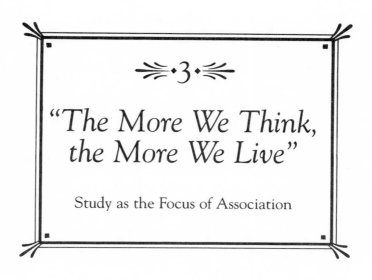

≈·3·≈

"The More We Think, the More We Live"

Study as the Focus of Association

"The place was in a state of transition, the old and new breaking up into cliques, social, religious, and political."[1] The locale and the situation are universal and timeless: Athens in the fifth century, London in the seventeenth. But for America in the three decades after the Civil War, in the throes of the economic and social changes brought on by industrialization, commercialization, urbanization, immigration, and the explosions in transportation and communication, the description is especially apt. The tension existed not just between the forces of the old and the forces of the new. Often the themes coexisted within one individual: the young Pennsylvania livestock farmer who used his profits to buy land in Decatur, Illinois, and to set himself up as the town banker, bringing his eighteenth-century agrarian values to the new railroad center, which he financed with modern capitalistic schemes; the eastern preacher's academy-educated daughter turned schoolteacher who married such a man. That women, feeling the need to organize, chose education as the focus of their associations may be explained in part by just the very times in which they lived. Education provided both a means of maintaining traditional forms and values and a means of expressing the stirrings and spirit of the new age.

"Genius without education is like silver in the mine," wrote Benjamin Franklin, and from the country's earliest days Americans prized learning. This country's fervent, almost passionate, belief in education as a right and as a ladder to dreams was captured at its peak by Ralph Waldo Emerson writing in 1884:

> We have already taken, at the planting of the Colonies . . . , the initial step, which for its importance might have been resisted as the most radical of revolutions, thus deciding at the start the destiny of this country— this, namely, that the poor man, whom the law does not allow to take an ear of corn when starving, nor a pair of shoes for his freezing feet, is allowed to put his hand into the pocket of the rich, and say, You shall educate me, not as you will, but as I will: not alone in the elements, but, by further provision, in the languages, in sciences, in the useful and in elegant arts. The child shall be taken up by the State, and taught, at the public cost, the rudiments of knowledge, and, at last, the ripest results of art and science.[2]

The establishment of women's clubs for the purpose of education was only one more current within the mainstream of American thought and certainly was hard to fault in the generally expansive and progressive mood of the late nineteenth century. As the populace became less physical and more cerebral, as leisure and discretionary money increased, an appreciation spread for the culture that education could provide. In 1870 the adornments of midwestern writer Hamlin Garland's three-room prairie home of pine and rough plaster were "a little picture on the face of the clock, a chromo on the wall, and a printed portrait of General Grant—nothing more";[3] before long the Gilded Age would leave hardly a domestic surface unembellished. The symbol of the "rise" of William Dean Howells's Silas Lapham was the house he built on Beacon Street in Boston, and it was the second-floor library which swelled him most with pride, although he had to ask a young Harvard-educated employee for the titles that would fill the shelves. Though Americans were likely to judge an education by its utility (hence little needed by women in their proper sphere), even as early as 1849 an occasional women's magazine piece urged education for its own sake: "The first reason for the education of every mind should be its own development. We are too much inclined to urge the enlightenment of women, as a sure means of improving man, rather than as in itself an intrinsic excellence, with the conviction that every mind should be educated for its own development."[4]

As the life of the mind gained in popularity, club women coupled it with another revered American ideal, self-reliance. Born of frontier necessity and nurtured by the idealism of the Concord philosophers, self-education was much admired—Abraham Lincoln with his fireside slate is an example that still finds its way into American classrooms. While some clubs, particularly in the cities, invited guest lecturers, the vast majority chose to educate themselves, convinced, perhaps, that their intuitive model of cooperative education was better suited to them than was the hierarchical and adversarial male model. Even programmed self-study existed as a precedent for women's clubs to follow: in the 1830s Elizabeth Peabody brought out a three-volume series of questions and answers entitled *Key to History.*[5]

For as long as many in the postwar decades could remember, the lyceum had been part of the landscape; its demise after the war left a void that women's study clubs filled almost without notice. "Self-education," wrote Josiah Holbrook, the lyceum's creator, "is, in all the departments and all the operations of the lyceum, its most prominent feature."[6] Established in 1826, the lyceum was a series of lectures and public forums, presented at first by local and later by traveling "authorities" and designed, according to the *Boston Recorder,* "to cultivate . . . intellectual and moral faculties [and] to elevate and dignify [the participants'] minds."[7] By 1830 lyceums offered their "regular courses of study," as Holbrook called them, in sixteen states and three thousand towns and villages.[8] The content of early lyceum courses was decidedly factual—"The Character, Customs, Costumes, Etc., of North American Indians," "The Sources of National Wealth," "Geology"—but more cultural topics eventually superseded the strictly informational ones, a pattern that the "curriculum" of study clubs later followed. In the 1856–57 season a New Haven lyceum offered, among other courses, "4 lectures on 'English Authors and Literature,' 2 'conversational lectures and readings by that celebrated declaimer George Vandenhoff,' and 6 lectures on 'Italian History and Reformers.'"[9] Although women appeared rarely as lyceum lecturers, they made up a large part of lyceum memberships. Accustomed to regular attendance at educational outings, women found mutual cultural instruction through clubs a natural activity in the wake of the departing lyceum.

Just as the lyceum, designed originally for artisans and farmers, was seen as harmless because it posed no threat to higher economic classes,[10] so intellectual self-improvement as a focus for organizing women into groups was one of the few rationales clubs could have chosen without greatly threatening the status quo. "Piety was linked to learning, and education to formation of moral character";[11] an attack on education per se might as well have been an attack on the Ten Commandments. College education for women was open to criticism because it could be viewed as a vehicle to move women from their proper sphere, but a biweekly ladies' club meeting conferred no academic degree or formal elevated status; it did not challenge boundaries. Most of the discomfort the clubs aroused came from the mistaken linkage of clubs with the Woman Movement, a notion Helen H. Santmyer captures in her recent novel ". . . *And Ladies of the Club*":

> "We're going to meet around at each other's houses and tell each other what we think of Milton and Shakespeare."
> Her father nodded. "Well, that's harmless; it ought to keep you out of mischief."
> "Harmless?" [queried her mother.] "I don't know. . . . It sounds like Woman's Rights to me."[12]

By eschewing religion, politics, and other controversial topics, as did the lyceum, and by disavowing in particular any connection with the suffrage issue, study clubs with their conservative goals tried to deflect potential opposition from outside their ranks and to reassure those within that they would leave intact the symbols which women themselves had developed as "substitute gratifications for their lack of real power."[13]

Echoes of the Protestant work ethic may be heard as well as women with increasing leisure time chose study as the focus of their clubs: "America is the only country in the world where one is ashamed of having nothing to do," wrote a European traveler in 1890.[14] Although leisure had become a status symbol, idleness was still the devil's playground. Free time should be used for improvement, and the earnestness with which club women later addressed their programs leaves no room for an interpretation of mindless pink-tea sociability. In their leisure, many women turned to reading to fill idle hours. Though the sixty-four women's magazines which began publication between 1830 and 1850[15] offered little beyond fashion plates and sentimental fiction, they were dedicated to self-improvement and, especially Sarah J. Hale's *Ladies' Magazine* and *Godey's Lady's Book,* supported female education.[16]

Study clubs buttressed tradition in yet another way by addressing a major requirement of True Womanhood—an *educated* mother to train the future citizens of the nation, a familiar theme now expanded. If women were supposed to acquire culture for their families and to pass it on, they needed weekday clubs "to acquire knowledge of earth . . . to supplement the Sunday clubs where they acquired knowledge of heaven."[17] And, as Julia Ward Howe asserted, their knowledge of earth needed to be extended beyond the four corners of their homes: "Women, while building firmly and definitely the social fabric they decide to rear, must yet build it with a tolerance of things foreign to their individual experience, which their combined and corporate wisdom may better explain, and whose final adoption or rejection is not to be made without reason sufficient to the best judgment of all concerned."[18]

While the province of culture was deemed woman's by instinct, concerted study gave her in addition some sense of cultural authority.[19] It also gave her the discipline and structure for self-directed learning which her patchy educational background had seldom instilled. Even M. Carey Thomas, with a strong Quaker boarding school background and an even stronger determination to learn, deplored her lack of self-discipline in the rigorous preparation she was making for admission to Cornell's first coeducational class: "it is so impossible to get the highest culture by one's self."[20] With just a bit of modification, club women must have agreed with William E. Channing: "[Wo]men, it is justly said, can do jointly what they cannot do singly."[21] Even after self-improvement lost its primacy among the goals of the General Federation of Women's Clubs in the mid-1890s, the organization continued to urge self-study on its members: "A mother does not wish to be a back number among her educated children, and she surely will be unless she keeps up her studies to a certain extent, for, even though she be college-trained, she will become rusty and forgetful without *systematic intellectual* work."[22]

Other articles of faith in the dogma of True Womanhood fit well with the study focus of clubs. Despite the efforts of Amelia Bloomer to free women from their literal (and metaphoric) stays and the introduction of calisthenics classes in women's colleges, the prevailing medical opinion in the latter half of the nineteenth century was that women's biological characteristics permitted them to pursue only special nonstrenuous activities. While the mental exertion required of college students was thought to have deleterious effects, club life, often satirized as little more than an efficient means of gossip, held no such threat. As delicate creatures no longer sought after in marriage for their working capacity but for their ornamentation and conversation, women could turn to clubs to give them the intellectual "finishing" only a few were able to acquire in academies or female seminaries. And as to ornamentation, the General Federation of Women's Clubs at its 1896 convention brought its members good news:

> It is a great scientific truth that intellectual work is actually a life-giving process, and rejuvenates the worker to a remarkable degree. Those who have studied statistics know that the greatest longevity is attained by scholars. . . . A proper course of study not only prolongs [woman's] life, and keeps her up with the times, and makes her a comfort to her friends even in her old age; but . . . it will actually refine her features and illuminate her eyes. It will change the expression of her face, and have a tendency to smooth out the old wrinkles which have come in consequence of keeping the mind in a rut, and thinking continually along the same lines.[23]

In addition, although the Cult of Domesticity gave woman few opportunities to develop her talents and self-confidence outside the home, its doctrinaire insistence on her exalted position within her sphere cultivated notions of personal integrity and self-worth, necessary components and often primary stimulants in the quest for further education.

While study as the *raison d'être* of women's clubs sat foursquare within a homegrown American geometry, it also encompassed emerging angles that would in time take the study-club movement off center. The point of convergence of these new ideas was gender. Although women's study clubs were not avowedly feminist, it is difficult not to see in their purpose some general stirrings of emancipation. As is the case in such movements, education is often the first step, as Jane Croly recognized:

> The quickening of moral and spiritual life in our day . . . addressed itself with signal significance to women. It came not only as an awakening, but as an emancipation—emancipation of the soul, freedom from the tyranny of tradition and prejudice, and the *acquisition of an intellectual outlook*. . . .
>
> The cry of women emerging from a darkened past was "light, more light," and light was breaking. Gradually came the demand and the opportunity for education; for intellectual freedom . . . ; for cultivation of gifts and faculties.[24] [Emphasis added]

Nascent feminists among club women may have divined, as did the first generation of women students at Girton College, Cambridge, who scrupulously observed "ladylike deportment," that conventionality was the best possible shelter for new aspirations.[25] Even though the discussion of politics was banned in most clubs, the sense of eventual suffrage was in the air, and Federation historian Mary Wood averred that, unconsciously or not, women would strive to measure up as intelligent, educated voters when the time came.[26] As the study of black history developed in the civil rights movement of the 1960s to reinforce the concept of racial identity, and as the study of women's history emerged in the 1970s to reinforce the concept of gender identity, the programs of some women's study clubs suggest a similar process at work. Few clubs called attention to their feminist interests as did the Mary Arden Shakespeare Club of New York City,[27] but club programs included the study of "Women as Rulers," "Famous Women of Rome," "The Homeric Heroines: Helen and Penelope," "A Year of Celebrated Women," "The Position, Influence, and Dress of Women in Ancient Egypt," and "The Queens of England in Chronicle, Song, and Story."[28]

By the later decades of the nineteenth century, education not only had become "morally improving" as it set the learner's sights on "higher" matters, it was also beginning to enhance social status, as the unlettered Silas Lapham had discovered. To have a daughter in an academy or a son in college implied discretionary income that was unavailable to children who remained at home to work on a farm or at a mill or who journeyed to the city to clerk in the new emporiums. Education was becoming a commodity in a developing consumer society, and as wealth vied with Mayflower ancestry as the conveyor of social standing, education was one more conspicuous acquisition. Women, now consumers rather than producers, and surely aware of their diminished economic importance in the family and their attendant loss of status, could cancel some of the losses by acquiring education.

Intellectual development held another new appeal for post–Civil War women. Those who had been forced, on the death of a husband or father in battle, to become wage earners had little time for clubs, but their plight did not go unnoticed by women who had been more fortunate. Total dependency on others was foolhardy in a world so rapidly and unpredictably changing, where the family was becoming more nuclear and where property rights of women were uncertain at best. Study-club programs would not, of course, give women marketable skills, but they would quicken their minds, foster a sense of independent achievement, and lessen their isolation from the social and intellectual mainstream of American life. "The idea of clubs for women," wrote Jane Croly (with marvelous ambiguity, for she was far more feminist than most in the club movement), "was to rid them of the system of exclusion and separation." [29]

While their generalized needs for association and their ancillary needs satisfied by study most often went unarticulated within their ranks, women's desire to educate themselves did not. On page after page of individual club histories chronicled by Jane Croly, the purpose remains unvaried:

- Mutual improvement on literary lines. (The Aurora Literary Club, Caribou, Maine)
- To promote the intellectual growth of its members. (The Athene Club, Bangor, Maine)
- The study of the writings of Charles Dickens, the creation of a greater interest in them, and the promotion of a united intellectual and social alliance. (The All-Around Dickens Club, Boston, Massachusetts)
- To read and study the best literature and to promote in-

terchange of thought and opinion among members.
(The Casmian Club, Springfield, Massachusetts)[30]
- To enlarge the mental horizon as well as the knowledge of our members. (Fortnightly, Chicago, Illinois)[31]
- To obtain intellectual advancement. (The Owl Literary Society, Brooklyn, New York)[32]
- Realizing the advantage of a thorough and systematic course of study of the principles of true art, and of the benefit gained by united effort, we, whose names are hereto appended, do form ourselves into a society for such study. (The Students' Club, Columbus, Georgia)[33]

Club mottoes underlined the message:

- Knowledge the wing wherein we fly to Heaven. (The Students' Club, Columbus, Georgia)
- More light. (The Woman's Club, River Forest, Illinois)
- Read not to contradict and confute; nor to believe and take for granted; nor to find talk and discourse; but to weigh and consider. (Over the Teacups, Indianapolis, Indiana)
- Knowledge rare, we seek and share. (The Woman's Reading Club, Fort Wayne, Indiana)
- Study to be what you wish to seem. (The McRae, Muncie, Indiana)
- The test of knowledge is choice of what you want to know. (Ladies' Literary Club, Cedar Rapids, Iowa)
- Thought once awakened does not again slumber. (The Tourist Club, West Union, Iowa)
- And in these cities there are not only men who pride themselves on learning, but women also. (The Nineteenth Century Club, Minneapolis, Minnesota)[34]

As if to fill a void suddenly recognized, women wanted to learn. Speaking to the First Woman's Congress in 1873, Julia Ward Howe urged her audience to address themselves "to the work of our generation: education, consolidation, inspiration."[35] Even by 1905 "the work" was not done: "The stirring of woman's unrest may be heard down the ages by the ear placed close to the heart of hidden things. Woman by reason of her environment has developed to excess on the emotional side. Now the infinite law of equilibrium demands a reaction to the neglected intellect."[36] However infinite that law of nature might be, it needed help from human hands if equilibrium of education were to be achieved between the sexes. Sarah J. Hale recognized that fact as early as 1838 when she advised her *Godey's* readers that reform and improvement in their education would not come from "without." She urged them to demonstrate their desire and ability to learn by starting a planned program of reading which would address the gaps in their knowledge, and she supplied them with a bibliography. Recognizing the importance of writing as a means of clarifying one's thoughts, she advised them to correspond with a learned friend to whom they could give accounts of their everyday lives as well as their ideas.[37] Study clubs, incorporating some of Hale's suggestions, finally began thirty years later to work from "within."

Until the nineteenth century there was scant outside educational opportunity for American girls; economically, formal education could be justified for their brothers, but learning at mother's knee or in a dame school sufficed for the daughters in a family. It was not lack of desire that kept girls and young women at home. Lucy Larcom recalls adolescent mill girls collecting money for the "education of indigent young men to become Western Home Missionary preachers. There was something almost pathetic in the readiness with which this was done by young girls who were longing to fit themselves for teachers but had not the means."[38] Again mainly for economic reasons, girls gradually were sent along with boys to master's schools to help portion out the salary paid to the male teacher. Although the 1820s saw the beginnings of the common school, little provision was made for girls beyond the eighth grade, and if the "ladies of the club" in the 1880s had had more than an elementary school education it would have been at a female academy or seminary. With some notable exceptions, such as Emma Willard's in Troy, Catharine Beecher's in Hartford, and Mary Lyon's in South Hadley, few academies offered a rigorous curriculum. There were no entrance examinations, the average stay was a year or two, and uniform standards for graduation did not exist: "I entered at 15 years and 6 months and graduated at sharp 17. I took the entire course, also lessons on the piano and guitar," commented Rebecca L. Felton of her Georgia academy days.[39] The purpose of these academies, according to Thomas Woody, whose 1929 *A History of Women's Education in the United States* remains the standard overview, was the development of "Christian religion and morals, domestic training, maternal influence and social usefulness, training for the teaching profession, accomplishments, physical health, intellectual enjoyment, and mental discipline."[40] The Cult of True Womanhood was not threatened by such goals. The courses most frequently studied were modern languages (particularly French), literature, history, geography, rhetoric, arithmetic, botany, chemistry (usually under the guise of "scientific cooking principles"), and music.[41] "Accomplishments," not achievements, won the day. One of the arguments against the opening in the late 1880s of the Woman's College of Baltimore City (later Goucher College) was that "there was not one school in Maryland and very few in all the South that could prepare young women to enter a first-class college."[42] Nor was the South an educational desert or an anomaly: female academies existed there in profusion, a number of them rated in 1870 by the commissioner of education as "superior."[43] In New England, upon the opening of Wellesley College in 1875, of the 314 entrants, 284 had to be enrolled first in the institution's preparatory department. Smith College in the same year refused applicants who were not fully prepared for a college curriculum equivalent to men's and opened with a freshman class of 14. Despite the uneven preparation offered by academies, women were beginning to be educated, but the numbers were small. At the height of their existence just before the Civil War, there were approximately two hundred female academies and seminaries.[44] If Mount Holyoke Seminary is used as a measure (although it is on the high side), the average academy graduating class in the 1850s numbered 100.[45] In 1850 the number of females between fifteen and nineteen years of age was 1,292,111.[46] If 2,000 young women were graduated each year, then only 7 in 1,000 young women in America were receiving the equivalent of today's high school education. By 1870 that number had climbed to 20 in 1,000.[47] Although the latter figure includes a growing number of graduates from public schools, by far the major share of secondary schooling throughout most of the nineteenth century was done by academies for the white, middle-class daughters of families who could afford the tuition—much the same population that swelled the membership rolls of women's study clubs.

College education for women comparable to men's was virtually nonexistent before the Civil War. The beginning of college education for women in the United States is often considered to be 1837, when four young women were accepted into the Collegiate Department of Oberlin College. In 1889, historian Richard G. Boone noted that Oberlin "from the first . . . has been an ultra-radical— since 1835 no distinction being made either as to sex or race."[48] But the description, at least as regards sex, is too sweeping. The college, which opened in 1834, began with two departments: a Collegiate Department for men and a Female Department, which offered a diluted and abridged version of the men's curriculum.[49] Jill K. Conway contends that the admission of women was prompted not by emancipated vision but by the need for a domestic work force to accompany the men's required four hours of manual labor each day on the college grounds.[50] While the men tilled college gardens and stoked classroom stoves, the women served meals to students and laundered and mended students' clothes.[51] They were in college, to be sure, but by 1857, twenty years after its founding, only 20 women had entered the degree-granting Collegiate Department while 299 had taken the "ladies' course."[52]

Although a few midwestern state colleges also opened their doors to women, it was through their own institutions that women made the most progress. Even by 1870 in the forty-eight public and private coeducational institutions of higher education only 800 women were enrolled.[53] Mary Sharp College in Tennessee, established in 1851, is Thomas Woody's nomination for the first women's institution worthy of the name "college."[54] Mary Sharp required both Greek and Latin in a four-year course leading to an A.B. degree, but most other early women's "colleges" were outgrowths of academies and offered at the most a junior college curriculum.[55] Four years after Mary Sharp was established, Elmira (New York) Female College notched the ratchet one level higher by opening with a curriculum roughly equivalent to that of Amherst College. In the first ten years of its existence, however, Elmira averaged only ten graduates a year.[56] Even after the opening in 1865 of Vassar College, which was neither an upgraded academy nor a downgraded men's institution, college alumnae were rare. Writing of her childhood in a prosperous upper-middle-class home in Baltimore in the 1860s, M. Carey Thomas, second president of Bryn Mawr College, noted: "I had never known a woman who had gone to college nor seen any one who had seen a woman who had gone to college."[57] The historian of Fortnightly, a Chicago women's club formed in 1873 whose members "gained a reputation for brains," takes special note of charter member Josephine Dexter, "that rarity of her time, a college graduate."[58] Speaking in 1916 to women of the College Club in Boston, a founder of the club recalled her young college days in the 1880s:

> You younger women can hardly realize what it meant to be a college woman 35 years ago, when, after 16 years of existence, Vassar had only about 500 graduates; after 6 years, Smith just 41 and Wellesley perhaps a few more. I do not know the statistics of the other colleges graduating women; but there were not very many of us, all told. . . . A college woman was such a curio that it was almost impossible to escape self-consciousness. Other women and men, too, were afraid of us, and set us on such a lofty pedestal that we were in constant fear of falling off. We were anxious to be a credit to our Alma Mater and to uphold her dignity and superiority against all comers. We were expected to do great things—to have a career![59]

The speaker did not romanticize the past: in 1870 approximately 750 bachelor of arts degrees were awarded to American women; two out of every thousand in their age cohort could call themselves college graduates.[60]

Even with an increasing number of college doors open to them, women did not rush through. Vassar struggled valiantly in its early years to maintain its standards and its enrollment. "There were simply not that many young ladies with the necessary preparation, the ambition, the willingness to flout public opinion, and the broad-minded parents who were able and willing to meet the costs," maintained Vassar professor Mabel Newcomer.[61] Lack of preparation may readily be deduced from the numbers of academies, public high schools, and their enrollments and from examination of representative curricula. Lack of ambition, however, is open to question, suggesting as it does a purposeful laziness. That great numbers of women wanted to be educated is borne out by study-club membership alone, but society offered to the college graduate few opportunities not open as well to her "finished and accomplished" sister. Teaching did not require a bachelor's degree; women in the professions were rare and generally reviled; business was a walled street unless one were a typist, stenographer, or department store clerk. Female college graduates had few compatriots and even fewer role models.

But it was not just the absence of positive stimuli that kept women from entering college in greater numbers; it was, as Newcomer states, their lack of "willingness to flout public opinion." Helen Santmyer's ". . . *And Ladies of the Club*" opens in 1868 with the commencement exercises of Waynesboro (Ohio) Female College. Graduates at seventeen (the academy rests its claim to "college" only on the inclusion of Latin in the curriculum), Sally Cochran and Anne Ballard are now among the "well-educated"; there is no thought of further education, and both young women are married and become mothers within two years. Amanda Reid, who has just returned from Oberlin College with "a man's degree," becomes an isolated, androgynous creature for whom there is no place in Waynesboro except the college, where she teaches Latin without enthusiasm. Her advanced education has made her not a Truer Woman but only an object of flawed respect and condescending pity because she has overreached her natural bounds.

In real life, newspapers of the time chronicled the fate of those women who persisted in the extreme. By 1869 a few women had gained grudging admission to the clinical lectures at Pennsylvania Hospital. The *Philadelphia Evening Bulletin* recorded their reception: "When the ladies entered the amphitheater they were greeted by yells, hisses, 'caterwauling,' mock applause, offensive remarks upon personal appearance, *etc.* . . . During the last hour, missiles of paper, tinfoil, tobacco-quids, *etc.* were thrown upon the ladies, while some of the men defiled the dresses of the ladies near them with tobacco juice."[62] Fifteen years later as a few young women of Rhode Island attempted quietly to use the resources of Brown University, their "unnatural acts" were remarked upon. The *Bruinian* carried the following student letter:

I'm glad Brown isn't "co-ed" because if I met on campus and in recitation and in society, the right kind of
girls—the womanly, tender, emotional kind—I'm afraid
I might get interested in something besides study, but if
we had a lot of those coldly intellectual females—those
prospective old maid doctors and lawyers who are all
very useful members of society no doubt—the glorious
"co-ed" influence in polishing my manners, *etc.*, would
amount to just about nothing at all, for I don't admire a
manly woman or a womanly man. [63]

Even in the midst of the celebration of the first commencement
exercises of Smith College in 1879, a cautionary note was sounded
by the graduation speaker, Charles W. Eliot, president of Harvard
University: "The college education of young women is an experiment the issues of which can be completely revealed only after the
lapse of many years, or even of generations." [64]

The question of the intellectual capacity of women was slowly
put to rest, but even into the twentieth century debate was waged
over the possible deleterious effects of college attendance on the
health of young women. Decidedly, a woman had to become a flou-
ter of public opinion in the last half of the nineteenth century if she
wished to attend college, but she could learn and could educate
herself through unremarkable means—through study clubs.

The college and university metaphor laces the writings of club
members. (A heightened use of metaphor, Carroll Smith-Rosenberg
contends, often occurs during times of radical social transformation.) [65]

The [study club] meant a school where [women] might
teach and be taught, a mutual improvement society,
which should educate them and lead them out into better hopes, nobler aspirations and larger life. [66]

The school is mother to the club, as college is to university extension. Those fortunate enough to be educated
wish to keep their intellectual activities in practice, and
those not situated desire a post-youthful education. [67]

What college life is to the young woman, club life is to
the woman of riper years, who amidst the responsibilities

45

and cares of home-life still wishes to keep abreast of the times, still longs for the companionship of those who, like herself, do not wish to cease to be students because they have left school. . . . Club life supplies in some degree the place of higher education to those women who have been deprived of the advantages of a college course.[68]

The club is the postgraduate for the individual woman.[69]

The club has not come to fill vacant spaces in empty lives, but rather to give women already crowned with zeal and labor in the great interests of humanity, a share—limited, indeed, but keenly appreciated—in the intellectual training . . . offered to younger women in the universities.[70]

Accounting for the rise of study clubs in Iowa after the Civil War, a member of the Conversation Club of Dubuque wrote for Croly's *History*: "Women in Iowa read of Anne Jemima Clough's work in England for university education for women and said: 'Our university must be in our homes. This country is too large to go to a place or a professor. The learned, inspiring minds must come to us.'"[71]

It was not only members who saw themselves as college women without a campus. Asked where the national university should be, Bronson Alcott replied:

It is already begun; it is everywhere; it is where two or more are uniting for mutual help and inspiration. The university of this republic! Why, it is in the parlors of appreciative women. There will be colleges out-of-doors, by the lakeside, on the mountain, as in the first century. When spirit has a new word for mankind, you will note some prophetess knows about it before the high priests; and the birth is always in unexpected time and place. The germ of a great system for general education of the people is already here. Women are nourishing it in their parlors. As in the first century, there was no welcome for the new word in the great buildings and recorded systems of the time.[72]

Not only the pull of demand made study the focus of women's clubs; the push of supply was at work too. The best of the academies had stressed lifelong learning, and women who had attended semi-naries became an important source of leadership for study clubs,[73] as did the increasing number of women who as teachers before their marriages had dedicated themselves to the principle of education. For those unusually motivated young women who had gone to college, whose sense of mission had been encouraged by their teachers, and who now found few outlets for the fruits of their dedication, clubs restored a sense of fellowship and purpose.[74]

"Defeat never converts. It is to the defeated what persecution is to the persecuted. The cause becomes daily more precious." These are the words Santmyer gives to the speaker at the 1868 commencement ceremonies of Waynesboro Female College. The speaker is referring to the civil strife just past, but he might have been referring as well to the forces that had denied higher education and equal opportunity to women. While a few brave flouters battled the establishment, women in study clubs, asserted Jane Croly, quietly began "to work out their objects in their own way."[75]

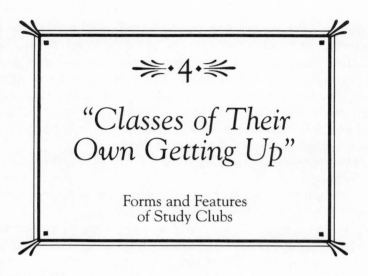

≈·4·≈

"Classes of Their Own Getting Up"

Forms and Features of Study Clubs

Although atypical in some of its aspects, Sorosis, the association whose inauguration set the study-club movement rolling, established fundamental features to be found with slight variation in later clubs across the country. The club was organized in New York City in 1868 by Jane Cunningham Croly, a women's page journalist known as "Jennie June." When she was not issued a ticket to a dinner honoring Charles Dickens, hosted by the New York Press Club of which she was a member, Croly conceived of a society composed only of women "that should manage its own affairs, represent as far as possible the active interests of women, and create a bond of fellowship between them."[1]

Prolonged debate over the name of the club suggests the uncommon step these women were taking. The first name proposed, the Blue Stocking Club, was opposed on two grounds: (1) that it would make the club too literary—the club must be "hospitable to women of different minds, degrees, and habits of work and thought";[2] and (2) that the word *club* allied it with the spirit of men's clubs ("smoking, drinking, and playing cards"), which the women found alien.[3] A second nomination was the Woman's League. Already the target of men's criticism for "tipping the teapot," the twelve charter members were not about to ask for more of the same with a name suggestive of suffrage leanings. In addition, with that title it was "expected

to cooperate with and receive the patronage of a male organization—this was more than the membership had bargained for."[4] Poet
Alice Cary then suggested Sphynx, but that term "appeared to hide
a mystery," and the members felt it imperative "to do things openly
and without concealment."[5] Finally, "for its full, appropriate signi-
fication, its unhackneyed character, and sweet sound, which seemed
. . . full of all gracious meaning," the club chose Sorosis, a botanical
term for plants with an aggregation of flowers that bear fruit—"a
growth to culmination," suggested Croly.[6] If it meant as well to hint
at the Latin *soror*, for sisterhood, the club notes are discreetly silent.

By the second meeting and even before its name had been decided, Sorosis had a constitution which delineated its purpose: "The
object of this association is to promote agreeable and useful relations
among women of literary and artistic tastes. It is entirely independent of sectionalism, or partisanship."[7] The constitution also regulated business protocol ("Members are elected by ballot. The initiation fee is $5") and etiquette ("Ladies receiving an invitation to any
meeting will return answer of acceptance or declination three days
previous to the date of meeting").[8]

By the end of the first year, eighty-three members wore the gold
club pin, a Roman *S* inscribed with "Sorosis" in Greek characters,
and recited the club pledge before the biweekly luncheon meetings
at Delmonico's restaurant. Prospective members, said Croly, should
be women "who had been seized by the divine spirit of inquiry and
aspiration, . . . who were interested in the thought and progress of
the age, and in what other women were thinking and doing."[9] Sorosis included among its eighty-three members "6 artists, 22 authors, 6 editors, 1 historian, 11 poets, 9 teachers and lecturers, 8
well-known philanthropists, 2 physicians, 4 writers on science, besides others who were contributors to periodicals."[10]

Without precedent and "working by instinct,"[11] Sorosis divided
its meetings from September through June into two types, literary
and business. At each meeting a chairwoman was elected in order
to "'educate' the members generally for the business of presiding
officer."[12] The focus of the literary meeting was a paper delivered by
a member, followed by a question for discussion. Topics often reflected public issues—women's dress, health, and wages—not the
cultural inquiry of later clubs. (In its high initiation fee, public
meeting place, and illustrious membership roster, Sorosis was also

unlike the study clubs that came after.) Although the first year saw "conversational disquisitions and literary exercises of a high order,"[13] by the second year the club had decided to institute a "regular system or classification of work" and to elect one president for a year to ensure greater continuity.[14] Still, it did not adopt a continuous class study. Instead it formed four committees—literature, art, drama, and music—which were responsible in rotation for the literary programs. No matter what the field, almost always it was studied in relation to women:

> Our membership is divided up into Committees, the work of which is to keep *en rapport* with whatever belongs to their department, especially when it relates to the doings of their own sex; and in bringing the results to the social meetings of the Club—presenting summaries of the facts, and discussing the questions that grow out of them, so that the knowledge of one and the opportunities of one in any direction shall, in a certain sense, become the knowledge and opportunities of all. . . . We do not paint pictures, perhaps, but we want to know all about those who do, and if it is a woman, what kind of pictures she paints, and if she gets more money than she would for making a shirt or dress. As a club we do not get up dramatic entertainment, but we want to know how the drama affects the interests and welfare of women, socially, mentally, morally, physically, and pecuniarily, and whether we want to train our daughters in that direction for a livelihood.[15]

Although the club on occasion invited an outside speaker such as astronomer Maria Mitchell, members prided themselves on their own (if not decidedly original) efforts.[16] In the Sorosis-sponsored organizational meetings for the First Woman's Congress in 1873, one of the first resolutions adopted was "That self-help is the best help; and that the elevation of women must come from within and not from without,"[17] a crisp echo of Sarah Hale's magazine advice 35 years earlier. Delivering her inaugural address in 1868, first Sorosis president Alice Cary underlined this aim: "We have, then, to begin at the beginning, proposed the inoculation of deeper and broader ideas among women, proposed to teach them to think for

Lucy Larcom's career as an educator and author began with her membership as a girl in the Lowell Mills' "Improvement Circles," study-club forerunners of the 1830s.

Elizabeth P. Peabody, an early advocate of programmed self-study, anticipated study clubs by a half-century with her 1827 "Historical School" and participation in Boston's "Reading Parties."

Margaret Fuller held weekly "Conversations" for women in Elizabeth Peabody's bookshop in the 1840s. She encouraged members to organize their thoughts on paper before speaking in front of the group, a practice later widely adopted by study clubs.

The Fauntleroy home in New Harmony, Indiana, was the meeting place of the Minerva Society in the 1850s. Members chose the club's name "because we wished to become wise."

In the parlor of the Fauntleroy home Minerva members debated "Are We Made Happier by Education?" and wrote a novelette to which each young woman contributed a chapter.

Friends in Council of Quincy, Illinois, had its own clubhouse and library. In the 1870s when its founder, Mrs. Denman (right), asked Mrs. McMahan (left) to join, the initiate later recalled, "The offer of a seat in the Cabinet of the United States would have surprised me less."

The Bee of Cambridge, Massachusetts, held an early annual outing in 1863.

Club members, like students at early women's colleges, enliv-
ened their "lessons" with "clever entertainment." The Bee in
1890 continued to record its playful sisterhood.

By 1900 only nine members of The Bee remained. Lifetime
commitment to a study club was common, one member observing, "No effort is made to increase the membership as old members drop out, the club having arrived at that condition of acquaintance where it seems like a family and hesitate about
taking in strangers."

Newspaper columnist Jane C. Croly, denied an invitation in 1868 to an all-male dinner for Charles Dickens hosted by the New York Press Club, in response founded Sorosis, later acclaimed "the mother of study clubs." Sorosis, Croly wrote, "has represented the closest companionship, the dearest friendships, the most serious aspiration of my womanhood."

Julia Ward Howe, a founder in 1868 of the New England Women's Club, traveled widely across the country encouraging her audience of True Women to establish their own small, local study clubs.

*Young Laura and Maud Howe took their mother's advice and
founded the Saturday Morning Club in 1871. Following a club
lecture on* Antigone *by Harvard's Charles Copeland in 1890,
the members enacted it, here well disguised as seven Theban
elders.*

themselves, and get their opinions at first hand, not so much because it is their right as because it is their duty."[18]

The tone of Sorosis meetings was serious: "We have proposed to enter our protest against all idle gossip, against misuse and waste of time, saying and doing what we are able to say and do, without asking leave and without suffering hindrance."[19] The group was earnestly dedicated to self-improvement: at each meeting three critics reported on "all violations of business, order, incorrect speech, faulty manners."[20] Nevertheless, Sorosis made a specialty of elegant anniversary celebrations and receptions honoring women of achievement, the latter "to offset the social marks of distinction bestowed by men upon men."[21]

Throughout its history, Jane Croly called on Sorosis to act on matters of reform, from female labor to sanitation to public education. The members readily agreed to amass facts on the issues and to suggest solutions, but, except for one occasion when the matter concerned higher education for women, they steadfastly refused to initiate concrete reform programs.

Sorosis, from its beginnings, was viewed with suspicion by the male establishment, especially the male press, whose conscience perhaps pricked uneasily. Not only was this the "first purely women's society"[22] in the city, it had from a male perspective no overt purpose (and, thus, perhaps, a covert one somehow aligned to "the woman question"). During the first months of its existence, an editor of one of New York's daily newspapers prophesied Sorosis's early demise; if it lived out a year, he wrote, "many men would have to recant their opinion in regard to women."[23] The editor himself "recanted" seven years later at a Sorosis May festival to honor distinguished women as well as men.[24] Even at that date, however, Croly hoped that the male guests upon firsthand acquaintance would recognize "that a Woman's Club is nothing monstrous or unnatural."[25] In the intervening years, Sorosis had been subjected to "sneering comment and vulgar would-be wit on the part of men,"[26] the *New York World* having announced in 1868, "Woman has laid down the broomstick to pick up the club."[27] Members took solace in the fact that "from women all over the country came eager questioning of our aims, methods, and possibilities"[28] and in the understanding that "sarcasms are, after all, but so many acknowledgements of our power."[29] After a Sorosis dinner to which the men of the New York

Press Club had been invited, those original godfathers to the club gave it their public blessing:

> We believe we violate no secret when we say that the gentlemen were most agreeably surprised to find their rival club composed of charming women, representing the best aristocracy of the metropolis, the aristocracy of sterling good sense, earnest thought, aspiration, and progressive intellect, *with no perceptible taint of the traditional strong-mindedness.* [30] [Emphasis added]

One wonders if the members of Sorosis were, after all, quite pleased.

With little fanfare Sorosis marched its quiet, determined way, opening doors for those who would follow. By the end of its first year, the club had filed articles of incorporation and had granted women of two other cities the right to organize under its name. [31] Later, women students from the University of the City of New York and the University of Michigan established Sorosis clubs on their campuses. [32] In 1873 at the urging of Jane Croly for a parliament of women, Sorosis issued a call to which four hundred women responded and formed the Association for the Advancement of Woman (AAW). The object was "not to secure an enlarged membership, but to gather the earnest few who should constitute a deliberative assembly upon the best interests of their sex." [33] Papers from the First Congress of the association in 1873 included "How Can Women Best Associate?" ("Every city, town and village in this country should have a Woman's Club") by Julia Ward Howe, "The Higher Education of Woman" by Maria Mitchell, "Kindergarten" by Elizabeth Peabody, "On Endowments for Woman's Colleges" by Catharine Beecher, and "The Relation of Woman's Work in the Household to the Work Outside" by the Reverend Antoinette Blackwell. [34] The AAW was dubbed the "John the Baptist" of women's clubs, stimulating the formation of local clubs wherever its sessions were held.

In 1876 Sorosis made its exception and went a step beyond its usual study of an issue and presented a petition to the University of the City of New York and to Columbia University "praying that Test Examinations be organized for women on the basis of those offered by Harvard, and that, further, these schools should grant the advantages of their curricula to young women as well as to young men."[35] Despite endorsement by Frederick A. Barnard, president of Columbia, the proposal remained just that, but it secured public notice.

Finally, in its most newsworthy legacy, Sorosis was responsible for the formation of the General Federation of Women's Clubs in 1890. To celebrate its twenty-first anniversary in 1889, the club invited representatives of all other women's clubs of which it had knowledge (only ninety-seven) to talk about their clubs and their work. Sixty-one clubs sent delegates; thirty-six others sent reports.[36] Geographically the distribution of the eighteen states which were represented was broad; delegates came from California, Indiana, Kansas, Colorado, Louisiana, and Tennessee as well as from eastern seaboard states. Ten representatives came from cities which had hosted annual AAW conventions. The proposal of the formation of a national organization of clubs elicited no debate; the need was felt, and recognition was immediate. Mary Eastman of the New England Women's Club expressed past, present, and future hopes:

> While the organization and the clasp of hands have been like a beautiful dream to me, I have rejoiced in the manyness of us more than in almost anything else. Today I felt the joy of the *vast intellectual wealth* in us, and it has been like a shock of electricity. . . . We must learn sympathy, learn unity, learn the great lesson of organization. I am sure we never have begun to dream of what will yet appear. . . . These clubs have made a new world, and we have got to adapt ourselves to it and to educate the world around us.[37] [Emphasis added]

Although the names of Sorosis alumnae are not household words, they were, as Croly's first-year roll call indicates, notable in their day. They were active women—doers in their own right. One of the founders, along with Jane Croly, was Ellen C. Demorest, a pioneering businesswoman, who through *Demorest's Illustrated Monthly Magazine* and *Mme. Demorest's Mirror of Fashion* became the "chief arbiter of Parisian fashion for middle-class women."[38] Forty-four when Sorosis was organized, Demorest, in addition to her periodical, ran a dressmaking and millinery establishment, helped her husband run his pattern-making company, and raised two children. She was a graduate of Schuylerville Academy in New York State.[39]

Alice C. Fletcher and Erminnie P. Smith, like Demorest, were graduates of girls' schools. Both were interested in the welfare of the American Indian and became noted ethnologists. Smith, who went on to take two years at the School of Mines in Freiberg, Germany, raised four sons along the way. Each woman was in her early forties when she joined Sorosis.[40]

Alice and Phoebe Cary, self-educated and prolific authors, especially of verse, shared the abolitionist views of most Sorosis women, including Celia Burleigh, although such political sentiments formed no part of Sorosis's agenda. The sisters were in their mid-forties when Alice was elected first club president.[41]

Other writers included Olive T. Miller, Phebe C. Hanaford, and Sara P. Parton. Miller, whose early education had been sporadic but included "a select school" in a small college town in Ohio, was a nature writer and author of children's books. She raised four children and joined Sorosis at the age of forty-four.[42] Hanaford, a cousin of Lucretia Mott, had been educated in public and private schools on Nantucket and at age sixteen began teaching on the island. After the birth of her two children, she wrote biographies and poems for children until her ministry in the Universalist church took her outside the home.[43] Parton, whose pen name was Fannie Fern, was America's first woman newspaper columnist. A graduate of Catharine Beecher's seminary in Hartford, she was fifty-seven when she joined Sorosis and had reared three children.[44]

The unusual number of Sorosis "sisters" who pursued self-supporting occupations outside the home may be related to the high number of widows and divorcées in the lot. Among the latter, along with Parton, were Mary F. Davis, a graduate of Ingham University in New York and a spiritualist lecturer,[45] and Clemence S. Lozier, an alumna of Plainfield (New Jersey) Academy. Lozier at age forty was graduated from Syracuse Medical College in 1853 and later helped establish, with both financial and moral support, the first women's college of medicine in New York.[46]

The courage one needed to become a "first," to join the only women's organization in New York City (and, as far as they knew, in the country) surely must have skewed the membership rolls as well. Anne L. Botta, who was fifty-three in 1868, had graduated from

Albany (New York) Female Academy with highest honors in 1834. As a young woman in Providence, Rhode Island, she compiled an anthology of local verse and prose; later in Brooklyn, she taught English composition at an academy for girls, wrote for various periodicals, and with her mother began evening literary receptions for which she later became famous. In 1855 she married Vincenzo Botta, a professor of Italian at the University of the City of New York.[47] Mrs. Professor Botta, as she is named in Jane Croly's accounts of Sorosis, was one of the original four women to whom Croly broached the idea of a women's club. It was Botta at the first meeting who suggested "'taking the bull by the horns' and calling it the 'Blue Stocking Club.'"[48] Despite her enthusiasm and verve, Botta by the second meeting had asked that her name be withdrawn from the roll upon "the opposition of her husband."[49]

Both in the midst and at the head of these notable women stood Jane Cunningham Croly. Born in 1829 in England, Croly at age twelve arrived with her family in Poughkeepsie, New York, her only education being what she acquired for herself at home, reading books from her Unitarian father's small library. After a brief stint teaching school, she went to New York City, where her first article was accepted by the *New York Tribune*, and a lifetime devoted to journalism was begun. At twenty-seven she married fellow journalist David G. Croly, another self-educated writer, whose irascible temperament and financial naiveté made his wife the primary breadwinner despite the birth of four children between 1859 and 1873. In 1868 at age thirty-nine, she founded Sorosis. In addition to managing the women's department at the *New York World*, she contributed drama and literary criticism to the *Weekly Times* and for twenty-seven years was chief staff writer for *Demorest's Monthly Magazine*. In 1889 she founded and was elected president of the Woman's Press Club of New York. Croly devoted the final years of her life to compiling her history of the women's club movement.[50]

Although she espoused the cause of women, Croly was no radical: "The radical woman has found no place in the women's club, but club life has reached beyond these to the women who most need this lever of progress, and the homemaking women of the country are its nucleus."[51] While she admired Susan B. Anthony, she herself believed that in woman's right to work lay the key—"All the rest will follow."[52] Croly urged women to become competent in whatever area they chose—household, school, or office—with the club serving as crucible.

In a memorial to his sister, John Cunningham said that in her "a potency was apparent." He mentioned her small stature "full of vivacity and abounding in natural intelligence."[53] Others in the same remembrance wrote of her as "spirited," "enthusiastic," and "cheerful." With a sense of mission and "a firm hand," Croly "guarded Sorosis always with love and with the same eager interest with which a mother contemplates the development of a child . . . steering it over rough places, bringing harmony out of discord, . . . sacrificing personal feelings for the good of the whole."[54]

Croly's feelings about Sorosis ran deep. In a letter to the club in her seventieth year on the eve of her departure for England, Croly wrote in words reminiscent of those reverently spoken by women's college alumnae about their alma mater: "What is the secret of the strength of Sorosis? What is its value to . . . the world at large? It is, as a centre of unity. This is our Holy Grail,—and this we are bound never to defame, or defile by thought, word or deed."[55] Whether or not "the world at large" profited from the "centre of unity" that Sorosis and later study clubs provided, individual women certainly did. In their weekly gatherings, club members began building a sense of intense community much as did the all-female professoriate at Wellesley College and students at the Seven Sisters.[56] Like their collegiate counterparts, club women found themselves bound together not only by a common interest in education but also by the dawning "consciousness of their common identity."[57] Croly in the same letter expressed the profound bonds of sisterhood that developed in the "school of the middle-aged woman": "[Sorosis] has represented the closest companionship, the dearest friendships, the most serious aspirations of my womanhood." Later, from England, Croly again addressed her club: "O my beloved Sorosis, you are the core of my heart."[58]

Although the founders of Sorosis were perhaps unaware of the power they were harnessing "on the simple basis of their common womanhood,"[59] they had well understood the power of language. Their search for just the right name for their club proved prescient; their "aggregation" did indeed "bear fruit" as Sorosis grew into sorority nationwide.

Few study clubs were formed in response to a single event as was

Sorosis; more often they developed from informal reading circles. Friends in Council of Quincy, Illinois, one of the pioneer "Light Seekers," grew out of weekly gatherings begun in 1866 of twelve women "for education purposes." During the first year they read aloud Lecky's *History of the Rise and Influence of the Spirit of Rationalism in Europe* and from Child's *Progress of Religious Ideas*. For the following two winters they read and discussed Plato. "During the progress of this disciplinary study," its secretary reported, "it became impressed upon the minds of all that with a form of government which would secure unity and method, a permanent society for mental cultivation might be successfully established."[60] In the spring of 1869 an official club was constituted. The Lewiston (Maine) Reading Circle drew its name from its origin: in 1892 three women met to read Draper's *Intellectual History of Europe*; friends asked to join them, and in 1895 they became a club.[61] The Springfield (Massachusetts) Woman's Club grew out of a nucleus of three women who met in the spring of 1894 to read and study Tennyson's "In Memoriam." The exercise was soon complete, "but the meetings had been so pleasant that the ladies resolved to take up some other study in the autumn for the purpose of keeping together and doing some improving work."[62]

The founding of many other clubs was like a candle-lighting ceremony, one from the other. Twenty-one women from Iowa who attended the thirteenth Congress of the Association for the Advancement of Woman in Des Moines in early October 1885 joined the association and by October 14 had organized as founding members of the Des Moines Woman's Club.[63] The Marshalltown (Iowa) Woman's Club had the same source of inspiration, and by 11 December 1885 had a complete board of officers and a membership organized by the "departments" in which they proposed to work: home and education, philosophy and science, travel, philanthropy, and applied Christianity.[64]

The Century Club was organized in 1888. "A number of progressive women of San Francisco" had already taken some tentative steps toward forming an association, but a visit by Julia Ward Howe in June of that year "crystalized the sentiment . . . into actual fact."[65] Howe was a peripatetic recruiter. The Woman's Club of Evanston, Illinois, came into being in 1890 after she delivered her original 1873 AAW speech "How Can Women Best Associate?" to women in that city.[66] Jane Croly was another effective organizer. After her visit to Atlanta, where she addressed "fifty of the leading ladies" on the advantages of club organization and was accompanied by Estelle M. Merrill of Cambridge, Massachusetts, who spoke about the work of the Cantabrigia Club, the Atlanta Woman's Club was born.[67] In the autumn of 1882, a member of the Lynn (Massachusetts) Woman's Club, Mrs. F. G. Keen, visited Skowhegan, Maine. "The club life of women was then hardly known in Maine, but Mrs. B. F. Eaton becoming interested in Mrs. Keen's description of the work, of the broader outlook upon life, and the intellectual companionship, invited some of the progressive and intelligent women of the town to her home to meet with Mrs. Keen and discuss the subject."[68] The Skowhegan Woman's Club began meeting in November of that year. Two women residents of Thomaston, Maine, were guests at a meeting of the Travellers' Club of Portland and later at field day exercises of the Portland Literary Union. They returned home to found Great Expectations, a club devoted to the study of English literature and history up to the Victorian era.[69]

Women often took their clubs with them when they moved. The name of the Social Science Club of Terrell, Texas, had nothing to do with its purpose. One of its founders had belonged to the Social Science Club of Kansas, and the Texans adopted the name along with the organizing principle, although they proposed to study English and American art, history, and literature.[70] The active and relatively independent Sorosis members were especially productive seed sowers. Abby M. Fuller, a physician, who had been a member of the New York club, founded the Woman's Club of Ellsworth, Maine, after she moved north.[71] The Nantucket Sorosis resulted from mitosis. First organized as a branch of the New York club by Rebecca Morse, who had moved to the island,[72] the club soon established its independence as difficulty in rapid communication in the early 1870s made coordination unwieldy.[73]

"Daughter" clubs were born in imitation of their elders. Often founded by daughters of women in the "mother" club, the clubs rounded out their membership with younger friends and acquaintances. In some instances the clubs were totally separate, as was the Saturday Morning Club, founded by Maud and Eliza Howe, from the New England Women's Club, in which their mother, Julia Ward Howe, was a leading force.[74] The Mary-Martha Club of Muncie,

Indiana, sponsored a daughters' "contingent" with no specific name of its own.[75] The more typical relationship was that of the Young Ladies' Art Class of Decatur, Illinois, to the Decatur Art Class, which enrolled many of their mothers. While the younger group established its own identity, programs, and tone, the subject of study was the same in both clubs, and they often enjoyed joint projects and anniversary celebrations.[76]

In one instance, at least, a study club was founded by fiat; it accompanied the building of the Panama Canal. After yellow fever had been controlled and the men employed in building the canal were able to move their families to the isthmus, morale appeared to worsen rather than improve as the government had expected. Sent by the National Civic Association to look into labor conditions in the Canal Zone, Gertrude Beeks diagnosed one of the primary causes of discontent: the women were lonely and lacked intellectual and cultural stimulation. Responding to Beeks's recommendation that a women's club be established, the government sent Helen V. Boswell to Panama in 1907 with that mandate, and the Cristobal Woman's Club was founded. Because the needs of its members were somewhat different from those of women in the States, social activities played a greater part, but not to the exclusion of study. Although outside speakers (often prominent men passing through) frequently took the place of members' papers, the study of Shakespeare and the production of his plays were the focus of more than one year's program.[77]

Beginning in the 1890s women's magazines began reporting on and extolling women's clubs, and newspapers began listing their activities. When members of the newly formed Milwaukee Club read about the Saturday Morning Club in the *Boston Post* and decided that the aims and composition of the two clubs were similar, they wrote to Boston, asking for a copy of the previous year's discussions and lectures. The information was sent "together with a letter expressive of friendly feeling on the part of the Saturday Morning Club."[78] *Harper's Bazaar* shortly after the turn of the century urged all women, but especially those "in the country," to avail themselves of the "civilizing influence" of a women's club.[79]

Not only was the impetus for the founding of Sorosis different from that of most clubs, the nature of the motivating event, exclusion of women from the Dickens dinner, gave Sorosis a decidedly, if low-key, feminist cast that was absent from most other clubs. Reading over club purposes as set forth in their constitutions, one would be hard pressed to find gender-specific goals. The charge was simply education. A portrait of Lilian C. Streeter, founder of the New Hampshire Federation of Women's Clubs, serves as a frontispiece to a volume of the history of that organization and suggests its aims and tone. She is an imposing figure, seated stately and without smile. Against a dark background she wears a black, elegantly severe garment resembling an academic robe. Two shafts of light in the portrait pick up a small graceful band of the richly brocaded cream-colored gown she wears underneath the robe and the book she holds in her hand.[80]

Although the membership of the New England Women's Club, founded in Boston in the same year as Sorosis, comprised ardent reformers and fewer career and literary women than did Sorosis, its mandate was to facilitate learning. Caroline M. Severance, Abby W. May, Mary A. Livermore (all of whom had had significant responsibilities in the Union's Sanitary Commission during the Civil War), Julia Ward Howe, Ednah D. Cheney, Lucy Stone, and Elizabeth Peabody worked for their causes *outside* the New England Women's Club, whose purpose was "to establish and maintain a place for social meeting and for the prosecution of literary, scientific, and artistic purposes."[81] Even when the New England Women's Club took active measures on behalf of women, they were generally in aid of education: the establishment of a horticultural school for women; the donation of a piece of apparatus to the Massachusetts Institute of Technology (as soon as women were admitted); scholarships for women at Boston University and Vassar College.[82]

The educational aims of study clubs ran the gamut from the breadth of the mission statement of today's liberal arts college to the single objective of one course. In the preamble to its constitution, the Woman's Club of Greencastle, Indiana, announced its reason for being: "With a desire to extend our knowledge by study, to investigate for ourselves the leading questions of the day and to attain and enjoy a higher intellectual, social, and moral culture, we . . . do constitute ourselves a society."[83] The Hawthorne Club of Galesburg, Illinois, was organized "for literary study." Its intention, wrote its secretary to Jane Croly, was well expressed in the words of Ralph Waldo Emerson: "'The use of literature is to afford us a platform whence we may command a view of our present life, a purchase by which we may move it. We fill ourselves with ancient learning, install ourselves the best we can in Greek, in Roman houses, only that we may wiselier see French, English, and American houses and modes of living.'"[84] More succinctly, the Nineteenth Century Club of Northampton, Massachusetts, stated its purpose as "mutual improvement and conscientious study."[85] The Monday Afternoon Club of Dubuque, Iowa, was "essentially a study club, with the object of gaining that which all well-directed study gives when aimed at—the apprehension of truth."[86] The study club, wrote Croly, "proved a means for the acquisition of knowledge, the training of power; and the working of a spirit of human solidarity, a comprehension of the continuity of life: its universal character and interdependence."[87]

At the other extreme was the club of narrow focus. The Lewiston and Auburn (Maine) Parliamentary Club with a membership of twenty-four declared that "the sole work of the club has been the study of parliamentary law and usages, supplemented by readings from Bryce's 'Commonwealth.'"[88] The Clef of Lewiston, Maine, organized "as a strictly musical club, having for its object the study of ancient and modern composers, with selections for practice, both vocal and instrumental, at each meeting."[89] The Portia Club of San Francisco included several women lawyers who acted as teachers of the majority who were lay women interested in law and government.[90] "To interest members in Robert Browning's poems, hoping thus to promote a higher culture" was the object of the Browning Club of Somerville, Massachusetts.[91] The Heliades of Chicago was inspired by the interests of its president: "I have long wished to make the world a study, to take every country and learn its geography, history, and present life, so that I can feel at home in it. This can best be done in a class, and it means work. Are you ready to undertake it?"[92] The members accepted her challenge and traveled with the sun, "seeing all that he sees, of waters, lands, and peoples, [beginning with] New Zealand at 180 degrees longitude to 170 latitude."[93]

The Beecher Club of Portland, Maine, devoted itself to studying the theory of evolution after hearing a series of talks on the subject by Miss A. M. Beecher, niece of the Reverend Henry Ward Beecher. The secretary reported to Jane Croly that "although the members of the Beecher Club are not all evolutionists, the study has cured many of superstitions, and broadened their mental outlook."[94] Clubs devoted to the study of Shakespeare were common: Minneapolis; Woonsocket, Rhode Island; Dallas; Cambridge, Massachusetts; Bath, Maine; and Barnesville, Georgia, were a few of the host cities.

However limited their original focus had been, most clubs expanded their inquiry over time. The Reading Club of Auburn, Maine, started as a Browning club; after the first year it included the study of several related authors and finally made literature in general the basis of its work.[95] The Whittier and Waverley clubs of Orono, Maine, followed the same expansion, as did the Reading Club of Auburn, Maine.[96] The Clio Club of Carroll, Iowa, took for its curriculum the study of the states of America in order of their admission to the union. After "exhaustive investigation," the club broadened its scope to include other countries and "some interesting comparative work."[97]

A club without an improving purpose was the exception, so much so that when the Mayflower Club of Cambridge, Massachusetts, declared that it met only for "rest, food, and congenial social contacts," the *Boston Transcript* of 3 May 1893 took note:

> The experiment of a woman's club for club reasons only will be watched by people of a sociological turn of mind. The members of the Mayflower Club say frankly that they have no "object"; they wish it to be distinctly understood that they have no literary, scientific, or even social reason for being, except their own sweet will to have a club that has no cause. For nearly a quarter of a century Boston has been beset with women's clubs of varying charm and usefulness, organized in fervent spirit and for various purposes. These societies have grown and flourished and have long ago passed through those early stages of development where the Puritan passion for visible usefulness was expressed by crochet work, those eras when a woman could scarcely listen conscience free to a Dante reading or a paper on reincarnation without having her fingers employed with needlework while her mind reached after ideas.
>
> Knitting work has vanished even from suburban fingers and even at Symphony rehearsals. And now lo! in

the fullness of time, the idea of life for the sake of life, taking no account of even mental endeavor, blossoms and the Mayflower Club is opened. Will it succeed? Are women as clubable by training and heredity as men are by instinct?[98]

Most groups of women ascertained their purpose for organizing before they decided on a name. Sorosis was not atypical in the care it took in choosing the title by which it would be known to the public. Although the derivation of the word *club* from the German *kleben* ("to adhere") and the Anglo-Saxon *clyppan* ("to embrace") had no sinister roots, it had developed connotations with which the conservative True Woman felt uncomfortable. The Ossoli Circle of Knoxville, Tennessee, while devoted to the study of that "advanced" woman thinker Margaret Fuller Ossoli, was not so forward-reaching in selecting its name in 1884: "In so conservative a city the idea of a society exclusively for women was decidedly an advanced step. 'Club' was not to be thought of and no one dared propose the name. Friends smiled incredulously, assured that the new fancy would be short-lived."[99] Like Sorosis, Fortnightly of Chicago, founded in 1873, solved the problem of its name by eliminating the noun after one husband had objected that *club* was "a masculine label."[100] The New England Women's Club, on the other hand, deliberately chose *club* to indicate a break with tradition; it did not want to be associated with good-works societies.[101]

It was not just the early clubs that trod gingerly. The Norway Lakes (Maine) Woman's Club was started in 1895. "It was at first called 'Norway Lakes Ladies' Social Circle,' in deference to the fears that 'Club' was too bold and too pronounced. The name was conceded by the more modern and progressive element, as it hoped to make it a neighborhood enterprise, in which all who desired an opportunity for improvement might unite."[102] Before long, "ladies' social circle" would come full circle and take on a derisive connotation. Even after the General Federation of Women's Clubs had been in existence ten years, the term *club* was a prickly one, not so much for its quality of "sounding advanced beyond gentility"[103] but because it suggested a lack of seriousness:

The name of the organization [General Federation of Women's Clubs] is admitted by all to be an unfortunate one since the word "club" as applied to a body of individuals has come to mean . . . an organization which exists largely for purposes of entertainment and amusement. The term as applied to men's clubs, whist clubs, country clubs . . . is in no wise applicable in the same sense to woman's clubs. These exist not at all for entertainment, but rather for the mental, moral and social improvement of the members. . . . The woman's club . . . is neither constructive nor destructive . . . it exists neither to inaugurate some notable reform nor demolish an existing evil. The woman's club has no policy, no creed.[104]

While a number of clubs called their group a *society, circle, association,* or *guild,* some chose the term *class,* leaving no doubt about the seriousness of purpose, except perhaps for the A.B.C. Klass of Deering, Maine.[105] From today's perspective, the use of *class* suggests rather poignant wishful thinking, an emulation of the college classes out of reach of most club women.

Club names ran the gamut of inventiveness from the prosaic to the fanciful. The later and larger clubs generally chose the generic Woman's Club, a term perhaps too unmistakable for the earlier groups, which chose genderless titles. The more descriptive names often called attention to the object of their study: the Nineteenth Century History Class of Atlanta, the Ruskin Art Club of Los Angeles, the Fern Club of Deering, Maine.[106] Some clubs honored their geography: the Methebesec of Rockland, Maine, used the original Indian name for a local mountain.[107] Others celebrated "godmothers" or founders: the McRae of Muncie, Indiana, saluted Emma M. McRae, an English professor at Purdue, a "scholarly woman whose influence is still felt in Muncie."[108] The women of the May family of Lewiston, Maine, clearly had a field day choosing the name of their club, the Mayfield, whose founding officers were Ada May Carter, president; Ellen J. May, vice-president; Ellen May Wheelock, treasurer; Kate May Andrews, secretary; and Julia Harris May, club poet.[109] The Wednesday Club of Jacksonville, Illinois, and the Fortnightly Literary Club of Indianapolis followed a common practice of naming by meeting day schedule.[110] Always to be found among the more businesslike titles were the whimsical. Over the Teacups of Indianapolis immortalized the occasion of its founding, a tea, the invitation to which bore these words:

"To be or not to be"—a club,
"That's the question." [111]

The Mustard Seed of Brunswick, Maine, was, of course, a small club, limiting membership to the original twelve. [112] The Forthian Club of Somerville, Massachusetts, derived its name from the Old English word *for,* meaning "to advance, to progress." [113] The Phalo Club of New York City used an acronym denoting the scope of its study—philosophy, history, art, literature, and oratory; [114] later, when the members discovered that *phalo* was a Greek word meaning "superiority," they "hoped that it might prove significant" and inscribed it on the helmet of Athena as their badge. [115]

The process of public organization was unfamiliar to most women. Missionary societies were run by men; women's rights leaders were learning slowly through trial and error. The Sanitary Commission had given its women leaders the opportunity to develop and practice management and organizational skills, but the rank and file, as usual, had merely carried out orders from above. The speech "How Can Women Best Associate?" given by Julia Ward Howe before the First Woman's Congress was a primer, almost a step-by-step manual, in the methods of establishing a club. Howe's audience was not only the unsophisticated True Woman (although for twenty years Howe continued to deliver the same speech across the country to that constituency); it included Catharine E. Beecher, Elizabeth C. Stanton, Maria Mitchell, Caroline M. Severance, the Reverend Antoinette B. Blackwell, and Dr. Mary E. Jacobi. Nevertheless, Howe delineated and defined in elementary terms a constitution and by-laws; officers and executive committees, their duties and reporting lines; membership fees; and appropriate meeting places. [116]

However unfamiliar women may have been with parliamentary procedure, they soon wore it like a mantle. Individual club histories painstakingly and lavishly detail the drawing up of each organization's constitution. Understandably so. A constitution announced solidarity and proclaimed legitimacy in the public sphere. It suggested a serious and important purpose. It provided the club with a rational and legal means of operation easily recognized and respected, one which would hardly harbor subversives. It imparted an outward sense of order on an endeavor whose substance and outer limits were not yet clear even to its participants. That women eagerly employed parliamentary procedure is not surprising. It was analogous to their daily routine—keeping their house in order. Most women were uncomfortable with the use of power except in the family arena where they were expected to wield control over domestic details and to preserve household harmony. As they met in each other's parlors, surrounded by familiar symbols of family life in which they each played a strong and unquestioned role, they found in Robert's Rules of Order a vehicle through whose guise they could extend the leadership traits they had unconsciously developed in their own homes.

Officers in most clubs consisted of the usual four, elected through annual balloting. In a number of clubs, however, like the early Minerva of New Harmony, Indiana, officers were more frequently rotated, often alphabetically, through the membership to give executive experience to even the most retiring woman. The Goldenrod Club of Nantucket elected its president and secretary to serve for four successive meetings, none being eligible for reelection. "The motive in this is to give each member a training in the work of presiding and taking notes."[117] The practice may also have reflected an internalization of the stricture of True Womanhood against competition or, at the other end, a rejection of male hierarchical forms. Quite clearly it was, in addition, an attempt at inclusiveness, an ideal much expounded by club leaders. Julia Ward Howe had urged women as a first principle of club organization "to draw the circle so that it shall not strengthen the divisions of society already existing, sundering rich from poor, fashionable from unfashionable, learned from simple."[118] The tenet was incorporated into a number of club constitutions. One aim of the Woman's Club of Santa Barbara was "to bring the narrow cliques of a small town into friendly and intelligent relation, and by regular meetings and mutual interest in some intellectual work cultivate friendships of . . . value."[119] Most clubs that experimented initially with frequent rotation of officers suffered, as did Sorosis, from the lack of a unified and coherent leadership vision, especially necessary in formative days, and they eventually adopted yearly elections.

Almost all clubs began by limiting the number of members. This practice appears less exclusionary than practical. If each member was expected to participate at each meeting, even a membership of twenty-five was a bit unwieldy; and most clubs wanted to hold the meetings in members' homes. The rigorous, determined insistence on small size suggests some subliminal factors at work as well. Women were not used to an audience or to playing an active role in a nonfamilial group. And, on a larger scale, they were witnesses to explosive growth and unsettling change throughout the country. A small, fixed circle of acquaintances satisfied a number of needs at once. Clubs which held tightly to their membership limit established a waiting list containing names submitted to the club by current members. "The membership limit [of the Cambridge Club of Brooklyn] is 50, with an impatient waiting list, whose complaint is that the members of Cambridge never die or resign."[120] Most often the applicant needed a unanimous vote of approval before she could be added to the waiting list and admitted to the club when a vacancy occurred. In a number of instances women impatient of waiting formed their own clubs; such was, in part, the origin of the Decatur (Illinois) Woman's Club. Clubs without a membership limit (mainly city clubs) quickly became "department clubs," clubs within a club, where a member confined her work to one section (art, philosophy, Shakespeare, and the like).

The succession of meeting places over the years of the Woman's Club of El Paso, Texas, represents a pattern frequently found among study clubs. Organized in 1891, the club met first in the homes of its members. As its numbers grew beyond fifteen in 1898, meetings were moved to a member's private library room in a commercial building and then to the rectory of the Episcopal Church. Finally, in 1909, the club built its own quarters.[121]

For both philosophical and practical reasons, most clubs did not follow the lead of Sorosis, which held its meetings in Delmonico's, a public restaurant, where a woman alone would not venture. Study clubs grew out of gatherings of women in their homes, where women felt most comfortable and inconspicuous, and that is where most of them remained. A majority of clubs limited their membership to twenty-five for beyond that, even in more commodious days, public quarters had to be sought. Clubs with larger memberships often met in church halls and in libraries, where the presence of women was not considered out of place. Later, clubs which outgrew these accommodations rented rooms in public buildings. The Forthian Club of Somerville, Massachusetts, rented a meeting room in a local hotel; the management provided hot water, the officers supplied tea, and each member brought her own cup, saucer, and spoon.[122]

Club houses were the exception, but where they existed, their symbolic importance to club members was striking, members' feelings for their "home" akin to those of alumnae for the Gothic towers of their alma maters and, perhaps, to the passionate pleading of Virginia Woolf for "a room of one's own." Club houses ranged in size from the tiny one-room cottage of Friends in Council of Quincy, Illinois, which housed six hundred volumes and mandated a membership limit of forty,[123] to the imposing Peoria Woman's Club building with its library, committee rooms, dining room, kitchen, and auditorium seating five hundred.[124] Clubs which erected buildings describe at length and in great detail the process and the product. The endeavor, which often involved the bold act of forming a stock company composed only of women, brought women into the public domain decorously and in the most natural way—through building a home. Although the Decatur (Illinois) Woman's Club rented "for business purposes" the basement and first two floors of its building, completed in 1890, the club rooms on the third and fourth floors were "homelike and elegant" with closets "filled with tasteful china and linen."[125]

In addition to the academic discipline of regularly scheduled class meetings, required attendance, and assignments to be completed at home, clubs adopted many of the trappings of women's colleges. Some, like the Century Club of San Francisco, sang their club song with member-written lyrics and music on anniversary occasions.[126] Others renewed club loyalty with a pledge at the start of each meeting: "I consider my membership in the Woman's Club of La Grange (Illinois) a helpful and ennobling factor in my life; and pledge my support and loyalty to the club, its work and its reputation."[127] Clubs had official colors and flowers. Often their mottoes were in Latin: the Peoria Woman's Club selected "dux femina facti" from Virgil's *Aeneid,* and "vis unita fortior" was the motto of the Chicago Culture Club.[128] Insignia ranged from simple ribbons in club colors to elaborate badges. The Rhode Island Woman's Club badge, designed by a member, was made of oxidized silver: "From a bar is suspended by a ribbon, old gold in color, a metal. . . . The design is a pair of scales, having in one a distaff and in the other a book, a palette, and a musical instrument. As the scales are perfectly balanced, it typifies the principle that the club together with the home, tends to make the perfectly developed woman."[129] Titles were conferred. Caroline M. Severance, first president of the Friday Morning Club of Los Angeles, became president emeritus upon her retirement,[130] and most clubs included a few honorary members (not infrequently, Jane Croly).

Traditions developed quickly. However spartan club meetings might be throughout the year, anniversary days were celebrated lavishly, most often with luncheon or dinner banquets and some form of entertainment. An annual memorial day was commonplace: for the Peoria Woman's Club, reported its secretary, it was a day "given to special remembrance of club members who have gone before—a day of loving, tender recollection, not gloom."[131]

Seldom, even in the midst of celebration, was the educational purpose of the club forgotten. During May of each year the Ebell Society of Oakland, California, held its rose day: "A paper is given upon the rose and its family, and a fine display of choice roses of many varieties turns the beautiful assembly room into a veritable rose garden. *But the purpose of the club is not even secondarily social; it is seriously studious*" [emphasis added].[132]

Like the college year, the club year generally ran from September through May. Monday through Saturday, weekly or biweekly, morning or afternoon, the clubs met. A few associations of working women, predominantly teachers, met at night, but evening meetings demanded a measure of independence that most club women found difficult to muster. "I feel rather 'streaked' to be seen coming to the depot alone and coming out alone at nine o'clock," confided Harriet J. Robinson to her diary in 1869 after a New England Women's Club meeting.[133] Almost invariably, meetings lasted two hours, a brief business session preceding the study program. As did most clubs, the Woman's Club of El Paso fined members for unexcused absences; three consecutive derelictions resulted in expulsion from the organization.[134] Membership fees were small, often one dollar a year to cover the costs of printing the program. While fees and fines underlined the serious purpose of the club and imparted a sense of legitimacy, they were kept at the break-even point to avoid any taint of unwomanly commercial venture or of socioeconomic exclusion.

By the 1890s and with the founding of the General Federation of Women's Clubs, newspapers began reporting on women's club activities, but until then most clubs shunned publicity. "The club is a larger home, and we wish to have the immunities and defenses of home; therefore we do not wish the public present, even by its attorney, the reporter," declared Julia Ward Howe.[135] Public criticism of "strong-minded women" was harsh, and educational endeavor, far from absolving one of untoward aspirations, might be suspect: Lucy Stone and Antoinette Brown had to meet secretly at Oberlin College to form a debating and speaking society.[136] For fear of censure, many members refused to have their names listed in an official register or directory.[137] It was not only fear, however, that drew women to the image of leaven with which they often described themselves—"working like silent leaven" were Elizabeth Agassiz's words.[138] Women had not been taught individualism; rather they had been taught selflessness, the living of a half life through others. Through inconspicuous club life, women could take a step outside while still clothed in anonymity.[139]

The membership of study clubs, whether limited to twenty, as was that of the Decatur (Illinois) Art Class, or to three hundred, as in the Chicago Woman's Club,[140] was remarkably homogeneous. A slice down the middle of each club reveals essentially the same ingredients. Club women came from the comfortable middle class: "The general air was one of modest prosperity," wrote an observer at an early Federation convention.[141] Chronicler Mary I. Wood described her compatriots as "a great throng of earnest, eager women who are neither forced by the exigencies of their fortune to add to the wage-earning capacity of their families nor are they willing to give themselves up to a life of personal indulgence." They were women well aware, she continued, that with leisure came responsibility.[142] In an attempt to solicit advertisers for her short-lived women's club magazine, Helen M. Winslow wrote: "The quality of our circulation is above all rivalry—because it is exclusively limited to influential women of brains in easy financial circumstances."[143] The amount of "ease" enjoyed by club women varied somewhat, but certainly working-class women were precluded from membership, as were those at the other end of the economic scale. Although few married working-class women were employed outside the home, (four percent of women wage earners,[144]) they did not have the leisure afforded middle-class women through household conveniences such as hot running water and through hired help. The names of upper-class women, the socially elite, especially in the East, were also seldom found on study-club rolls. Maria Mitchell cited one reason for their absence in her speech before the First Woman's Congress in 1873: "Painful as it may be to admit it, we have very few thoroughly educated women. Public sentiment does not yet require learning in women, and 'society' is decidedly opposed to it."[145] In the West and Midwest, with a less entrenched social establishment, the case was not so clear-cut. There, "'prominent clubwoman' was often synonymous with 'social leader.'"[146] The speeches of leaders in the study-club movement and the constitutions of many of the clubs themselves are heavy with the rhetoric of democracy:

> The study club affords equal and independent terms of membership; every member being allowed to find or make her own place, regardless of church affiliation or social prominence. The club is a common center where there is a social, natural, and equal division of interests . . . ; character, not social position or wealth, is the basis of club aristocracy.[147]

Within the club, their ideals ring true—performance was what counted—but especially in the small clubs, which were by far the majority, the waiting list for admission scarcely ever contained a name not known to all members. To be sure, there were exceptions to homogeneity. Lemoore, California, in 1884 was a town of six hundred inhabitants in a county as large as Connecticut and Rhode Island combined. The club there consisted of "farmers' wives, and the wives of professional and business men in a scattered community. They are widely separated from each other, do their own work, and often have to drive [by wagon or carriage] several miles to reach their club. Frequently they bring a baby with them."[148] Then, too, even within the homogeneity of "circumstances," there existed diversities that often introduced heretofore sheltered women to new elements: women of different denominations and political parties and occasionally self-supporting women (mainly teachers and professional women).

The membership of study clubs was predominantly white, Anglo-Saxon, and Protestant. Although a number of clubs voted, as did the Chicago Woman's Club in 1895, "that no one can be excluded from membership on race or color lines,"[149] black women generally formed their own organizations, which more often had religious and benevolent purposes. The Alpha Home Association, founded in Indiana in 1883, was just such a black woman's organization, dedicated to helping the sick, poor, and aged.[150] Because the Catholic church strongly advocated home as women's "proper sphere," Catholic women seldom broadened their affiliations beyond those of the parish.[151]

Generally study-club women were married and, like Sorosis members, in their forties and fifties. Of the twenty-four charter members of Fortnightly in Chicago, only three were single;[152] of the presidents and recording secretaries of the member clubs of the General Federation of Women's Clubs for 1893–94, seventy-eight percent were married.[153] The majority were mothers: the Cosmos Club of Lewiston, Maine, reported that ninety-five percent of its members "are mothers and housekeepers,"[154] and sixty percent of all members of the Massachusetts State Federation of Women's Clubs in 1900 were mothers.[155] For the most part these women joined a club only after their children were grown or nearly so. It was not only the ethic of True Womanhood that kept club women at home during their twenties and thirties. The rigors of childbirth and childrearing were real. Activists before their children were born and after they were out of childhood, Lucy Stone and Antoinette B. Blackwell went into "retirement" during the intervening years.[156]

The pages of Croly's *History* carry not a hint of the apology or self-consciousness that the term "middle age" has so often evoked in later years. These were women, declared Mary I. Wood, "who have already entered upon the serious work of life."[157] The Wintergreen Club of Boston admitted no one under the age of fifty, and the club was composed mainly of presidents and vice-presidents of other local clubs. In tribute to the members, a young guest wrote:

> Those dear old, cheery old, Wintergreen girls!
> Still steadfastly playing their parts;
> They stood by the cradle when we were not—
> Yet today they have evergreen hearts.[158]

"Generally middle aged, she is gradually becoming younger"[159] was meant as a metaphorical description of club women in 1892 when it was written, but it gained literal truth as the movement grew. Although some young women joined their mothers' clubs, most formed their own. The Panvosac Club of Skowhegan, Maine, no doubt elicited smiles when it was organized in 1883 "by little girls of ten or twelve years" who derived the name from the "Sophie May" stories in which Skowhegan was fictionalized as Panvosac. Nevertheless, the club was still going strong fifteen years later with its original membership limit of fourteen. The members, "who have now become women—most of them married—of thirty, more or less," continued their study of history and literature.[160] The Goldenrod Club of Nantucket described itself as "a literary and debating society of young girls"; the Waverley Club of Orono, Maine, required that its members be "young unmarried ladies"; the Athena Club of Dorchester, Massachusetts, was known as the "bachelormaids'" club.[161]

The Saturday Morning Club of Boston, while not wholly typical, represents a kind of "young ladies' club" that warrants a closer look. A delightful introduction to the club is the following newspaper article, headlined "Feminine Philosophers—Mount Vernon Street on Saturday Morning," which appeared in the *Boston Post* in 1871:

> Clubs are on the increase. Whether Bostonians are essentially a clubable people, whether there is a magic in east winds tending to develop that peculiar quality, or whether it is a mania run mad, certain it is that new clubs are constantly springing into existence. . . . The latest of these—and by no means the least important— is the Young Ladies' Club that meets every Saturday morning, and whose members devote themselves not to the discussion of beaux . . . nor the perplexed question of Spring costumes, after the manner of girls generally; but to listen to essays and talks from the distinguished men and women who are either in Boston or a part of it, and afterwards to discuss the questions that the essays and talks may suggest, with seriousness and earnestness. . . . Mount Vernon Street is the headquarters of these youthful metaphysicians, embryo reformers, and predestined philosophers. They are students of Plato rather than Demorest, more interested in Kant than "Die Wodenwelt," talking of science when their sisters of

Gotham would talk of clothes. . . . Worthy daughters of Boston are they, following the lead of their mothers and elder sisters of the Woman's Club. . . . Emerson, who ought to be a good authority on audiences, says they are keenest in perception, the most appreciative of good things, of any audience he ever spoke before, and after reading a paper for them one morning, and finding them so quickly responsive, he begged the privilege of reading his new papers to them before they were read elsewhere because he wanted to test them by the effect they had on these girls . . . ; ever since there has been an idea very prevalent among them of transferring the title of "Brain Club" from the Woman's Club to their own. . . . Very few of these girls have reached their twenties. . . . Alcott has talked to them about Plato and the dialectic. . . . Collyer came to them . . . bringing the strength and breadth of Western prairies. . . . Not all days are devoted to essays; every alternate Saturday is left open for a discussion of the subject introduced the week previous. "We don't like to express ourselves before those people who talk to us," said one girl shyly: "our ideas are too crude and we don't like to be criticized, and, besides, some of the girls won't talk." . . . One of the leading spirits of the Club is Miss Abbie L. Alger. . . . Miss Alger published, a short time ago, a very fine translation of Von Wasielivski's *Life of Robert Schumann*, which has been very successful, and is an important addition to the musical literature of the day. . . . There are other members of the Club who will one day achieve success in literature, and they are laying the foundation for their future in this novel and attractive Saturday Club.[162]

As the article suggests, the club was founded in the home of Julia Ward Howe at 28 Mount Vernon Street on Boston's Beacon Hill by Howe's two teenage daughters. The purpose of the society, similar to that of the New England Women's Club of which the girls' mother had been a founder in 1868, was "to promote culture and social intercourse."[163] The girls did, in fact, suggest Junior Brain Club for a name as well as Boston Association for Intellectual Improvement; both were vetoed by Mrs. Howe as "too pretentious."[164] The club met weekly at members' homes; addresses recorded in the minutes—Louisburg Square, Beacon, Pinckney, Chestnut, and Marlborough streets—suggest their Brahmin connections. By 1874 with an average attendance of forty-four and a new membership limit of seventy, the club began renting "Mr. Hooper's school room, 69 Pinckney Street" for five dollars per meeting.[165] The club pin depicted an open book. By-laws stipulated the usual fines (ten cents for tardiness, five cents for absence) and inducements to regular attendance ("Two wilful absences in two months shall deprive a person of membership"). *All* outsiders were excluded on discussion days, when the members themselves performed; on lecture days the hostess might invite three friends, the lecturer two, and a member might bring a friend staying with her on lecture day if she had notified the president of her intention beforehand. Simple parliamentary practice was spelled out: "Should two members claim the floor at one time, the chairman will decide which shall have the priority."[166]

The program format of the Saturday Morning Club differed substantially from that of most other study clubs, outside lecturers alternating with club discussion of the topic that had been introduced at a previous meeting. In the early days discussion was spontaneous and free-form, often taking the line of least resistance. In December 1871 two lecturers followed in succession without the usual intervening discussion day: Mr. J. W. Champney read a paper on the Passion Play at Oberammergau, and Mr. J. H. Skinner spoke on "The Education of English Girls." The minutes of the following meeting are candid: "It was moved and seconded that as very few of the young ladies thoroughly understood the Passion Play, the meeting should be given to the discussion of Mr. Skinner's lecture on 'The Girls of the Period.'"[167] Even the redoubtable Julia Ward Howe, who was an honorary member, could not always kindle an intellectual fire. After a lecture by Professor T. Sterry Hunt on "The Nebular Hypothesis," Mrs. Howe led the discussion. Her opening remarks were followed by "dead silence," and then the discussion "drifted away into the regions of theology."[168]

It was not lack of ambition or serious purpose that produced discussion "drift." With experience (and perhaps frustration), passivity and lack of self-confidence began to disappear. In 1874 "the President Miss Grey made an earnest appeal for better work." By imposing something like a classroom discipline on themselves, the members produced more focused work. The by-laws were altered. Subjects for discussion, not necessarily linked with previous lectures, were given out two weeks in advance; four members (appointees if not enough volunteered) prepared papers on the topic not to exceed seven minutes each; two members were responsible for leading the discussion. A later change in by-laws gave more lead time for preparation and stipulated that the six discussion volunteers meet at least two weeks before their appointed day. They were to choose a leader, who would assign subtopics, "call as many meetings as may be desirable, and invite the President to attend any or all of these meetings." Without stick or carrot, however, classroom rigor could not be maintained; if a volunteer begged off reading her paper, the president would do so, preserving the writer's anonymity.[169] Some discussion topics enabled members to improvise if they chose: "Is Character Independent of Circumstances or the Result of Them?" could easily be covered by personal anecdote or literary recollection. Many, however, demanded some sort of "research": "How Far Were the Writings of Milton Influenced by the Times in Which He Lived?" "How Have the Ancient and Modern Poets Differed from Each Other in the Treatment of Nature?" "A Comparison Between the Ancient and Modern Drama in the Matter of Simplicity and Elaboration of Stage Setting."[170]

Emerson and "The Nebular Hypothesis" were not exceptions among the club's programs; neither medium nor message was lightweight. The only topics barred were "religion, suffrage, and politics." Lecturers were unpaid: "For the simple dole of a ride and a flower / They gladly our knowledge extend" was part of a club tribute in rhyme written by member Ada T. Cushing.[171] Richard H. Dana, Oliver Wendell Holmes, Sarah Orne Jewett, Alice F. Palmer, Edward Everett Hale, Henry James, Alice Longfellow, and Vida Scudder lectured before the club. In the 1880s the club, like the Annex (later Radcliffe College) in Cambridge, benefited from Harvard faculty: George T. Baker, Charles T. Copeland, John C. Ropes, Ernest Fenollosa, and Harvard President Charles W. Eliot are listed in the minutes.[172]

The young club members had a larger pool of women lecturers to choose from than did clubs in most other locations, but they heard only a few. Likewise, few discussions touched on women's issues, none before 1873. The progression after that year, while too few in number to lead us to conclusions, is nevertheless interesting. Selected weekly program topics included the following:

1874   The Weak Points of a Girl's Education.

1875   To What Extent Has a Girl a Right To Work Out Her Own Life?

1876   (1) Should Women Interest Themselves in Politics?
       (2) Men's Women and Women's Women.

1878   (1) Do American Women Give Enough Attention to Their Own Physical Development? Boston Girls Especially.
       (2) To What Extent Ought We to Resist the Rule of Fashion in Dress?

1879   Have the Recent Novels of James and Howells Presented the Character of American Women in a True Light?

1880   What Are the Advantages and Disadvantages of a Professional Life for Women?

1884   The Conflicting Claims of Home Duties and Duties in the World at Large.[173]

The change in members' word choice from *girls* to *women* and in perspective from one girl's education to the world at large suggests, along with maturation, a growing consciousness of their gender and its roles.

In the 1890s, lecturers and discussions on women's higher education began to appear. Vida Scudder of Wellesley College described the college settlement house movement; Alice F. Palmer, Wellesley's president, spoke on "Recent Educational Methods"; James C. Ropes examined the adaptation of English university extension to American needs; Harvard's Charles W. Eliot gave "The Presidential Aspect of the Education of Women in Universities." Members' discussion included "How Can We Best Carry Out the Higher Education of Our Women?" and "What Is the Effect of College Training Upon Women?"[174]

However intellectual the members considered themselves by comparison with their peers, their work was not profound, especially lacking any unified, systematic progression. The summary of an early discussion suggests the unsophisticated level of thought:

> The discussion on Elizabeth of England and Mary Stuart was opened by Mrs. Howe, who thought that the character of each should be considered. The part Mary did, or did not take in the murder of Darnley was discussed; Elizabeth's part in Mary's execution and in the executions of many of her ministery [sic]. The general opinion seemed to be that Mary was the weaker but more fascinating woman and Elizabeth more cruel, ambitious, vain while as a sovereign she was stronger and wiser.[175]

The members can be credited more for their effort than for the results. In 1873, for example, reluctant to lose the year's momentum and enthusiastic as always, the young women formed study groups over the summer break. They tackled metaphysics, Dante in English, Dante in the original, art, botany, and cookery.[176] Perhaps for perspective it should be noted here that in the year of its founding, 1871, the Saturday Morning Club preceded by four years the founding of Wellesley and Smith colleges; the former opened with the majority of its enrollment assigned to the preparatory department and the latter, refusing the preparatory function, opened with only a handful of students.

In tone, the Saturday Morning Club was like that of literary societies in women's colleges, its serious purpose intermingled with "clever" entertainment. The final meeting of the year often featured charades, original short stories, song, and self-spoofing poetry. An annual "theatrical" soon became a tradition. One year, inspired by Charles T. Copeland's lecture on *Antigone*, the club performed it. Another year, "with apologies to J.A.," they presented scenes from *Pride and Prejudice.* Often they wrote their own script, such as *Developments* in 1874, "a play in two acts written expressly for the occasion by members of the S.M.C. and performed by a celebrated troupe of imported artistes." One of the Howe sisters took the role of Miss Regina Sinclair, the heroine. Other dramatis personae were Miss Serathina Whirlgay, Mrs. Lovelorn, Mr. Grosvenor Lovelorn, and Mr. Augustus Lovelorn. Act I was set "in a Bawston Drawing-Room"; Act II "in a Skipmonk Kitchen." In 1885 the "troupe" performed "The Princess,"[177] an adaptation of Tennyson's narrative poem about women's higher education. Behind all the jollity, and giving shape to it, however, was a backbone of intellectual seriousness. In a play written to celebrate the fiftieth anniversary of the club, "Wisdom" speaks:

> Lectures remarkable, and discussions many;
> Study and papers—no escape for any!
> Each would-be member must, however frightened,
> Pass the stern test to prove herself enlightened.[178]

Although mothers and daughters were generally to be found in different clubs, it was spirit more than a divergent outlook that separated them: most club women, whatever their age, were conservative.

> Women are not creators: they are not discoverers: they are not inventors: they are not warriors. The function of man seems to embrace the creative, inventive, exploring, and fighting qualities. But whenever man has entered new fields, either of country or of thought, he has brought woman with him to conserve and preserve the good of the new life. . . . In all times and ages, this high calling of conserver and preserver has belonged almost exclusively to woman.
>
> It is upon this fundamentally true basis that the Woman's Club movement is founded: there was no great scheme of distinct and separate work laid down by founders of the club movement.[179]

The formation of most clubs (Sorosis is an exception) did not represent a startling departure from convention—women had always moved in quiet little circles—but even this slight deviation was taken slowly and at times with trepidation. Harriet J. Robinson (who felt "streaked" appearing on the street at night alone) was elected a member of the New England Women's Club in February 1869. Two weeks later she attended her first meeting and noted in her diary that it was the first time in twenty years that she had spent an evening away from her husband, Tom. At the next meeting Kate Fields read a paper on "Woman as Lecturer." Robinson recorded her reaction to the speaker:

Tom says she would make a good reporter and I think she might but she makes the mistake of most clever women who are ambitious of literary honors. She expects to spring full armed into the arena, ignoring the long season of training which men go through before they can make their mark. I was not pleased with her. If we aim to be equals of men we must be trained . . . disciplined and educated.[180]

It was not until April 1871, two years after she joined the New England Women's Club that Robinson revealed in her diary that she had spoken at a club meeting for the first time.[181] Cautious and conditional though her steps may have been, Robinson nevertheless conceived of women becoming "equals of men," a value clearly evolving in her mind, even if the transformation was unconscious. And she makes clear the link between women and equality—education.

Even had they not encountered opposition, criticism, and satire aimed at their clubs, women knew that they were moving forward. Women's clubs "hold neither the aggressiveness of the suffrage movement nor the limitations of church and charity associations," wrote one observer.[182] While they were ready to acknowledge that they had outgrown the narrowness of benevolent societies, they were not ready to face the public or themselves with a new persona. A participant in the 1889 gathering which led to the General Federation of Women's Clubs recalled the reaction of women at the time. When the Sorosis call came, "suggesting that women might meet in the open and hold public discussions, [it started] a fluttering in the dovecotes. . . . Might we not be chronicled in the daily papers as standing for progressive ideas we did not approve?"[183] While she was learning writing, speaking, and organizing skills that might later lead to her achievement of professional status, the club woman clung to her amateur standing: "As a rule she is pre-eminently a religious woman, and, though gifted with facility in verse and prose, she is seldom a novelist or historian, but is always a good housekeeper."[184] Not surprisingly, study-club women had many of the same characteristics seen today in women entering continuing education programs: a background of traditional mores, anxiety about departure from convention and insistence on conservative goals, and lack of self-confidence compensated for by earnest, dedicated, and unobtrusive hard work.

The conservative nature of the family as an institution was replicated in the study club, and, indeed, family lines tended to run strong in these associations. Sisters, cousins, and in-laws abounded. Of the twenty-five members of the Clionian Society of Vernon, Indiana, seven were Vawters and three Barnums.[185] A member's association with her club often lasted her lifetime. Ten young college alumnae in Brunswick, Maine, started a Shakespeare Club in 1876. Twenty-two years later at the time Croly wrote her *History,* the society had lost one member through death; the rest had carried on.[186] Through their club ties, unrelated women often developed a kind of family loyalty. The Casmian Club of Springfield, Massachusetts, organized in 1877, limited its membership to twenty. By 1898 it had only eleven members: "No effort is made to increase the membership as old members drop out, the club having arrived at that condition of acquaintance where it seems like a family, and hesitates about taking in strangers."[187] And a family affection for their clubs developed along with members' loyalty. On the seventeenth anniversary of the Bloomington (Illinois) History and Art Club in 1896, the secretary recorded simply: "We still love our society."[188] Julia Ward Howe, according to her daughters, often called the New England Women's Club " 'my dear Club,' no other organization brought such a tender ring to her voice."[189]

Some women, especially in larger towns and in cities, belonged to more than one club. These women were often instrumental in founding a new club after some experience in the old. Katherine Merrill, a teacher and an early member of the Indianapolis Woman's Club, organized in 1875, founded the Katherine Merrill Club in that city in 1885. Based on the report of its members, Croly noted that the club "has always been strictly literary in its work and ways. For its members it has been a post-graduate course in literature, more thorough and of finer quality than can be found in many universities."[190] Although the large urban associations like the Indianapolis Woman's Club subdivided themselves into departments to meet members' interests and the aim of active participation and "work," it is doubtful that members felt the press of individual responsibility and productivity that they did in smaller, single-purpose clubs. The motto of the Katherine Merrill Club suggests perhaps the lessons drawn from her club experience: "God had sifted three kingdoms to find the wheat for this planting. Then had sifted the wheat, as the living seed of this nation."[191]

The historians of most study clubs pay special tribute to a dynamic and inspiring founder, such as Jane Croly of Sorosis. Reading circles without such a woman in their midst often record several years of regular meeting before embarking on constitutional organization. The woman who was recognized as "the good genius" of the Century Club of San Francisco was Sarah D. Hamlin, "from the first the moving spirit, the active worker, . . . a woman of broad intelligence and great personal magnetism."[192] The Lemoore (California) Woman's Club acknowledged that "the impetus to organize came in the beginning from the Rev. Sarah Pratt Carr. To her energy and organizing ability the club is largely indebted for its birth."[193] In Gardiner, Maine, the History Class met weekly for eight years at the home of its president, Laura E. Richards. Upon her resignation, the club ceased to meet for a year until some of the former members convened and reorganized as the Current Events Club.[194] That some spunk and spark were required to organize a club is understandable when, looking back in 1898 on her own experience, even the dauntless Jane Croly acknowledged that "thirty years ago, for women to form a club of their own in any community meant 'to array themselves against the prejudices of society.'"[195]

In Rhode Island, the woman with the courage of her conviction was Elizabeth R. Churchill. "Her confidence that an association [for literary purposes] could be formed and would live stimulated others who had the desire, but not the faith, to lead them to take so radical a step as the formation of a woman's club demanded in a conservative city like Providence in 1875."[196] Churchill held meetings with friends to explore organization; to one gathering she invited Jane Croly, who spoke on "The Work of Sorosis." "That such organizations had become desirable no one doubted; but the feasibility in Providence was questioned. Mrs. Churchill's faith, however, removed mountains, and five ladies associated themselves with her in calling a public meeting." Perhaps because the meeting was held at the rooms of the Irrepressible Society, the birth of the Rhode Island Woman's Club was assured.[197]

In 1891, speaking about what recently opened Barnard College was doing for the young women of New York City, Annie N. Meyer,

Barnard's founder, reminded her audience of the women Barnard could not help:

> You have no idea of the hundreds of ill-trained, or rather untrained, women that come to us, women of all ages, women with husbands and often families, that come to us aimless, ignorant, hopeless, with one cry, "Tell us what to do! Give us something to study! Do something for us!" And I tell you the tears come in our eyes when we answer, "Too late! we can do nothing for you." [198]

Although the women who joined study clubs were seldom "aimless, ignorant, and hopeless," they were women for whom the colleges of that time could in fact "do nothing." There were few enough colleges which accepted women and certainly no provisions for students beyond the traditional college age. A few colleges, such as Wellesley and Barnard, in their early days accepted "special students," but these were generally women in their mid- or late twenties preparing to teach or upgrading their teaching skills. In 1875 as study clubs began to proliferate, women who were then forty had come of college age in the early 1850s, when Oberlin was the only college with a national reputation that offered a bachelor's degree to women. In 1895, in the study-club heyday, women who were then forty had come of college age in the early 1870s, when Vassar was five years old, Cornell was accepting its first women, and Wellesley and Smith were still in the planning stages. Not much beyond an academy, seminary, or normal school education had been available to the women who formed study clubs, and it is understandable that in 1898 the Conversation Club of Muncie, Indiana, identified with obvious pride its young president, Harriet W. Kitts, as "a graduate of Vassar College in the class of 1884." [199] In Brunswick, Maine, the Crescent Club asserted that in 1898 its twelve members were all "school graduates," also an apparent matter of pride. [200] Although the accounts in Croly's *History* are replete with references to the activities, talents, and personalities of individual women, the Crescent Club and the Conversation Club stand out as rare references to educational attainment:

> "Not one of us was a college woman," wrote Harriet Wilkin, a charter member of The Coterie, founded in Fay-

etteville, New York, in 1885. "We were all well acquainted with 'the coarser plants of life.'" (The last
phrase was part of The Coterie motto, a line from Washington Irving, "In America, literature and the elegant
arts must grow up side-by-side with the coarse plants of
daily necessity.")[201]

Among the early members of Sorosis, many were graduates of
female academies, but Jane Croly was self-educated. By the 1890s,
the self-educated club woman had virtually disappeared, and
normal-school training was quite common, as the following list of
presidents of the Indiana Union of Literary Clubs in the 1890s suggests:

1893   Mary H. Smart: Normal School at Fredonia,
       New York
1894   Alice P. Dryer: taught before her marriage, no
       information on education
1895   Virginia C. Meredith: Glendale Female College
1896   Annie K. Conner: Ohio Female College
1897   Merica E. Hoagland: Vassar College
1898   Anna L. Saylor: Indiana State Normal School[202]

"Always life learned, [the study club woman] is now often college
trained," wrote one observer in 1892.[203] Once they were "college
trained," women at the turn of the century transformed their study
clubs into social service groups, but until then their clubs were their
alma maters. While they hardly constituted an intellectual elite or
an avant garde, club women chose to identify themselves first and
foremost with the life of the mind. Said one participant: "The clubs
are selected by natural law from the women who think."[204]

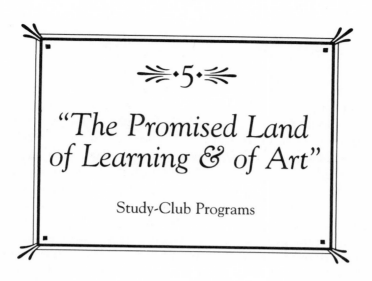

5

"The Promised Land of Learning & of Art"

Study-Club Programs

The range of study-club women's thought is suggested by the following two assessments by members of study-club programs:

> In ancient days when Monday came
> We used our clothes to rub,
> And set them boiling on the stove,
> And stir them with a club.
> But, Oh, our Monday Club today
> Is quite a different stick;
> For we've abandoned household toils
> And learned a better trick.
> And yet a not less potent rod,
> Is our new Monday Club,
> For with it we the poets prod
> And all prose authors drub.
> And with it, just as Moses did,
> We drive the waves apart,
> And enter on the promised land
> Of learning and of art. [1]

Were Plato alive today, his auditors
would be chiefly women. . . . Women are
grappling with the problems of pure
thought that underlie all other

problems, seeking to remove the
limits of the unknown but not the
unknowable.[2]

Jane Croly asserts that "the knowledge that club women sought
was not that of a limited, sectional geography, or a mathematical
quantity as taught in schools, but the knowledge of the history and
development of races and peoples, and of the laws and principles
that underlie this development."[3] Although there was no one starting point either in time or in content for study clubs, their overall
tendency was to begin with the ancients and progress chronologi-
cally (and slowly) toward the modern age. Most clubs took their
first bite in the part that looked juiciest or most nutritious—Dickens's novels or the philosophers of early Athens. Where they started
mattered not as long as the topic was what Matthew Arnold defined
as "culture . . . the best that has been thought and said in the
world." The Home Reading Club of Leadville, Colorado, which
confined its study to English and American literature, asserted that
"the club has found that moral and social culture, with all of their
humanizing influences, are contained in this study of the best literature."[4] Study clubs operated on the elective principle that was then
jostling the classical curriculum on college campuses. Theirs was
not a prescribed education for an elite, but, like most adult education since, it fostered a diffusion of knowledge, meeting students on
their level and engaging them in content compatible with their interests.

Study of literature and history predominated. Among Maine
clubs listed in Croly, thirty-seven percent took up literature (mainly
English and American), fifteen percent history, and sixteen percent
literature and history combined—over two-thirds, then, in those
two fields alone. Other areas studied in Maine included astronomy,
art, travel, current events, music, French culture, botany, and numerous permutations of these.[5]

That study clubs focused primarily on literature, the arts, and
history is not surprising. Reading, especially literature, had long
been a way for girls and women to compensate for their limited
intellectual opportunities.[6] These were traditional women, not
groundbreakers, and they studied disciplines to which women had
been traditionally linked. Elizabeth Peabody believed that "history

is the proper study to unfold the intellect of woman. . . . As Emerson has said, we can judge our own characteristics, and those of others when they are displayed on the page of history, without personal pique. The same passions that play around us in our neighborhood, have determined national events."[7] Peabody's recommendation was given a boost in the late 1880s and early 1890s by the upsurge of nativism, which helped make historical study a popular topic among women's clubs.[8] It was also natural for club women to continue studies begun in their academy training, where the arts and humanities had been emphasized.

Practical considerations played a hand as well in the selection of study texts. Although current events clubs relied on newspapers and magazines for source material, the work of most clubs rested on books, which, in the era before the public library, were in short supply outside major cities and were limited to only the most common areas of inquiry. Even dictionaries were far from common household appurtenances: in the 1880s, a service provided to members of the Chautauqua (New York) Literary and Scientific Circles was a reference bureau to which they could write for pronunciation of a word or the identification of a name merely alluded to.[9] While the occasional club studied botany (usually limited to collection and identification of specimens), other sciences were virtually ignored; the sciences were fledgling fields of study within school and college curricula, they required apparatus, and, like mathematics, they were deemed not appropriate fields of study for women.

For the first few years of a club's existence, the value was often to be found not so much in results, but in aim and effort. The experience of the Skowhegan (Maine) Sorosis was typical:

> The first year's work was desultory. Like most young things, the mere sense of life was sufficient cause for exultation and enjoyment. It had to learn how to use its energies. At every meeting a sketch of the life of some favorite author, with a synopsis of his or her best works, was given, or papers on the government, manners, and customs of some foreign nation. Those who were asked cheerfully undertook to tell in fifteen minutes great facts concerning greater matters that might well have occupied months. There is nothing like the optimism and capability of youth. "Not for worlds," says the historian,

"would one of us forget the pleasure and profit that came to us day by day; and if we have come to view great questions more deliberately, we can never be more in earnest than we were then."[10]

Much of the ridicule and criticism leveled at study clubs was generated by women's unaccustomed attempts at self-education, which stimulated learning but often did not teach; there was much to learn, and these middle-aged women had already lost time. Thoroughness was often sacrificed for breadth. The heroine of *The President of Quex* reminisces at the turn of the century: "She had been the founder of the club and had led the members carefully into *the shallows* of literature according to the methods of women's clubs of years ago" [emphasis added].[11] The comments of Le Baron Briggs, dean of the faculty at Harvard College, about female academies apply as well to the early days of study clubs: "Academy training for girls in the middle of the nineteenth century was a sort of bluff at literary and artistic culture. . . . But even such an education gave access to great works of literature. . . . Out of these crude academies came women of a sensitive, though narrow culture . . . such women as today go to college if they can and, at any sacrifice, send their daughters."[12]

These were the days when "The History of Art in the Renaissance" was polished off in one afternoon program;[13] the Current Events Club of El Paso, Texas, studied in one year Roman history interspersed with papers on "Sanitation in the Home and Community," "Women as Rulers," and "Can Criminals Be Reclaimed?"[14] And the Forthian Club of Somerville, Massachusetts, devoted one meeting to "What Can Be Done with the Chafing Dish."[15] Selma White, the heroine of the 1915 novel *Unleavened Bread*, spends "three forenoons" with "an encyclopedia and two handbooks" for her study-club "research" debut; the topic is "The Inferiority of European Dynasties to the United States."[16]

Women delved into encyclopedias, digging reports out full-blown, "not daring to believe that their own ideas, being feminine, could be worth while."[17] Untrained in sustained composition (never mind critical analysis), women *had* been "trained to silence"[18] and often had to be regulated into discussion. One common icebreaker was response to a roll call. When her name was called, the member was obliged to answer with a current event, a quotation, a figure of speech, a fact recalled from the topic of the previous meeting, an anecdote about a famous person, a description of a unique custom in a foreign country, a selection from a seasonal poem, or an epigram.[19] One club in Rochester, New York, used an "Ignorance Book" to elicit oral work. At the beginning of the meeting, a member wrote in the book any question on which she desired information. After the program the book was opened, and the questions were read. If a member had an answer, the matter was concluded; if not, the question was assigned to a member at random, who became "the specialist" and was required to report an answer at the next meeting.[20]

The growth and development of study-club programs and members' self-confidence and skills are well illustrated in the story of Friends in Council of Quincy, Illinois. Beginning in 1866 twelve women met regularly to read aloud and discuss the subjects suggested by their reading. After one season of miscellaneous selections, the group spent two years on Plato. In 1869 the women organized officially into a club and in 1873 voted to study "one general subject continuing throughout the year, with subdivisions assigned to individuals." In 1875 Friends chose "a course of historical study"; the program committee drew up "thirty topics, covering the important epochs in the Christian world, and these were assigned by lot, one to each member." Two-hour papers began with "State of the Roman Empire at the Appearance of Christ," continued through "Attempts at National Organization—Cortés of Spain—States General of France—Parliament of England," and concluded with "Present Aspect of Russia."[21] While it is easy to deprecate an attempted overview of Christian world history in sixty hours, in the same year Vassar College announced in its catalogue a year-long history course which "proposes to make the students acquainted with the chief facts of universal history, and to give them besides, in a series of generalizing lectures, a synoptical view of the development of human civilization and culture in literature, science, philosophy, and art, as well as in the course of political events."[22] It was just this sort of overview that so delighted Lucy Larcom, when, after leaving the Lowell mills, she moved west with her sister and enrolled in the Monticello (Illinois) Seminary in 1849. After years of patching together the remnants of information she had gathered in her

Improvement Circle, she praised the survey approach: "Our principal's method was to show us the tendencies of thought, to put our minds into the great current of human affairs, leaving us to collect the details as we could, then or afterward."[23] The numerous overviews and surveys that constituted a year's study suggest that nearly thirty years later, club women felt the same need for structure. In 1877 Friends in Council once again narrowed its focus. It adopted a textbook, Green's *History of the English People*; the president chose a portion of the book to be reported on by two members, "elaborating or condensing, as found convenient."[24]

In 1892 President Anna B. McMahan recalled growing up with the club:

> Looking over the period of my membership in Friends in Council, a period which dates back to the very early days of the organization, and covers just half the whole number of years of my life, I realize that the society has been in that life one of its great shaping forces. It calls forth my most loyal and grateful feelings, and I am moved to linger awhile among its pleasant reminiscences.
>
> To this day I recall every detail of the interview in which Mrs. Denman, of blessed memory, the founder of the society, called to announce to me my election to membership. The offer of a seat in the Cabinet of the United States would have surprised me less; these ladies, so much older than myself, of whose meetings I had heard, seemed to me like Virgil's women, all "goddess-born." I remember regretting that I should happen to be wearing an apron at such a momentous hour, and I asked timidly what was required of members. Mrs. Denman explained that generally some book was read aloud, that remarks were made or papers written on questions that might come up. I assured her that never, no, never, could I speak to such an august company, nor could I write much. She kindly reassured me, and called for me on the following Tuesday to mitigate the trying ordeal of a first appearance.
>
> I can only mention a few of the epochs of those early days, such as when I was asked to read a chapter from Cousin's "History of Philosophy," the usual reader being

absent; also, when I gained courage, though with quaking limbs and trembling voice, to read aloud something of my own selection. It was about the Middle Ages. In those days we never mentioned anything more modern than medieval times, and more commonly we tarried in Egypt or ancient Greece. My first original contribution was called "Method of the Study of Mind." I remember that one member praised this very much, saying that "it was so good, that she could scarcely believe that any woman wrote it." The dear old lady may well have indulged her doubts; had she been at all familiar with Maudsley's first chapter of the "Physiology of the Mind," she would have discovered a similarity too great to be accidental. I am not sorry for my sins at that time, nor ashamed to confess them. I am glad, however, for the oblivion which time mercifully grants, and that papers are so little remembered except by the writers thereof. I should be grieved, indeed, if compelled to defend the position which I expounded so glibly twenty years ago. Being absolutely ignorant of the arguments on the other side, I was an easy convert to Maudsley, and maintained that the only way to study mind was through a physiological knowledge of brain and nerve tissue. Monstrous doctrine! But fortunately it shocked no one, possibly because the listeners recognized as little as the reader what out-and-out materialism it was.

In the fall of 1873 the general subject was "The History of Painting"; my special topic, "The Venetian School." Think of it, friends! A person who knew nothing of art principles, who had never seen a painting, nor perhaps even an engraving of any work of the Venetian school, with such a theme!

Those who had been abroad and knew something about the subject at first-hand were very good not to laugh in my face. But at least I was industrious. Never before had I spent so much labor in the preparation of anything, nor, I presume, shall I ever do so again. Everything that I heard or saw seemed somehow to bear a relation to Venetian art, and into my paper it all went.

Neither was fine writing nor flight of rhetoric wanting, for the spell of Ruskin was upon me. The reading of this paper took nearly two hours. Few subjects in heaven or earth were left untouched, but almost any title beside Venetian art would have been equally fitting. Still even such an omnivorous compilation was a decided gain over the Maudsley cribbing.

. . . Yet I am not deriding these old days of second-hand work. They were a necessary step in the evolution of our club life; they gave us the habit of expressing ourselves on paper; they taught us not to fear the sound of our own voices; they made us acquainted with each other's mind and thoughts, since even a compilation gives an opportunity for the expression of individuality. With the year 1883 we entered upon a new epoch. The course of study was not limited to one topic, but four subjects were outlined. This arrangement took account of the diversity of tastes, provided for some originality of treatment, and is the one which still continues in favor after nine years.

In this new departure we had fairly entered upon the period of original thinking. It is too much to claim of Friends in Council that all of the work done now is of the truly student-like or creative order, but it is not too much to say that a great deal of it is really admirable, and worthy of the larger audience which some of its papers have gained through subsequent publication in journals and magazines. If I read the signs of the times aright we are at least on the right road and travelling in the right direction.[25]

Accustomed to a passive role outside their homes and living in the heyday of the public lecturer, women in some clubs, especially in urban areas, began their studies primarily as listeners. This was true of the New England Women's Club and Fortnightly of Chicago. The latter for the first two years after its founding in 1873 alternated between afternoon meetings at which a member gave a paper and evening meetings which featured a lecture by "some well-known gentleman."[26] By 1875 the gentlemen had disappeared from the programs, and the club embarked on a study of ancient Greece and Rome.[27] One club in New England varied Fortnightly's early procedure slightly. Every two weeks the thirty members met in a private home for the presentation of original papers and discussion. On alternate weeks meetings were held in a church hall for two to three hundred "honorary members" (paying guests) to hear a professional lecturer.[28] Outside lecturers were not lightweight entertainers. Academicians often dominated a club's list of speakers. William R. Harper, G. Stanley Hall, Josiah Royce, and Alice F. Palmer were a few who addressed the Chicago Woman's Club.[29] The Saturday Club of Brunswick, Maine, drew on the faculty of Bowdoin College, among others, for its lecturers.[30] The use of lecturers was atypical, however, and quite soon was abandoned by most, especially as they were urged on to active member participation by club women of national prominence. In her club manual published in 1891, Olive T. Miller, an early Sorosis member, assailed the lecture system: "This plan destroys the vital interests of its members, and the club is apt to become cold and dead. Unless each one herself takes a part, or may take a part in the exercises she comes to regard the club meetings with . . . indifference."[31] Explaining Sorosis's abstention from philanthropy, Jane Croly highlighted as well the study-club imperative that each member be actively involved, no matter how slight or tentative her initial contribution: "The results of individual benevolence must always be temporary and partial, since it is a law that everything thrives in proportion to the development of its own powers."[32] The Tuesday Club of Marlborough, Massachusetts, founded in 1891, recorded seven years later that its "members have emerged from their original attitude as listeners to writing original papers well thought out and well expressed."[33]

Papers prepared by members were the staple of study-club programs. Like everything else in this new venture, they evolved with time. Chroniclers of the Chicago Woman's Club validate the progression confessed to by Anna McMahan of Friends in Council: members at first produced "a manuscript that the paper might at least have the effect of originality"; next came "collated matter presented verbatim"; and, finally, "original productions from Club members."[34] Length of the papers varied from ten minutes to two hours. At each meeting of the Social Art Club of Syracuse, New York, two papers, each an hour in length, were read with a short break for refreshments. Once or twice a year husbands were invited to the meetings; on those occasions three papers were read with a break for supper, entailing a marathon meeting of seven hours.[35]

Of course, the quality of the paper depended on its writer, but neither commentators nor participants claimed any "bragging rights" for the early compositions. Even by 1915 instructions such as "How to Start a Club" in Caroline Benton's *Complete Club Book for Women* set minimal expectations for intellectual content. Benton suggested that the club start with a popular author whose books were available; Dickens was a likely choice. Next the club would be divided into two, each group given one novel to read. The president would prepare a summary of Dickens's life with pictures of places associated with him. Each group in turn would then present papers telling the story and describing the characters (including why they admired or disliked certain characters). Finally, sections illustrating the main point of the novel would be read aloud.[36] For clubs with more self-confidence, experience, and greater access to reference books, Benton gave a sample program on Ruskin. The presenter was to "read something on his life . . . the more she can read, the better paper she will write." The paper should discuss "(1) his home, his early education, the influence of his mother, and his gradual growth into his place in the world; (2) what he did; his travels, his interest in painting, architecture, economics, and sociology; his friends, his controversy with Whistler and its outcome, his contact with Oxford, and the books he wrote; (3) a resumé of what Ruskin actually accomplished; the value of his work to society and his influence on social problems." The paper was to raise the question of whether Ruskin's views had contemporary relevance. "The paper should include brief readings, anecdotes, and estimates of others." Benton reminded her readers that "the value of a discussion after a paper cannot be overestimated. One joins a club not so much to acquire information, because that can be done at home, but rather to learn to express oneself readily and intelligently."[37] Benton's formulas suggest the methodical nature of club papers, which is, however, not to deny the careful work that went into them. Members of the Social Art Club of Syracuse, New York, "were required to be able to recite from which book, page, and paragraph any quotation was derived."[38] One is reminded of Jencks and Riesman's comments about students at women's colleges in the late nineteenth century: "They were relatively willing to do large quantities of academic work in a fairly methodical way."[39]

Many study-club women found it all they could do initially to get up and read their papers, "quaking," as Anna McMahan remembered. It was not only that they were engaging in an intellectual and social exercise foreign to them, but also that they were unaccustomed to an audience and, often lacking the ego strength acquired in establishing an independent identity of their own, they were overdependent on the approval of others. While sister members played the role of sympathetic classmates, the presenter was faced with one member who assumed the teacherly function of critic. At the conclusion of the paper, the critic pointed out and corrected errors in pronunciation, content, and presentation. The Vassar College catalogue for 1875 describes a similar ordeal for students in the English composition course. Seniors were required "to read original productions in the presence of faculty and fellow students. Criticisms from the instructor are minute, personal, and free."[40] As club women, through constant practice, grew more comfortable in speaking before the group, emphasis on oral work increased. Although some clubs continued throughout their history to rely solely on papers, many later looked back on their paper-writing period as merely a first step, part of a weaning process. Margaret Fuller in her Conversations had used writing in such a way:

> When they [women in her Conversation groups] have
> not been successful in verbal utterance of their thoughts,
> I have asked them to attempt it in writing. At the next
> meeting, I would read these "skarts of pen and ink"
> aloud, and canvass their adequacy, without mentioning
> the names of the writers. I found this less necessary, as I
> proceeded, and my companions attained greater command both of thought and language; but for a time it
> was useful. . . . Great advantage in point of this discipline may be derived from even this limited use of pen.[41]

The increase in oral work may also have been due in part to women's growing willingness to envision themselves as participants, however minor, in the public sphere. With their overwhelming insistence on a serious intellectual purpose, it is likely too that they were trying to pattern their procedures after those in academe. Harvard pedagogy was still based on recitation, arising from the tradition of rhetoric which prepared men for the pulpit and the bar. Women at Vassar in the 1870s were given instruction in elocution two times a week during half of each of their four years.[42] In an attempt to re-create their academy days or in a gesture of wish fulfillment, study-club women brought the classroom experience into their homes.

The movement from reading papers to oral presentations was not a retreat from rigor. The Clio Club of Hastings, Minnesota, whose specialty was ancient Greek history, observed that "papers are allowed, but oral work is much preferred, as it trains thought, memory, and conciseness in expression."[43] The Cochnewagen Club of Monmouth, Maine, highlighted another benefit: "The papers increase in value, but a still further advance has been made, as members gain freedom by substituting oral work for the written."[44] The two presenters at each meeting of the Philosophy Club of Cambridge, Massachusetts, were allowed to use only notes as their prompts: "The object in avoiding prepared papers is to teach fluency, self-control, and consecutive thinking."[45] In Bloomington, Illinois, the Mosaic Club, whose purpose was "to collect bits of information and piece them into mosaics of knowledge," scorned members who read rather than referring to their papers: "If a member is seen to do so, the President and other members are to look out of the windows and turn their attention to anything beside what the member is saying."[46] Some spartan clubs such as the Saturday Club of Columbus, Ohio, required memorization.[47] The Boston Political Class represented the extreme in oral work, reflecting, perhaps, its atypical choice of current politics as the subject of its study. "Some work is done on previously announced topics, others unannounced in order to encourage women to think on their feet and to speak extemporaneously."[48]

That women gained in confidence and skill in their oral presentations may be seen in the actions of the Tuesday Club of Marlborough, Massachusetts, which reported its steady progress from members as listeners to skilled paper writers. Each year the club chose two papers to be delivered in public and noted that they "are as warmly appreciated by as large an audience as is given to any speaker from out of town."[49]

Before too long clubs introduced variety into their program format. The section of the New England Women's Club which studied art supplemented its book study with trips to the Museum of Fine Arts.[50] Many clubs were armchair travelers, reporting on foreign countries, but the Ashmont (Massachusetts) Tourist Club took its "imaginary journeys" with well-known guides. *A Thousand Miles up the Nile* accompanied them to Egypt, the *Marble Faun* to Rome, and *Romola* to Florence.[51] The All-Around Dickens Club of Boston studied carefully the topography of the English country where Dickens laid his scenes as well as the author's great themes and characters.[52] The Carpe Diem Club of Findlay, Ohio, started each year's historical study with a chart lecture based on a member-prepared map of the country under discussion. Several times throughout the year the club appointed leaders to lead "table-talks" on the day's topic at a luncheon following the meeting. While studying the history of France, Carpe Diem held an Evening at the Court of Louis XIV during which each member gave a short account of some part of the reign, discussing important personages and events. In the same year, to help in locating and understanding the historical cities of France, "each member traveled, in a paper, from one city to another, describing the same, the country and the manner of traveling, locating the historical points with an accuracy of one personally familiar with the facts mentioned."[53] To improve both their oral and written skills, a rural Iowa club held each week a "Better Speech drill based on lessons in a pamphlet textbook." The drill covered "pronunciation, the use of words with slight differentiation in meaning, and common errors in syntax."[54]

Debates made their appearance in a number of clubs and came highly recommended for their instructional value and for countering women's reported subjectivity and lack of critical judgment. "We know all too well that women are not naturally logical," wrote one female commentator; "debating soon shows one how easy it is to think in a hazy, indefinite way, and how difficult to say clearly and concisely what is to be said."[55] The Fortnightly Club of Bath, Maine, reported that "it took a little time to develop debates and debaters, but these have now assumed much importance. The first question proposed for open discussion was 'Resolved, that Howells does not faithfully portray the average American,' and excited lively interest."[56] The Committee on Formal Debate was accorded "much praise" by members of the Century Club of San Francisco. "The discussions cover a wide and varied field; politics and theology being alone prohibited. These debates are conducted with marked ability. The most timid of the club's members have developed a surprising readiness in addressing an audience with clearness and conviction."[57]

Dramatics in various forms gave study-club women opportunities for cooperative work and enhanced their feeling of unity.[58] Shakespeare clubs often read aloud from the work they were studying. Skowhegan (Maine) Sorosis held "private theatricals" each midwinter.[59] In the year it studied English history, the Literary Union of Lewiston and Auburn, Maine, held an elaborate entertainment consisting of "a reproduction by tableaux, incidental music, and stage arrangement of scenes from the court life of the Elizabethan period."[60] The French Club of Bath, Maine, conducted its meetings wholly in French (its members were fined five cents for every word "in any other language") and once a year presented "a bright little play . . . exclusively for the members."[61]

Clubs, especially those with younger members such as the Shakespeare Club of Bath, Maine, often encouraged creative efforts. Meeting weekly on Monday evenings to read an act or two "of a great play" and to discuss its "obscure passages," this small society of twelve spent the remainder of the time reading aloud original essays, poems, and translations from Latin poets.[62] The Old and New of Malden, Massachusetts, formed a writing group, limited to twelve, within the club. These women "were obliged to furnish a certain number of articles or contributions, many of which appeared in print; and at least four books in prose and verse have been published, which were first read at the group for its approval. The writing group was an inspiration to the *Original Magazine*, which has appeared annually since 1879, is edited and its articles all written by members of Old and New, and its cover and pages illustrated by 'our own artists.'"[63] Whatever intellectual activity the club offered, it was designed to get each woman actively involved. The Woman's Club of El Paso fined a member one dollar if she failed to contribute to a program as appointed,[64] and the hundred-member Indianapolis Woman's Club stipulated that only after membership in the club for eighteen years could a woman apply to be a "privileged" member, a status which excused her from participation in literary work.[65] As Margaret Fuller had pointed out, women had the intellectual ability, but under a bushel their light went unnoticed, even by themselves:

Women are now taught, at school, all that men are; they run over, superficially, even *more* studies, without being really taught anything. When they come to the business of life, they find themselves inferior, and all their studies have not given them that practical good sense, and mother wisdom, and wit, which grew up with our grand-mothers at the spinning-wheel. But, with this differ-ence; men are called on, from a very early period, to reproduce all that they learn. Their college exercises, their political duties, their professional studies, the first actions of life in any direction, call on them to put to use what they have learned. But women learn without any attempt to reproduce. Their only reproduction is for purposes of display.[66]

Like Sorosis, the Saturday Morning Club, and Friends in Coun-cil, most clubs plunged headlong into a miscellaneous program of study, following their members' interests or available resources. Many, like Sorosis and Friends, soon "settled down to some orga-nized plan of work."[67] They realized collectively what Lucy Larcom had discovered upon her enrollment in Monticello Seminary after her years of self-education: "A habit of indiscriminate, unsystema-tized reading, such as I had fallen into, is entirely foreign to the scholarly habit of mind."[68] Clubs prided themselves on their ad-vancement. The Rhode Island Woman's Club reported that during the first few years of its existence, papers "had no logical connection with each other. It is an indication of progress that the work has since been classified."[69] Members of the Indianapolis Woman's Club devised their yearly program by submitting lines of study they wished to pursue. The program committee attempted to find a common thread on which to string the various beads of interest. Failing that, they were scrupulous about the unity and coherence within individ-ual programs. They assigned two papers on "congenial topics such as 'The Homeric Heroes: Achilles and Ulysses' and 'The Homeric Heroines: Helen and Penelope'" and concluded the day with a "dis-cussion relating the two, 'The Relation between Homer's Men and Women.'"[70] Other clubs, like the Quid Nunc of Little Rock, Ar-kansas, were more compulsive; "dissatisfied with 'miscellaneous work,' it spent four years entirely on Greek and Roman history."[71]

Even by the 1890s, however, two strong warnings against miscel-laneous programs suggest their continued existence.

Women need to be trained to clearness of thought and accuracy of expression. Much of their work through life is necessarily disconnected; it lacks coherence and steadiness; it is, without fault of theirs, of the patchwork order. That club work which has in it the counter elements of unity and persistence, is not only what they most need, but what they most thoroughly enjoy. If the club offers to its members a desultory programme,—papers upon diverse subjects, magazine readings, addresses by invited guests, et cetera,—it may present a pleasing entertainment, but will it not foster the very mental habits which it ought to correct?

Amusement is easily obtained without organization. Let the club hold to something higher. It is this very stimulus of a formulated course of study, systematic and exhaustive, which most women need in order to find that they can study and that they like it. There is a fascination in going to the root of things, in personal investigation of a great subject, which is in itself a spur to continued and increasing effort.[72]

A speaker at the Third Biennial Convention of the General Federation of Women's Clubs in Louisville in 1896 reiterated the point:

It is not true that beauty is "only skin-deep," it is *soul-deep!* But in order to be effectual the training must be systematic.

The brain, like the body, is slow of development, and when men are trying to train their bodies up to the highest point, they do not take a little exercise today, and a ride next week, and punch the bag a little when they feel like it. Not a bit of it; physical athletes are not made in that way—the finest development of the physique is accomplished by hard and systematic work, and intellectual athletes must be made in the same way. I do not mean that we must give all of our time to study; the duties of life are too varied for that. But I do mean that, if we can give only one hour a day to intellectual work, it should be done systematically and along one line of thought, until we understand the subject we have in hand.

It is not enough to belong to a club, unless your club

is wise enough to take up some systematic course of study. We all know that the only way to accomplish anything is by doing one thing at a time and doing it well.[73]

The programs of Fortnightly of Chicago illustrate well the acceptance of the value of systematic work. Beginning with miscellaneous topics, by 1890 it had established two program committees, one for the "Continuous Course" and one for the "Miscellaneous Course," each alternating programs. Both courses, however, distributed their printed programs a year in advance to members, listing presenters and their paper topics along with the names of published authorities in each field.[74] By 1909, the Miscellaneous Course had been dropped. In that year the club studied seventeenth-century France and accompanied each topic with a suggested reading list of twenty to thirty volumes, including a large number of scholarly works written in French.[75]

Without an instructor to recommend source material, club women in the beginning relied heavily on encyclopedias, but during the 1890s they were aided by bibliographies from university extension courses and by commercial book lists. In 1895 Augusta H. Leypoldt and George Iles compiled and annotated for the American Library Association a *List of Books for Girls and Women and Their Clubs*. The list is divided by topic with no differentiation for age and is, therefore, a far cry from a scholarly reference. The list includes "acknowledged masters but also some which though widely popular are frivolous in ideas and defective in taste and skill." Those introduced with warning include Thomas Hardy, whose *Tess of the D'Urbervilles* "shows Hardy's confusion of mind in regard to decent standards of behavior," and Mrs. Mary Jane Holmes, whose "works are unknown to the cultured reader, . . . are prosy and dull . . . , and whose secret of long popularity has never been divulged by [her] readers." Among the twelve sources under the psychology heading is *Thinking, Feeling, Doing* by E. W. Scripture, described as an "elementary work, first book in the English language on the new psychology, based exclusively on experiment. No long words. Special attention to practical applications in every-day life. Copiously illustrated."[76] Even left to their own devices, however, most club programs occupied an intellectual level substantially higher than the American Library Association assumed.

Few people outside the clubs themselves attributed intellectual worth to study-club programs, which were often the butt of literary caricature and satire such as that of Sinclair Lewis in *Main Street:*

> "We will first have the pleasure of hearing Mrs. Jenson on the subject of 'Shakespeare and Milton.'"
>
> Mrs. Ole Jenson said that Shakespeare was born in 1564 and died in 1616. He lived in London, England, and in Stratford-on-Avon, which many American tourists loved to visit, a lovely town with many curios and old houses worth examination. Many people believed that Shakespeare was the greatest playwright who ever lived, also a fine poet. Not much was known about his life, but after all that did not make so much difference, because they loved to read his numerous plays, several of the best known of which she would now criticize.
>
> Perhaps the best known of his plays was "The Merchant of Venice," having a beautiful love story and a fine appreciation of a woman's brains, which a woman's club, even those who did not care to commit themselves on the question of suffrage, ought to appreciate. (Laughter.) Mrs. Jenson was sure that she, for one, should love to be like Portia. The play was about a Jew named Shylock, and he didn't want his daughter to marry a Venice gentleman named Antonio—.[77]

The record, however, shows that meetings operated on a higher level. Although a knowledge of their exact content is denied us, it is difficult to believe that during the four sessions which the Tuesday Club of Cambridge, Massachusetts, held on Emerson's essay "Poetry and Imagination"[78] the members confined themselves to pedestrian observations. Fortnightly of Chicago "deliberated for one whole afternoon" on "Music in Connection with Herbert Spencer's Essay on the Origin and Function of Music";[79] surely such an exercise must have stretched the minds of those involved. Although the Phalo Club drew its name from the philosophy, history, art, literature, and oratory which it proposed to study, it was philosophy on which the members concentrated. After they had explored "the different systems of philosophy . . . and investigated in conscientious studies . . . their comparative value and methods," they were ready for more integrative work: their discussions included "The Three

Cosmic Principles," "Theoretical, Practical, and Absolute Philosophy," "Occult Forces in Nature," "The Relation of Science to the Transitory Period of Philosophy," and "What Effect Have Metaphysics and Science on Practical Life?"[80] The Chicago Woman's Club prepared in advance a three-year program on English drama. The first year took the group through the middle of Shakespeare's career; the second year to the close of the Elizabethan period; and the third, after a brief review of Restoration and seventeenth-century drama, emphasized the various dramatic developments of the present era. This was not, however, an indiscriminate sweep. "The design was to illustrate the growth of dramatic art by a series of selected plays of Shakespeare, studied in comparison with some other work or works of the period, and considered as an exponent of the growth of Shakespeare's mind and art." Special bibliographies accompanied the study.[81]

Outsiders were not totally oblivious to the intellectual achievements of study-club women. Ralph Waldo Emerson stood before the all-male Boston Radical Club and praised the papers he had heard Julia Ward Howe deliver to the New England Women's Club.[82] The papers written by members of the Castilian Club of Boston, which studied exclusively Spain and its history, "are so exhaustive in character and so carefully written, that they are deposited in the Boston Public Library at the request of the curator"[83] (see Appendix 1). Herbert B. Adams, professor at Johns Hopkins University, and Daniel C. Gilman, president of Johns Hopkins, in 1893 publicly congratulated the Nineteenth Century History Class of Atlanta, Georgia, upon its completion of what amounted to a five-year graduate course in nineteenth-century history; both men had been consulted when the original plan had been drawn up. The club next went on to a university extension course in political history to which it devoted three years.[84]

Some club programs were overviews, to be sure, but they often had the intent of integrating previous studies. When the Ebell Society of Oakland, California, embarked in 1898 on a year-long study of English art, the club built on its members' prior work in English history and English literature. The following syllabus resulted:

  I. Early History of Britain, Celts, Danes and Saxons.
 II. Geography and Physical Features of England.

   III. Formation and Origin of the English Language. Bards and Poetry of Wales.
   IV. Early English Art. Druidical Remains. Illustrated MSS.
    V. English Gothic Architecture. Cathedrals of York, Salisbury, Gloucester, Peterborough, Canterbury, Old St. Paul's, Chester. Feudal Castles. Kenilworth, Windsor, Hampton Court. Stately Homes of England.
   VI. English Literature under the Norman Kings. Chaucer and His Followers.
  VII. 1213–17. Magna Charta. The Growth of the English Constitution. Foundation of Schools and Universities.
 VIII. The Early Masters. Holbein, Sir A. Moro, Oliver, Van Dyke, George Jamesone, Sir Peter Lely, Sir Godfrey Kneller, Sir James Thornhill.
   IX. The Reformation and Its Literature. 1540–53. The Age of Elizabeth. The Expansion of England, and the Beginning of her Commercial Greatness.
    X. Early Masters (continued). William Hogarth, Richard Wilson, Sir Joshua Reynolds, William Blake, J. M. Turner, Thomas Gainsborough, Sir Edwin Landseer, and artists of their time.
   XI. English Cathedrals. Durham, Lincoln, Oxford. Domestic Architecture. Old Taverns.
  XII. Spenser. The Rise of the Drama. Bacon.
 XIII. Oliver Cromwell and the Revolution. The Literature of the Puritans. The Cavalier Poets.
 XIV. The Restoration. Dryden. Drama of the Restoration.
  XV. The Ceramic Art of England.
 XVI. English Sculpture. Old English Customs. Punishments and Amusements.
XVII. The Literature of the Age of Anne. Pope and the Classical School of Poetry. English Philosophy. The Essayists. The Rise of the Modern Novel.
XVIII. English Abbeys. Tower of London. Houses of Parliament. Westminster. Palaces of London.
 XIX. History of English Theatres. History of English Funerals and Weddings. English Lighthouses.

XX. Kensington Modern School of Art, 1850–82. The Pre-Raphaelites (John Ruskin, Holman Hunt, Sir Noel Paton, J. E. Millais, D. G. Rossetti). F. Madox Brown, Burne-Jones. Landscape. J. F. Millais, David Cox, Mark Fisher, R. W. Macbeth, Edwin Edwards.

XXI. Ceramic Art. Etching and Etchers. Seymore, Haden, Whistler. Historical Painting. Sir Frederick Leighton, Alma Tadema. Genre Painting. Erskine Nichol, H. O'Neil, Thomas Faed, G. H. Boughton.

XXII. Modern School of Water Colors. English Caricaturists.[85]

A year before, the Chicago Woman's Club had formed a united study class out of its six departments. Reminiscent of core programs found on college campuses in the twentieth century, the class chose for its topic "Great Movements of Thought in the Nineteenth Century." Representative papers and discussion topics included "The Essential Idea (Social Unity)," "Proposed Solutions of Social and Industrial Problems," "What Are Biography and Psychology Doing for Education?" and "Nineteenth-Century Characteristics of Music and Painting."[86] In a similar manner the Colonia Club of New York City held a one-year symposium on "The Colonial Period of American History." The biweekly programs were presented by members of its various study departments: music and art, literature, science, home and social relations, history and civics, and education.[87] Jane Croly's observation about the Ebell Society could have been applied to a number of study clubs: "It may well be called 'a liberal education' for those who take advantage of its opportunities."[88]

Further definition of the intellectual achievements of some study clubs may be approached through their detailed study questions and paper topics. During its study of English prose fiction, the Chicago Woman's Club devoted two hours each to Thackeray's *Henry Esmond* and George Eliot's *Romola*. Assigned paper topics for the former were as follows:

Discuss the book from the following points of view:

1. As a story. Lacking in any great central situation, by what means does it take hold of the reader and leave its vivid impression on the memory?
2. As history. The art and method by which the spirit of the age is reproduced, so that we seem to live again in the time of Queen Anne.
3. As a philosophy of life.
   (a) The tedium of being placed on a pedestal (book i, chap. 7).
   (b) The tragedy of marriage as revealed in book i, chap. 11.
   (c) The latent power of loving in Beatrice Esmond, as described by herself at the close of book iii, chap. 7; its possibility in a woman of her nature and in her surroundings.
   (d) Truth of the statement that "women have an instinct of dissimulation."

For *Romola:*

Discuss this book from the following points of view:

1. The evolution of a beautiful soul in the character of Romola.
2. The analysis of deterioration in the charming personality of Tito.
3. The great historic background, including the character of Savonarola and the secret of his influence.

Discuss the following questions, raised by the text of the book:

1. Does Virgil paint a perfect traitor (chap. 4)? See Virgil's "Aeneid," book ii.
2. Qualities desirable for world leaders; causes of a pulpy condition of mind (chap. 39).
3. Comment on Romola's last answer to Savonarola (in chap. 59).
4. Discuss Romola as a type. Compare with Kingsley's "Hypatia" and Mrs. Ward's "Marcella."[89]

The Dallas Shakespeare Club devoted six months to the study of each of Shakespeare's plays, taking it act by act, scene by scene. The following questions answered by members of the club in connection with *Love's Labor's Lost* seem to ensure the engagement of members on several levels of analysis.

How old was Shakespeare when this play was written?
Why is it considered his earliest play?
What works of his had previously appeared?
When did Shakespeare's name first appear on the title-page of a play?
Was this play printed during the poet's lifetime?
What is meant by the "Quartos" and "Folios"?
What is the "First Folio," and what entitles it to be considered one of the most valuable works in the whole range of English literature?
Was the plot of this play original with Shakespeare?
Mention some of the books with which Shakespeare shows himself familiar.
Is there in "Love's Labor's Lost," as in all other plays of Shakespeare, a gradually increasing dramatic interest?
Is the climax satisfactory? Does the play seem to need a sequel? What "lost play" of Shakespeare's bears a title that would suggest it might have been intended for a sequel to "Love's Labor's Lost"?
What is the most dramatic situation in the play? The most humorous scene? The best acting scene of Holofernes? The most characteristic speech of Don Armando?
What character in the play may be taken as a prototype of the precocious infant of today? Mention some of his cleverest speeches.
In the name of what character in "Love's Labor's Lost" is there, possibly, an allusion to a glorious episode in English history which may have tended to make the play popular?
Mention the principal characters.
What characters in Shakespeare's later comedies are foreshadowed by Armando and Constable Dull?[90]

To answer these questions club members were required to range from a simple inventory of characters to a sophisticated consideration of the most dramatic situation in the play, a judgment involving both a definition of *dramatic* and a defense of their stand. (The list is also intriguing for its emphasis on people—the analysis of character, the direct equation of Shakespeare's life with his work, and the direct relation of his work to present-day interests—suggesting, perhaps, that it was first through the medium of people, both fictional and real individuals, that club women began to make meaning of the world.) A study of Tennyson's "The Princess" followed that of *Love's Labour's Lost* because Shakespeare's plot is said to have influenced the Victorian poet. The joint study ended with discussion of the question "The perfect independence of woman—its effects—is it to be desired?"[91]

The format of study-club programs was often dependent on the size of the club. When membership surpassed fifty, making discussion unwieldy, limiting individual participation, and increasing the variety of intellectual interests represented, most clubs created departments, smaller interest groups within the large organization. Departments often met three times a month, reserving the fourth for a meeting of the entire club at which one department was responsible for the program. Because the larger clubs were usually found in urban areas with greater intellectual resources and a more affluent population, departments often did their work in "classes" for which some hired an instructor and charged a nominal fee while others proceeded with the usual study-club method of mutual instruction or leadership from a club member.

Historians of the Chicago Woman's Club recalled that "our first activities were the formation of study classes in art and literature, and preparing ourselves for those classes as though we were at school. The Club became the mature woman's college. These classes served a two-fold purpose—they brought the members together in a more intimate way and stimulated them to continue to give attention to serious topics of study, and gave them a feeling of solidarity."[92] Members brought friends and acquaintances to classes in such numbers that the club voted in 1879 that "no person can properly belong to the Club community without first becoming a member of the Club."[93] Most women belonged to only one class, but for others, "the club seemed to be only an appendage to classes,"[94] and they enrolled in as many as their schedule permitted.

In 1898, Julia A. Sprague, historian of the New England Women's Club, wrote about the spread of classes: "I feel almost as if I were a centenarian when looking back I recognize the great change from the time when a woman's club was an unknown quantity and classwork for adult women (not in seminaries) was nonexistent. Now a half page at least of a prominent Boston newspaper is set apart weekly for a condensed account of women's clubs in a small district of Massachusetts, and each club has its quota of classes. Formerly I was beset by inquiries as to what the phrase 'classwork' meant; now I should smile in astonishment at the ignorance of the inquiry."[95] Her own club, the New England Women's Club, started a botany class in 1872 that continued for over twenty years. With fieldwork, books, and microscopes, "from elementary beginnings they have gone onward to the profounder scientific studies." In 1876 the botany class received permission to attend lectures given to teachers by Professor George Goodale of the Massachusetts Natural History Society.[96] In addition to its botany class, the club in 1897 offered three in English literature and one each in political economy, French, Italian, current events, Emerson, and Shakespeare; only one, French, required an outside instructor.[97]

Classes which hired professional instructors often were university extension courses in all but name. In the 1898–99 season, the philosophy and science department of the Chicago Woman's Club sponsored a study class in psychology under Professor James. R. Angell of the University of Chicago. Angell led the class again the following year in a course on psychological aspects of ethical problems.[98] Between 1890 and 1900, when university extension programs were still peripatetic and not based on a campus, they often relied on women's clubs for logistics and in good part for audience. In California, women's clubs procured the halls, publicized the offerings, and sold subscriptions for the University of California extension lecture courses given by "circuit-riding" instructors who generally made one-night stands over a period of six weeks.[99]

Whether they debated Spencer's theory of music, discussed the chafing dish, or followed a university extension syllabus, study-club members were, according to Croly, "studious, sincere, and somewhat conservative."[100] Like early college women, identified by President L. Clark Seelye of Smith College as "a particularly solemn set, in more need of being taught to play than to study,"[101] club women were sternly enthusiastic; they characterized themselves as "brainy and conscientious women."[102] According to her daughters, Julia Ward Howe more than once returned home from the New England

Women's Club with the comment "It was a thoughtful, earnest meeting."[103] Wearing hats and gloves and seated in a member's home, study-club women had no need to prove their homemaking skills or social graces. It was their intellectual ability that they were testing. The measure, moreover, was not to be a private, individual affair. Acting in concert, they were taking as well a stand, however "gentle the art of club-living,"[104] for the status of women and their future. The Century Club of San Francisco in describing the place of papers in its club work revealed its understanding of its gesture on behalf of gender: "that the number of papers increases year by year is the best proof of the power of women's clubs to educate and develop woman's ability. . . . Perhaps one of the pleasantest features of those occasions [when papers are read] is the pride evinced by all the members when a paper, denoting more than ordinary ability, is presented by one of their number."[105] The seriousness of those pursuing a cause shaped the attitudes of study-club women. While explicitly their goal was intellectual improvement, implicitly one senses the suggestion of a higher calling. The Dickens Club of Muncie, Indiana, was formed "for the study of Dickens." Its emblems, however, connote something beyond prose: "for its flower the ascension lily, and for colors green and white, signifying growth and purity of aim."[106]

Like college women, club women were immediately engaged in a task. There was no parading with banners, no agitating for change. The change was upon them, and they had to prove themselves not with promises but with performance. The Monday Club of Santa Barbara, California, attributed the respect accorded it in the community to "our moderation and quiet, non-aggressive policy."[107] As women's colleges eschewed the suffrage issue, desiring not to weaken their forces by fighting battles on two flanks, so too women's study clubs carefully avoided suffrage and other controversial topics. In most clubs, like the Friday Morning Club of Los Angeles, "the severe and the technical, the rigid and the hustling were conspicuous by their absence."[108]

Whereas women's colleges before the turn of the century emphasized the "familiness" of the college community, women's clubs prided themselves on the "schoolness" of theirs. The Ebell Society wished to be known primarily as "seriously studious."[109] The Mt. Desert Historical Club of Tremont, Maine, was formed by "educated women," the Monday Club of Westfield, New York, by "studious, intelligent women."[110] In Muncie, Indiana, the McRae was founded in honor of "a scholarly woman," and the Dante Club of the same city consisted of "ten young women of scholarly tastes."[111] It was not intellectual pyrotechnics that lighted study-club skies or hearts. They were not out to compete or to prove themselves "better than" anyone—only "capable of" and deserving of due accord. The "cardinal principle" of the Ruskin Art Club of Los Angeles was "not to hurry its investigations, but to pursue with careful persistence its line of work until it had finished the school or period it represented."[112] The Woman's Club of Greencastle, Indiana, prided itself on its "great zeal and thoroughness."[113] The motto of the Lewiston (Maine) Reading Circle was "No day without achievement."[114] In the same college town the twelve founding members of the Mount David Shakespeare Club agreed "that each one should perform the duties assigned to her to the best of her ability, and submit unflinchingly to the ruling of a critic."[115] The "beautiful garment" that was the Social Art Club of Syracuse, New York, was "woven from the warp and woof of patient study and constant effort."[116]

The meetings themselves were businesslike, disciplined by self-consciousness and parliamentary procedure. "Though there is little social life in the club," explained the Chicago Woman's Club, "our spirit is most cordial and friendly, and our atmosphere is one of hospitable sympathy with all women."[117] "Gossip and scandal are relegated to the background," an initiate to Quex is advised in Helen Winslow's novel.[118] Although it had descended from a sewing circle, the Wednesday Morning Club of Elmira, New York, allowed "handiwork" only at the meetings between Thanksgiving and Christmas.[119] Generally refreshments were not served except on special occasions. "We do not want to be seduced into seeing who can bake the richest cake," says a member of the Waynesboro Woman's Club in Santmyer's fiction.[120]

Spartan as the daily regimen might be at women's colleges (and it *was*, even in Wellesley's palatial surroundings), yearly traditions were paeans to the good, gracious, imaginative, and frolicsome life. So it was with women's clubs. On "Gentlemen's Night," an annual event in many clubs, earnestness was nowhere in sight. "The programme for those evenings at the Woman's Conversation Club of Marion, Indiana, consisted mainly of humorous responses to roll-call, conundrums written upon cards, music, and anything of a light and amusing character that could be devised to suit frivolous masculine tastes."[121] Anniversary celebrations especially were occasions for lavish food, dress, decoration, and entertainment. The club history was often summarized and satirized in poem, charade, skit, song, or tableau. Toasts frequently expressed in words the *esprit de corps*, the appreciation for "close friendships formed that can never be broken,"[122] and the affection for their club so "dear to the hearts of its members"[123] that were taken for granted throughout the club season. The last meeting of the year was frequently held outdoors as a garden party, picnic, or, for the Literary Union of Portland, Maine, a "field day" on the coast. There, after experiencing the "brilliant clearness brought together in Maine's air and sky and water," a luncheon of "generous and beautiful hospitality," and musical exercises, members returned home with a souvenir "set of leaflets decorated with a picturesque bit of Maine in water-color, tied with Union ribbons, and filled with an autograph collection of verses or mottoes, original and selected."[124]

"There is a sense of devotion to an Alma Mater that permeates the reminiscences of all the early Fortnightly members," wrote its chronicler.[125] While it is clear from their ubiquitous college metaphors and from the college trappings and traditions they appropriated that most club women wished to see themselves as collegians, it is equally clear that all their aspirations and efforts combined could not produce the equivalent of a college degree.

Not so rigorous as Smith, but more a college than seminary, Vassar's curriculum in 1875–76 presents a firm contrast to study-club programs. Candidates for the freshman class were examined in English grammar, ancient and modern geography, history of the United States, arithmetic (algebra and elementary geometry), Latin, and a choice of Greek, German, or French. In their first semester, all students followed a prescribed course of three "full studies" (courses with five recitations or lectures a week) and three "minors." The "full studies" were Latin (Livy), mathematics (a review of algebra and geometry), and a choice of Greek, German, or French. The required "minors" were lectures on physiology and hygiene, exercises in English composition, and elements of drawing. By second semester of their sophomore year, students had a choice (albeit limited) of "full studies." These included Latin, Greek, German, French, mathematics (general geometry and calculus), zoology, and chemistry. The "minors" consisted of English composition, elocution, and lectures on popular astronomy. "Full courses" offered in the junior and senior years in addition to languages were rhetoric, logic, geology, astronomy, physics, physiology, chemistry, medieval history, modern history, mental philosophy, and moral philosophy. In addition, seniors could substitute two or four "half-studies" for one or two "full studies." "Half-studies" included English literature, mathematics (an advanced course in geometry and calculus), geology (an advanced course), and astronomy (with "practical observing"). English composition was a required "minor" throughout the eight semesters; elocution was required during one semester of each year. Other mandatory "minors" introduced were lectures on Greek and Roman history and theory of art.[126]

Course requirements and titles alone point immediately to the wide gap between a college curriculum and even the most extended and meticulous of study-club programs. The Vassar graduate completed twenty-four "full studies" and nineteen "minors." With the college in session for thirty-six weeks each year, a "full study" course entailed ninety classroom hours in a semester. As most clubs met biweekly for two hours, a club season (usually nine months) would net a total of thirty-six hours, thus requiring more than two years to cover just one subject in equivalent college hours. While Vassar students did not declare majors, it is likely that they grouped themselves, as Smith women were required to, into a classical, literary, or scientific program. Even if they did not, their choice of subjects was narrow enough to ensure depth in several areas. Members of study clubs with a single focus like Shakespeare or Spain surely acquired some depth in their subject over the years, but, then, of course, they lost out on the breadth that the "minors" at Vassar helped establish. College and even seminary education provided what a study club could not: "For the one great thing she gave her pupils—scope—often quite left out of woman's education—I especially thank her," wrote Lucy Larcom of the "lady principal" of Monticello Seminary.[127] Although astronomy, botany, and physiology (women's) occasionally appeared in study-club programs, chemistry, physics, and geology did not. Mathematics was likewise absent, and the infrequent modern language clubs were designed mainly for practice in conversation and not, as were the more advanced courses at Vassar, for "the aesthetical and historical" elements.[128]

In common with adult education since its beginnings, the study-club curriculum included courses which would later be adopted into the "regular" college course of study but which were then consigned to the realm of "popular" inquiry, notably modern history, contemporary literature, government, economics, art, and music. The latter two could be found at women's colleges but were often sops to True Womanhood: Goucher College in Maryland opened in 1888 with offerings in art, elocution, and music but eventually dropped them in an attempt to emulate course offerings at Johns Hopkins.[129]

Although study-club programs had some of the ingredients of a college education, they lacked an essential catalyst, the professor. In urging club women to adopt university extension courses instead of their own self-study programs, a speaker at the Third Biennial Convention of the General Federation of Women's Clubs in 1896 capitalized on that omission:

> It is one thing to attain results that are pleasant and entertaining, and quite another to gain intellectual discipline and development. . . . It is not enough to have a good subject, to have access to the proper books; it is essential that we shall know how to treat that subject, how to use the books. . . . I do not mean to say that club women will not do very good work and end by having a fair knowledge of their subject, but I emphatically say that their knowledge will not be scholarly nor in any sense thorough.[130]

While it may be tempting to disparage study-club education, it is also well to remember the rarity of a truly college-educated woman at the end of the nineteenth century. Vassar in 1875–76 enrolled a total of 183; Smith and Wellesley together had 44 students in collegiate courses in the same year. Mount Holyoke was still a seminary; Barnard, Bryn Mawr, and Radcliffe were yet to be founded. Most women in higher education were students in "female colleges," a large majority of which were little more than finishing schools and offered only two years of instruction.[131] Goucher's first class in 1888 was "a heterogeneous group of students, almost incapable of classification . . . , many of whom were subfreshmen in one or more studies."[132] Rigor clearly existed in some colleges and even in some seminaries; social reformer Jane Addams remembered that in her junior year at Rockford Seminary she had to commit to memory

Paul's Epistle to the Hebrews, and "we analyzed and reduced it to doctrines within an inch of our lives."[133] But it is also easy to romanticize those early women pioneer scholars, bent over their books for long hours, wrapped in woolly rugs in dim, gas-lighted rooms. Vida Scudder, an early Smith graduate, acknowledged that Smith instruction was "the best then procurable" for women but recalled her instruction at Girls' Latin School in Boston as more demanding:

> Smith College did not educate me much. I look back at the four years spent there as the period in my whole life during which I was least interested in things of the mind. . . . I can not quite account for my lapse. It was due perhaps at the outset to the fact that we found freshman studies too easy. There was none of the severe discipline from which we had profited; no marks were given. . . . There was no denying it, freshman studies were . . . pretty dull for a clever girl.[134]

And while there were women such as astronomer Maria Mitchell and Wellesley professor and later president Alice F. Palmer on women's college faculties, even the president of Smith, L. Clark Seelye, admitted that "the early Faculty was not an imposing body." Smith had one full-time instructor, Professor Josiah Clarke, a former principal of Williston Academy, who taught Greek and Latin. Seelye himself taught English and biblical studies along with his administrative duties. Sarah W. Humphrey, daughter of a former president of Amherst, taught history and directed the social life of the students. The eight other men and women who made up the faculty came to the campus regularly to teach their courses but were not a sustained part of college life.[135] The year of Goucher's opening, 1888, saw one professor at the new college teaching psychology, philosophy, logic, biblical literature, and history.[136]

Despite the shortcomings of early college education for women and however thorough and demanding the best study-club programs were, there can be no valid comparison, intellectually, between the education offered by the two. Congruence did occur, however, in the company of women. In both environments women and their aspirations were not only taken seriously, they were encouraged. The criticism of professor or club critic was designed not to keep a woman in her place but to enable her to reach a higher level of performance, with the clear assumption that there was one. Surrounded by like-minded women, she could begin to shed the self-doubts often fostered by isolation from her kind. The *esprit de corps,* so new to most women, did more than produce class cheers and club songs. Morning prayer service at Smith promoted spiritual soundness, wrote President Seelye, but in addition "it was considered an inestimable aid to all members of the College . . . in the opportunity it afforded to emphasize their organic unity, to consider subjects of mutual interest, and to develop a strong and loyal *esprit de corps as a potent factor in realizing the highest academic ideal*" [emphasis added].[137]

Campus and club room alike provided women with new measures by which to judge their worth, new arenas in which to test their mettle. Intellectual accomplishments were rewarded and applauded, but there was also room to make one's mark in top leadership positions. Public speaking and a talent in dramatics earned more praise than did china painting and other "accomplishments." And both communities supplied role models other than the True Woman. Although the study of alchemy was listed neither in college catalogues nor in study-club programs, it was at work. A transformation was taking place; education, both formal and informal, was the "philosopher's stone."

≋·6·≋

"Difficulties & Delights" of Study Clubs

Public Ridicule & Private Satisfactions

Alchemy, while it was called "the art of arts and the science of sciences," from its beginning was suspect. If, indeed, it could turn base metal into gold, it would threaten the established order of the universe in which base metals occupied a prescribed and useful (if unlovely) place. Moreover, the outcome of the alchemical process was not assured; gold was promised, but might not scrambling the natural state of things produce the unexpected, an aberration, a monstrosity? Alchemists, said their brothers uneasily in the world of science, have delusions of grandeur; they have picked up some scientific jargon, but it's still all hocus-pocus.

Involved as they were with alchemy of a sort, women's clubs met with opposition of long standing. An early member of Chicago's Fortnightly recalled her first introduction to club life:

> I often played in a yard at the corner of the street where a kind woman lived who invited me into her yard. One day my father finding me there, was much shocked and forbade me going there again, saying that the woman who lived there was a dangerous person—she wore her hair short, she had most radical opinions, and, worst of all, she was the President of a Woman's Club. That woman was Mrs. Kate Newell Doggett, who founded and was president of the Fortnightly, and who

was, I suppose, one of the most cultured women Chicago has ever known.[1]

A threat to the established social order at any time will draw a response. The intensity of the repercussion varies with both the vulnerability of the social fabric and the nature of the threat. The timing of the study-club movement and the suggestions it held for gender reclassification ensured a loud, though not explosive, reaction. In part as a consequence of the political and economic upheavals of the 1860s, the years following the Civil War were witness to the shifting needle within the social compass. Class, genealogy, and tradition were losing their power to determine social position, and people clung to gender classification "as the last remaining insurance against social disorder."[2] Women's domestic bonds, which had ever held them secure, had already begun to loosen. Girls had left New England farms to work in the Lowell mills. Benevolent societies had brought upper-middle-class women face to face with squalid urban slums. The women's movement urged greater autonomy for all females. And, finally, the rising demand for teachers was pushing open for women the gates of higher education. Study-club women were one more manifestation of gender disorder, and in an attempt to keep club women in their proper place, critics cried out against the disintegration of the family, which, they said, clubs fostered. Upon the founding of the New England Women's Club in 1868, the *Boston Transcript* alerted its readers: "Homes will be ruined, children neglected, woman is straying from her sphere."[3] Edward Bok, editor of the *Ladies' Home Journal*, acknowledged the increase in women's leisure time but criticized activities that drew them away from "the great and fundamental problems directly touching the marriage relation and the home."[4] Seen as subversive of home and family, "clubbers" (a derisive term that "libbers" will recognize) proclaimed again and again their True Womanhood:

> No greater libel can be cast than the implication that club work detracts from the home. On the contrary, the fine club women of the country do not figure in the divorce court, and the home life of the club woman is, almost without exception, harmonious, well-ordered and happy.[5]

The club course of study is so attractive that each member of the club woman's family is interested, the tone of conversation raised, and the solidarity of the home strengthened.[6]

The marketplace knew better, however. The manufacturers of Electric Bitters addressed their advertisement in an El Paso, Texas, newspaper to "The Coming Woman, who goes to the club while her husband tends the baby, as well as the good old-fashioned woman who looks after the home."[7] Critics ranged from stolid President Grover Cleveland, who would have limited the activity of women to *Kinder* and *Küche*,[8] through the shrill Greencastle, Indiana, newspaper editorial which painted Elizabeth Ames, founder of the Woman's Club of Greencastle, as a temptress who "lured women from their duties as homemakers" to become members of that "unspeakable menace"[9] to the waggish husband who nicknamed his wife's Rhode Island Woman's Club the "Society for the Prevention of Home Industry."[10] Not only men were critics. Some women saw the movement of women outside the home as an indictment of the role they had themselves adopted. In response to efforts in Indianapolis to organize a women's club in 1875, one woman wrote, "I find my mission in taking care of my several little girls, and I do not wish for other work. Nor do I think I could either give or receive help by aiding your project." Another admonished, "I should think you could see that your God-given duties point in another direction."[11] Generally the southern woman was initially antagonistic to the study-club movement. Kinship rather than sex was the most powerful basis of a woman's self-identification in the South, and groups of independent women were slow to evolve.[12] In addition, the Cult of True Womanhood remained strong in the South. Writing in 1892, one club historian observed: "From the sacred home niche, where the pride and chivalry of Southern men had placed her, [the Southern woman] held herself aloof [from clubs]."[13]

Home was a "known"; in its isolation it fostered and preserved traditional ways of living and thinking. Study clubs broke through that isolation—for what? Study-club women were not part of the male classification system; they could not be pigeonholed or predicted—or controlled. Improvement of the intellect must surely be a means to some end—but what? The ambiguity was unsettling. As

Jane Croly said, if Sorosis had proposed to "do" something, it would not have been attacked on all fronts.[14] But "Sorry Sisters," one nickname for the club, had "no excuse for existence."[15] It was criticized by men as "too bold" and was feared to be in alliance with women's rights. It was criticized by women activists as "too timid" and scorned for its lack of militancy.[16]

Perhaps more threatening than the dissolution of women's bonds and the ambiguity of the purpose of the clubs was the perceived blurring of distinction between the sexes, a mixing of categories, which causes disturbance in any culture, an uneasiness summed up in 1888 by Dr. Morgan Dix, head of Trinity Church in New York City: "I disapprove of unwomanly tactics, of creatures who are not men and certainly not women."[17] The Boston club woman was cartooned as "aggressive, meddlesome, angular."[18] Consigned to the category of "strong-minded women,"[19] club members were admonished against becoming "mannish and losing the charms of womanhood."[20] College women and club women alike were warned that "intellectual activity tends to diminish their affectional power, and to diminish their regard for the graceful amenities of social life."[21] Both groups of women were accused of contributing to race suicide,[22] although the majority of club members were near the end of their childbearing years. The arguments were based on the theory of a closed energy system: a force expended in one function would not be available to any other. Use of the brain would drain energy from the reproductive organs.[23] Great caution was needed, proclaimed the *Quarterly Review* of the Methodist Episcopal Church South in 1881, "in utilizing the gifts and graces of pious, zealous, and intelligent women. Nothing can compensate for the sacrifice of feminine modesty: this must be guarded tho the heavens fall!"[24]

"The study club's most generous critics have been wont to look upon it as a violent departure from womanly ways and womanly traditions, aggressive in its tendencies," wrote Olive T. Miller, a member of Sorosis.[25] To counteract such censure, she continued, "an annual show of hospitality of some kind should be provided for, because so long as Women's Clubs are looked upon in any way askance, it is well to remind the world that even club women are ladies, and that being able to read a paper or make a speech does not prevent their remaining charming hostesses and admirable entertainers."[26]

Through their yearly lavish socials, most club women reminded "the world" (their husbands) that their club was not "advancing the rights of women to be men."[27] On those occasions men were generally entertained by the kind of accomplishments they expected of women—culinary and floral delights, music, and lighthearted verse. In a letter to a friend, an organizer of the New England Women's Club speculated on those who would attend the first meeting: "I think many will, who are dying of curiosity; some to see the monster."[28] The annual socials made every attempt to convince men that what they were seeing was what they were getting, that gender lines were still intact, that no "monster" was aborning.

Some of the same men who had urged their wives into Civil War work were the staunchest opponents of study-club participation.[29] (Had they been aware that their activities in aid of the war effort were sowing in women the same seeds of liberation already germinating in slaves, such men might have directed their patriotic zeal to other fronts.) Paradoxical on the surface, their dichotomous positions, however, were actually consonant. Selfless, anonymous charitable and benevolent work, rooted in a pious religious tradition and, until the Civil War, directed by men, fell within the simple, clearly drawn circle that comprised woman's world. Clubs, led and carried on exclusively by women, using the hitherto male tools of charters, constitutions, and parliamentary procedure, were another matter. Quietly and decorously, they were challenging the assumption of male authority over women. It is no wonder, as club woman Harriet Robinson wrote in her diary, that "Dr. Howe is averse to his wife speaking in public."[30]

Although perhaps the majority of men treated clubs with the condescension of amused toleration, one senses as well an edginess in their attitude, a defensive possessiveness about *their* domain of intellectual prowess. Oliver Wendell Holmes had once feared that even the old academy training "might make a girl intellectually too exacting for the young men of her own circle,"[31] and study clubs posed a similar possibility. In 1892 the alumnae of Abbot Academy in Massachusetts proposed the formation of "a scholarly club, which would form a sort of postgraduate course for the graduates of the academy. But this was crushed by Col. T. W. Higginson. Like most studious men, he advised recreation and entertainment for women's clubs rather than study; and the 'scholarly' idea was abandoned."[32]

Not much had changed in the fifty years since Dr. John Gregory had advised his daughters and their peers, "If you have any learning, keep it a profound secret, especially from men, who generally look with a jealous and malignant eye on a woman of great parts and a cultivated understanding."[33]

When study clubs failed to manifest recognizable feminist characteristics, criticism settled on their intellectual aspirations: "Mrs. Ballinger is one of the ladies who pursue Culture in bands, as though it were dangerous to meet it alone. To this end she had founded the Lunch Club, an association of herself and several other indomitable huntresses of erudition."[34] This opening of Edith Wharton's short story "Xingu," which first appeared in *Scribner's Magazine* in 1911, equated in caricature the educational goals of study clubs with the popular Victorian avocation of the acquisition of culture (a hobby practiced not only by women, as Howells had observed with Silas Lapham's "library"). "Culturine," it was dubbed by satirists of women's clubs,[35] among them Sinclair Lewis, who portrayed club members' intellectual efforts as the traditional feminine affinity for gentle "accomplishments" gone amok.

> "O Mrs. Kennicott, I'm in such a fix. I'm supposed to lead the discussion at the Thanatopsis Club, and I wondered would you come to help?"
> "What poet do they take up today?"
> "Why, the English ones."
> "Not all of them?"
> "Why yes. We're learning all of European Literature this year. The club gets such a nice magazine, *Culture Hints,* and we follow its programs. Last year the subject was Men and Women of the Bible, and next year we'll probably take up Furnishings and China. My, it does make a body hustle to keep up with all these new culture subjects, but it is improving."[36]

Women applied "culture" as if it were makeup, the critics complained, and not all detractors were to be found in fiction. *Club Woman* in 1898 ran an article entitled "Woman's Clubs from a Reporter's Point of View" by Josephine Woodward, who concluded that a women's club was "a body of women banded together for the purpose of meeting together."

> I have been reporting club meetings for four years and I am tired of hearing reviews of books I was brought up on. I am tired of amateur performances at occasions announced to be for the purposes of either enjoyment or improvement. I am tired of suffering under the pretense of acquiring culture. I am tired of hearing the word "culture" used so wantonly. I am tired of essays that let no guilty author escape quotation.[37]

Olive T. Miller of Sorosis devoted one whole section of her handbook *The Woman's Club* to relationships with the press. If reporters are barred from meetings, she maintained, they will make things up, and if they are allowed in, they will ridicule or misrepresent; she advised careful dispensing of "a little information."[38]

One suspects there was more truth to criticisms leveled at shallowness than at affectations of culture because club leaders themselves often admonished against "second-hand wisdom" and "encyclopedic rehearsals."[39] In their early enthusiastic attempts to digest a complete topic in one sitting, "club members writing on Plato and Dante, on the Language of the Iroquois, or the Trial of the Sarasens in Spain, found it difficult to improve upon carefully written and wisely edited pages of encyclopedias and historic tomes," admitted Mary Wood, looking back at her own club's history.[40] Some undoubtedly tried to disguise their uncertain knowledge with florid ornamentation: "The papers read at our oldtime club occasions were like sentimentally rounded periods, interspersed with flowery quotations and set in formal rows, a yard, if not two or more tiresome yards, in length."[41]

Study-club members were also an easy target for those who aimed their barbs at what they viewed as woman's inferior intelligence and her futile attempts at "higher" education.

> "I hardly see . . . how a book steeped in the bitterest pessimism can be said to elevate, however much it may instruct."
>
> "I meant, of course, to instruct," said Mrs. Leveret, flurried by the unexpected distinction between the two terms which she supposed to be synonymous. Mrs. Leveret's enjoyment of the Lunch Club was frequently marred by such surprises; and not knowing her own value

to the other ladies as a mirror for their mental compla-
cency she was sometimes troubled by a doubt of her wor-
thiness to join in their debates.[42]

Undeniably there is truth in the allegations of sophomoric scope
and self-satisfaction; the pride with which some clubs ticked off
their progression through the "greats" cannot help but elicit smiles
and frowns. Theirs was not a college education, no matter how
often members referred to their societies as "universities"; "scholarly" was a misnomer for their work. Many failed to realize what
Lucy Larcom learned when she attended a seminary after long years
of self-education: "Book knowledge . . . was not itself education,
not even culture, but only a help, an adjunct to both."[43] Criticisms
aimed at the study-club movement as a whole have a certain valid-
ity, but it became a movement only in retrospect. Its purpose lay
with individuals, and there lay its success.

In 1873 while pioneer study clubs through trial and error were
attempting to define an educated woman and to realize the concept
within their numbers, theologian John Henry Newman was describing the value of university training to the student:

> It shows him how to accommodate himself to others,
> how to throw himself into their state of mind, how to
> bring before them his own, how to influence them, how
> to come to an understanding with them, how to bear
> with them. He is at home in any society, he has common
> ground with any class; he knows when to speak and
> when to be silent; he is able to converse, he is able to
> listen; he can ask a question pertinently, and gain a les-
> son seasonably when he has nothing to impart himself.[44]

In their own less articulate, less professional, and less disciplined
way, study clubs were striving for the same effect and achieving some
remarkably similar results.

The first simple requirement of study clubs, that each woman
leave her private, accustomed sphere for several hours each month,
was the basis for all the benefits that followed. It meant that while
she could preserve her familiar True Woman identity and traditional
female ties, she perforce was exposed to lives (in the concrete and
in the abstract) different from her own. Within her own home,

nineteenth-century woman had experienced a "retarded social development [subject as she was to] the power and persistence of all those attitudes, customs, and traditions that are linked with the family and handed down by the very personal, very emotional contact with the primary group."[45] Early in the nineteenth century Mary Lyon, too, had understood that to educate young women "to a new direction" it was necessary to remove them from their homes and their "private concerns";[46] at the same time, recognizing the strength of family structure (and the necessity of allaying the fears of parents), she contrived to make Mount Holyoke Seminary as homelike as possible when she founded it in 1837. Fifty years later, meeting in each other's homes and allaying the fears of their husbands, club women found their own way to her formula.

A heightened energy surges through the writings of club women. It may have been in sole reaction to the ennui brought on by the sameness of their circle and their increased isolation as migration reduced the extended family and as the focus of their husbands' and children's lives, turned increasingly away from home, but it speaks convincingly to the revitalizing powers of club life. "I went to a Sorosis meeting the other day . . . and nothing ever impressed me so much. The fraternity, the versatility, and the spontaneity of those women was a revelation! A new life tingled through me from head to foot; my horizon broadens."[47] The woman's club, wrote Olive Miller, lifts a woman "out of the ruts into which she has allowed herself to settle, and surrounds her at once with fresh air and sunshine, in which the hobgoblins and chimeras which have haunted her—the spiritual bats and moles bred in darkness—cannot exist for a moment."[48] While American women were hardly Rapunzels locked in Victorian towers, most led severely circumscribed lives. If they belonged to organizations, they were generally societies of single purpose, founded on one dogma, opinion, or idea—societies which admitted no one of differing purpose. Again, Jane Croly's observation applies, this time without a feminist twist: "The idea of clubs for women was to rid them of the system of exclusion and separation."[49] Writing in 1954, Henry Taylor, former president of Sarah Lawrence College, underscored the educative instinct of unschooled Jane Croly: "Nothing very helpful can happen until the individual woman student learns to see life as something which extends beyond the circle of her own private interests."[50]

Immured in their homes with precious few books or magazines beyond *Godey's* or the *Ladies' Home Journal,* with a present and a future inhospitable to intellectual aspirations, women lacked the mental stimulus to draw their thoughts beyond household concerns. The result, recalled a club member, was often "solemn, arrogating, feminine, self-inclusive thinking."[51]

> During my married years [1876–1887] when life was more tranquil—and dull—I rarely heard women discuss anything but personalities, a fashionable novel, or some actress who was "the rage." They may have been dependent for happiness upon their husbands, but they took no interest in business or the professions, and lived their days in a small world of their own.[52]

In the process of forming associations, said Julia Ward Howe, women would shed "their tedious self-hood" and cast down "the idol of [their] own way."[53] "The constant personal note"[54] which had sounded throughout conversations about dress, children, servants, or neighbors was stilled during club programs. One club observer from abroad noted that "periodical meetings of this nature have a strong influence on the mind of women, on their powers of conversation, banishing frivolous and too personal subjects, accustoming them to listen attentively, to refute an argument logically."[55] Required in their club life to work in concert, women began to develop a sense of reciprocity and a respect for the will of the majority. Although women might run their homes with independent hands, club life was inimical to autocrats: "One of the first things a club president has to learn is that she must lay aside her likes and dislikes in the club."[56] Oliver Wendell Holmes once told Julia Ward Howe, "Mrs. Howe, I consider you eminently clubable," and added that he was not. Like his creation, he said, he was the Autocrat of the Breakfast Table and expected to do all the talking.[57]

Although it drew its membership almost exclusively from the middle class, the study club provided a social diversity unknown to most women, whose relationships outside the club were determined by kinship and by religious and political sympathies, associations with "our own kind."[58] While objecting to the amount of time

Smith College students in the 1880s spent in their literary clubs, President Seelye praised the same advantages that were accruing to their matronly counterparts: "They promote social intercourse between many girls who would otherwise not be associated."[59] Even coalescing around a common interest or talent did not neutralize differences in tastes, opinions, ideas, or habits. Frequently in Croly's history, clubs call attention to their democratic principles and practices. The interests of the Port Washington (New York) Woman's Club "have brought together the best elements in the neighborhood, harmonized conflicting ideas, and broken down sets and cliques."[60] In addition to its "studious and literary results," the Dubuque (Iowa) Ladies' Literary Association noted "constantly growing fellowship [and] the disappearance of the class spirit."[61] And, although it engaged in literary work, the Woman's Club of Santa Barbara, California, identified its primary aim as "[bringing] the narrow cliques of a small town into friendly, intelligent relation."[62] There were not just class and clique barriers to be breached. "Society women discovered that women who pursue serious objects do not, thereby, forfeit their social qualities, and the women who follow occupations and advocate causes . . . learned that they do not monopolize seriousness."[63]

As clubs matured, the spread in the ages of the members grew. Younger women "graduated" from "daughter" clubs, and recent college graduates often found the club an outlet for their trained, inquiring minds. The infusion of youthful ideas on an equal footing with elders' ideas was another means of jarring set ways and patterns of thinking.

> The club is a little world in itself. Women of varied types, temperaments and purposes meet in democratic equality in the club-room. Here is an opportunity for the study of human nature—and its consequent enrichment of the life of the student—never before offered to woman. Has she a talent which has long laid wrapped in a napkin? Here is the place to develop it. . . . The women are appreciative of one another. . . . The collegian brings her culture, the musician her songs, the artist her art, the wise woman her counsel, the woman-of-affairs her energy, and the commonplace woman what

she hath. Each lays her gift upon the club altar, and each
in turn partakes of the composite incense and is the better therefor.[64]

The study club was "a democracy of brains," wrote one midwestern club woman,[65] and as such it gave to many women for the first
time an intellectual basis for friendship. ("Now if Chloe likes Olivia
and they share a laboratory," wrote Virginia Woolf forty years later,
"[this] of itself will make their friendship more varied and lasting
because it will be less personal.")[66] It was not only desire for a
"broader outlook" but also for "intellectual companionship" that inspired the founding of the Skowhegan (Maine) Woman's Club.[67]
"What did club life give me?" asked Julia Howe. "Understanding of
my own sex; faith in its moral and intellectual growth."[68] The "vast
intellectual wealth in us" that had so electrified Mary Eastman at
the 1889 Sorosis convention paid for more than tuition.

It was necessary first for women to step outside their dooryards,
but more important in terms of benefits was where their direction
led, to a place which offered "some food for the mind, a quiet hour
when we can think and talk."[69] Club histories record differences of
opinion about the names of their organizations, about membership
limits, and about procedures. About their purpose, intellectual improvement, they record no disagreements; on that, club women
were in accord. This was a self-selected group of women, women
with a "mind hunger," wrote a club member,[70] women primed to
learn. What they needed was an incentive to study and encouragement in the development of disciplined thought. Even in the beginning when many did little but copy encyclopedia accounts of their
topic, women were forming patterns of study. Even then they were
becoming active learners instead of passive listeners. Even as they
cribbed, they were being exposed to orderly thoughts expressed in
logical sequence. And there was always the critic to take them to
account for accuracy, a trait which, along with breadth of thinking,
had seldom been required in the narrowly personal world of their
households. Into women's lives where "much of their work . . . is
necessarily disconnected, . . . lacks coherence and steadiness,
[and] is of the patchwork order,"[71] study clubs imposed a task which
demanded that the member "concentrate her faculties and focus
them upon the object to be attained, the purpose to be accom-

plished."[72] In addition, though their work may not have been profound, it was generally painstaking and seldom dashed off, as satirists would have had it. Participants thus began to develop a sense of the scholar's patience and perseverance, the habit of "deferring immediate and personal gratifications" that Julia Ward Howe counted among the benefits of study-club membership.[73]

While their methods of learning may have suffered from inefficiency, study-club women through trial and error were evolving a model of education strikingly similar to one recently proposed as especially effective in the teaching of women students. Called "connected education," the model is based on a study of "the academic experiences of ordinary women." For her education to proceed, the study asserts, "every woman, regardless of age, social class, ethnicity, and academic achievement, needs to know that she is capable of intelligent thought, and she needs to know it right away." She needs confirmation that she "can be trusted to know and to learn" and to be accepted as a person with something to say, no matter what her academic background. The experience of being doubted is for her not energizing, as studies have suggested that it is for men, but debilitating. Women, the study found, learn best when "teacher and student construct knowledge together, [when students are] not mere spectators [but] actively nurture each other's ideas, [when] no one apologizes for uncertainty [because] it is assumed that evolving thought must be tentative." A "connected class" works best when the group meets over a long period of time and gets to know each other well, "like a family, trying to work out a family problem."[74] In their "family" setting, finding among themselves the acceptance and encouragement of intellectual endeavors not proffered women by contemporary society, study-club members had the freedom to develop a pedagogy especially suited to their needs, one which would organically bridge the gap between where they were and where they wanted to be.

Just as club women found their own way to an effective method of learning, so too the content they chose took them out of the ordinary intellectual traffic of nineteenth-century women, introduced some system and organization to their reading, and generated a wider idea of what the world had to offer. As clubs grew more sophisticated in their study, in addition to the miscellaneous ideas of great thinkers, women in "core courses," yearly programs built around one theme, experienced the rudiments of liberal arts integration. In a company of like-minded women, "efforts otherwise desultory [when attempted on one's own] are given connection, purpose, and fruitage," advised the editors of a book list for study clubs.[75] "Solitude and silence are essential to philosophical insight," wrote club woman Ellen M. Mitchell in 1892, "but association and discussion with others . . . will dispel prejudices and broaden the insight gained."[76] With experience and growing self-confidence came the "development of the judicial faculty," observed club member Jennie M. Lozier.[77] Confronted with new ideas, opposing ideas, or those divergent from her own, the club woman was forced to evaluate and to learn a measure of objectivity, to find, as she was reminded at an annual meeting of the Massachusetts Federation of Women's Clubs, that she could be criticized or that she could disagree "and still be friends."[78]

> The constant interchange of ideas on every subject enlightens the club woman in regard to the books she should read . . . Sharing the matured thought of women who have spent their lives in one work be it art, music, literature, or philanthropy, helps her to new opinions, and shows her different sides of a subject. She expands mentally from day to day.[79]

Having found something to say, the study-club woman next needed the courage to say it. "Self-trust is the secret of success" was the motto of the Monday Club of Lafayette, Indiana.[80] In part, the substance of her idea provided an impetus; however shallow her work on Plato, Dante, or Shakespeare might have been, she was trafficking with weighty material, with words the world took seriously. Nevertheless, esteemed authors would not have been enough without the member's *self*-esteem. In a small, informal, supportive group of women and without the need first to win the acceptance of men, the study-club woman found her voice.

The advent of study clubs in homes is not unimportant as a contributing factor in the development of the self-confidence of these women. Although the message was different from the social visits they were accustomed to paying, the medium was much the same. Surrounded by everyday household trappings, they were anchored in the familiar as they cast about in new waters. "One of the greatest needs of women," wrote Sorosis member Celia Burleigh with apt imagery, "is an hospitable entertainment of their thought."[81] "Many of us mute, inglorious Miltons who had not the courage to speak our minds before several hundred in formidable array, expressed our humble opinions freely over the tea-cups."[82]

Having been told not to speak up in public, to avoid politics, and to defer higher education to their brothers, nineteenth-century American women were led to the conclusion that they were incapable of these things.[83] To unlearn this lesson took time and the mutual trust engendered by a newfound sisterhood. "Sorosis afforded me an atmosphere so genial, an appreciation so prompt, a faith so generous, that every possibility of my nature seemed intensified, and all its latent powers quickened into life."[84] "Instead of censure," wrote one club member, "women who seek to be and do something in the world now find within the club encouragement and generous sympathy."[85] Every woman in the club was entitled to an equal place, not through charity or toleration, but through consideration and respect. In their clubs, women found in a semipublic arena what they had experienced before only in the intimate world of intense, personal female friendships. As Smith-Rosenberg describes that private world, it was one "in which hostility and criticism of other women were discouraged, and thus a milieu in which women could develop a sense of inner security and self-esteem. . . . They valued one another. Women, who had little status or power in the larger world of male concerns, possessed status and power in the lives and worlds of other women."[86] The Chicago Woman's Club observed the results: "The most notable features of the general meetings are the freedom and ease with which so large a proportion of the members take part in the discussions and the high and earnest tone which pervades the same. This is a direct outgrowth of . . . the feeling of strong sisterly pride and affection which binds the members together."[87] Invested with a new sense of collective identity, even these conservative women were able to reassess the intellectual capabilities of their sex and of themselves individually. Alone, in a time when "they did not yet know each other,"[88] they had had neither the courage, the power, nor the opportunity to refute the female stereotypes.

Fueled every two weeks with small successes, club women quietly began to redesign the template of womanliness and femininity. In time, in addition to the new notches they cut for intellectual aspiration and achievement, they added other serious endeavors. Leadership, they found, was not synonymous with masculinity. Nor was public speaking and the assertion of one's own opinion. Women were capable not only of spending money, but of raising it—often in the large amounts needed to build club houses. Between 1888 and 1890, the club women of Indianapolis formed a corporation, with stock held only by women, and raised the $28,000 required to erect the imposing stone Propylaeum, which became "an indispensable and paying institution" for the city's women's clubs and other private organizations.[89] With their efforts, they built more than an assembly hall: "Men who have had control of material forces, who have built and owned since the beginning, cannot understand the thrill of satisfaction with which women see a work of their own, involving financial risk, begun in fear, brought to successful completion."[90] Quite unplanned, together in their study-club groups, women began to unfold the potential of their gender and to look inside themselves for signs of its being.

In the midst of the delegates massed for the First Biennial Convention of the General Federation of Women's Clubs in 1890, Jennie M. Lozier spoke of the first benefit of membership in a study club: "It gives to woman a sense of individuality."[91] Contemporary historian Daniel S. Smith would likely agree: "Education may be a proxy variable for the degree to which a woman defines her life in terms of self rather than of others."[92] The concept of an autonomous self was clearly absent from the ideology of the True Woman as, lacking a rite of passage, she melded from True Daughter to True Wife without opportunity to discover a true identity. Journalist Jane C. Swisshelm documented her conscious, but ultimately failed, attempt at selflessness:

> It was not only my art-love which must be sacrificed to my duty as a wife, but my literary tastes must go with it. "The husband is the head of the wife." To be head, he must be superior. An uncultivated husband could not be the superior of a cultivated wife. I knew from the first that his education had been limited, but thought the defect would be easily remedied as he had good abilities,

but I discovered he had no love for books. His spiritual guides derided human learning and depended on inspiration. My knowledge stood in the way of my salvation, and I must be that odious thing—a superior wife—or stop my progress, for to be and appear were the same thing. I must be the mate of the man I had chosen; and if he would not come up to my level, I must go to his. So I gave up study, and for years did not read one page in any book save the Bible.[93]

The True Woman lived for her family through *self*-sacrifice. Her club work allowed no such thing. With her developing ego strength, which unlike the individualism of the marketplace did not fuel itself on the exploitation of others, club work was something she did "just for me." It demanded of each woman *her* thoughts and opinions, *her* leadership and particular talents; years before in Seneca Falls, Elizabeth Cady Stanton had asserted, "Woman herself must do the work."[94] With a sense of individual identity, a new perception of self, the club woman began to define her own future. From that time on, higher education would be a part of it. As the motto of the Tourist Club of West Union, Iowa, proclaimed: "Thought once awakened does not slumber."[95]

=≈·7·≈=

"The Magic Circle"

The Decatur Art Class

Although one may deduce a family's history from a photograph album, carefully kept, it is the photographer's diary which can confirm or refute the viewer's thesis, can stimulate insights, suggest private effects, and reveal distortions through circumstantial or subjective overrepresentation or omission. So, too, with written history. With demographic tools, with public documents and utterances, one may trace an ideology or a movement. It is the diary or, in this case, a study-club's meticulously kept minutes, which provide a check on the overview. The close-up, detailed picture provided by the minutes of the Decatur (Illinois) Art Class, founded in 1880, conforms closely to the panoramic display of the study-club movement. More important, it allows us to view the effects of the overall pattern on individual lives and enables us to see things from the inside out.

October 14, 1899

The first business was an election of officers. A trial ballot for president was taken without nominations. So large was the vote for the former president no other name was considered and by vote of acclamation Mrs. Millikin was (considered) declared elected.[1]

So opened the twentieth year of weekly meetings of the Decatur Art Class from 2:30 to 4:30 on Saturday afternoons. In its meeting at the home of Mrs. J. F. Roach, the Class proceeded quickly and easily to fill the remaining offices for the year. The parliamentary ease of the members and the ready accession of the officers illustrate on a simple but fundamental level the growth in self-confidence achieved by the twenty "ladies of the club" in the central Illinois farm community. Without even a paragraph break, the minutes flow smoothly on to the next agenda item, the members unaware of the transformation that had occurred within their sisterhood of scholars during the first two decades of their club's existence.

The self-confidence which enabled the women of the Art Class to execute their middle-aged "cartwheels" and thus to view the world from a changed perspective had been pieced together slowly from the fabric of their everyday lives in the club. At the first meeting of the Class on 17 January 1880, the minutes reveal, despite some gentle bravado, a self-conscious insecurity. After the casting of secret ballots for the officers to fill a six-month term, "Mrs. President took her seat amid some confusion but with considerable ease and nonchalance. The address was short and full of point. She said she could not—as was usual on such occasions thank the class for the compliment—as she felt her want of experience so much."[2]

Ten years provided ample experience; by 1890 "Mrs." had disappeared from officers' titles, the officers filled in for one another without hesitation, and members felt secure enough to tease their leaders. "The President leaving the solid, substantial and improving for a trifling matinee at the Opera House, it fell to the lot of the Vice-President to conduct the meeting, which she did in a very acceptable manner, forgetting her duties and dignity not more than half a dozen times during the afternoon."[3] By 1898, elections had become old hat and had taken on a girlish playfulness and genuine nonchalance.

> It was the day and hour for distributing honors of the class and there being no hindrances, those present proceeded to put themselves into offices. Each with grace and sweetness desired to give the office to the other, and the other was too unselfish to desire the office. The election moved with magical smoothness until it came to a

selection for treasurer where the ladies like Diogenes took a lantern . . . and went out to look for an honest man. He was found in the person of Mrs. Roach. Mrs. Millikin having been busy ministering to Mrs. Quinlans [sic] bad cough, was surprised upon returning with a second glass of wine, by recieving [sic] a rising Salute as President of the class.[4]

Unsure in the beginning of their roles as students and as parliamentarians, founders of the Class had taken care, a bit defensively, to assert the seriousness of their endeavors: "the ladies conversed upon the various topics with much interest—much more than we are, even, supposed to talk upon the affairs of our neighbors."[5] The minutes of those early days rarely even hint at club conversation beyond the business and "lesson" at hand. Later, confident in their student identities, the group could admit to less than high-minded interests. The Valentine's Day meeting in 1905 began with a display of valentines made by pupils in Decatur schools.

That the atmosphere was visibly affected by these touching sentiments is not to be wondered at and many heart to heart talks followed before the lesson was entered upon. One being especially worthy of mention—the conversation between Mrs. Nelson and Mrs. Wells regarding the patent medicine prescribed for our good friend, Mrs. Roach who was unable to be present to act in self defense.[6]

The next sentence carried the Class right into Books X–XII of the *Aeneid*.

Another measure of the members' developing self-confidence, which enabled them to make effective use of their educational endeavors, revolved around the role of the critic. In the Decatur Art Class, as in most other study clubs, the critic's main task was the correction of pronunciation and grammatical construction. As one of the few immediately discernible marks of education, criticism in that area can understandably be threatening if one cares about such things, as members of a study club must have. The Art Class established the office of critic two months after the founding of the club. Upon the appointment of Miss Alice Judd to that position, the secretary noted that it was "another step in the right direction. It is complimentary to the class to be willing to be criticized. One of the brightest lights has said: 'We have ascended several rounds of the literary ladder when willing to be criticized.' " [7] The critic herself did not seem so sure as the secretary that her efforts would be viewed as complimentary.

> She seemed to manifest a little timidity lest she might offend. The Art Class will not be offended at having its errors pointed out. Any critic may rest assured that her criticisms will be most kindly received by each and all and the rest of the class concede the same priviledge [sic] to themselves—to criticize the critic—nor will she get offended. No one pretends to perfection and the one idea of this class is improvement and we all realize the fact that it is from our mistakes we learn the most. [8]

Miss Judd, however, had read the group correctly. For a while at least, they were content on the bottom round of the literary ladder, with their pride intact. After Miss Judd's critical report in her third week in office, "some little excitement followed—but it is well to have some folks stirred up. It is good for their advancement. Indeed it is good for us all. We need agitation to keep us from stagnation." [9]

Whether the critic learned tact or the members learned to speak with more accuracy, one year later the secretary's note on the critic's report was more positive: "It is encouraging to see that our errors are becoming more and more like 'Angel visits—few and far between,' consequently the report . . . was brief." [10] Before long, criticism had clearly become an uneventful part of the proceedings: "Some well deserved criticisms for interruptions and irregular discussions were made." [11] Still, sensitivities were yet delicate: "Miss Philips special critic made a brief report. The president then called for general criticisms. One lady stepped aside from the usual custom and criticized the grammatical construction of one of our poor members, but through pity and kindness wouldn't tell who, and no one was 'a going' to guess." [12] Nevertheless, members soon began calling for more rigorous criticism: "Mrs. Walston was appointed critic for another month with the request that she be very severe in the future." [13] By its tenth year, the Class was able to tease the critic as it had its officers:

The crowning feature of the afternoon was the report of the critic—she criticized without stint or mercy—neighbor or friend, officers or privates—grandmother, mother-in-law—Mrs. or Miss. She thumbed the dictionary from Alpha to Omega—she knocked at the storehouse of memory, and laid at our feet rules learned in "Auld Lang Syne"—she held up before us errors to which she had called our attention until her patience was threadbare.[14]

Seldom, however, did concern with pronunciation abate, although in later years initial edginess turned to pride or to the cavalier attitude of the sophisticate. When Mrs. Millikin returned to the Class after a winter's sojourn in Florida, the secretary touted the group's familiarity with Latin:

> A welcome glad awaited her
> Which she with grace acknowledged
> "Salute" it was, but not the one
> That's used by those who're "colleged."[15]

Over the years the Class "warmly argued" over the pronunciation of *acoustics* (*koo* or *kū*) and *Theseus* (*sē əs* or *səs*) and laughed over its difficulties with foreign names during a discussion of European revolutions of 1848 and 1849: "The critic was so faithful she taught us to say 'yellachick' and other names equally as barberous [sic] till we all refused."[16]

The saga of the Art Class and the Central Illinois Art Union perhaps best exemplifies the development of the Art Class members' self-confidence. In the spring of its first year, the Art Class was invited to the first gathering of local art societies for the purpose of learning something of each other's work and uniting "for mutual benefit."[17] The groups (the majority had exclusively female memberships, but the president of the Union was always a male) represented the towns of Bloomington, Champaign, Decatur, Jacksonville, Lincoln, Peoria, and Springfield. The yearly two-day gathering called for a welcoming address, the presentation of a thirty-minute essay from each club on topics assigned by a Union committee, musical entertainment, an art exhibition, and often a visit to a local site of interest.

Invited on April 24 to attend the first meeting of the Union on May 26, the members of the Art Class had little time to generate anxiety. On May 1, the Class elected Mrs. R. J. Oglesby, wife of a former governor of Illinois, as essayist to be accompanied by three delegates. The following week, two of the delegates declined their post, and the week after, Mrs. Oglesby abdicated her position. The secretary, "Mrs. Dr. Walston," was "appointed" in her stead and read her essay on "The Pleasures and Benefits of Art." Apprised by the returning delegates of the full attendance and the erudite essays of Professor J. H. Woods, Colonel D. C. Smith ("an authority on all branches of Art"), and Dr. T. J. Pitner, the Class the following spring was hardly exuberant about participation in the Union gathering. Mrs. J. E. Bering, the first nominee for essayist, declined, "saying it would be impossible for her to read in public."[18] Always helpful, the group moved that she write the essay, which someone else would read. Mrs. Bering refused their solicitation, and Mrs. Millikin, the founding spirit of the Class and a former teacher, agreed to the task. Perhaps hoping to catch members off guard or to give the essayist enough time to perfect her recitation to her satisfaction, the Class in 1882 decided to elect its essayist for the Union gathering months in advance. Miss Mary Wilder agreed to her election but recanted a month later. Miss Alice Judd, absent from the Class on the day of Miss Wilder's defection, was elected in her place.

In 1884, the Art Class offered to sponsor the Union's convention in May. After two more years' experience and perhaps feeling more secure on home territory, Mrs. Bering without a demur now found it possible "to read in public" and accepted the Class's nomination for essayist. For the welcoming address, however, the women looked beyond their ranks and gender and chose, without discussion or debate, Judge William E. Nelson of Decatur. In one point only did they depart from the procedure of the previous sponsoring organizations (three out of the four had been art societies whose presidents were male): they would suggest an essay topic for only the Art Class, allowing other clubs their freedom of choice. While not totally unambiguous, the wording of that decision in the minutes suggests an impatience with autocracy rather than a feeling of inadequacy to the job: the "Class did not feel it to be within their province to make suggestions farther than to their own essayist." From February on, lessons, though not abandoned, were often hurried to leave time for committee reports on site (the Christian Church), programs, music, decorations, entertainment, and finance (each member of the Class was assessed ninety cents following the convention to cancel all indebtedness).[19]

The success of the meeting and Mrs. Bering's debut did little, apparently, to alleviate the members' fears of the podium. Mrs. B. O. McReynolds was elected essayist to the next meeting, at Peoria, but "owing to extreme disclination [sic] on her part to perform the duties," the Class gave her a week to consider her decision; her "resignation" of the post came via written note. Upon her return to the group, however, Mrs. McReynolds agreed to write the essay provided someone else would read it. Because her name does not appear among the delegates, and no mention is made of the essay after the convention (it was usually read at the club meeting directly following the gathering), it is likely that the Art Class contribution in 1885 was strictly corporeal.[20] The next two years saw the usual resistance to publicly expressing their private thoughts and testing their public poise, but in 1888 the power of sorority solved the problem. The club decided on a "composite essay," all members contributing a section with the veteran Mrs. Bering reading the whole.[21]

In 1889 the roiling of impatience and the first signs of humor around what had now become the essayist issue signaled the change in tide that would occur the following year. Not only was Mrs. George Haworth nominated, "the desire of the class was most affectionately, sincerely and unanimously urged upon her." In a week "the President reported that Mrs. Haworth had rendered her decision and when known that it was in the negative, all were distraught, recognizing that she would ably represent the Class, and grieved that ill health would compel her to such a necessity." Because Mrs. Haworth was well enough to attend the convention and to report back vigorously on the proceedings, it seems a fair guess that the grieving was done tongue-in-cheek. Mrs. Haworth suggested as essayist in her stead a friend, who, although known to the women, was not a member of the Class. "While the ladies appreciated her generous and kind offer it was voted that the Class, if possible, be represented by one of their own members. Miss Elizabeth Jack became the unanimous choice of the class, but pleas, threats, entreaty, and taffy were alike unavailing." The secretary recorded her own exasperation that not 1 out of "20 ladies of at least average intelligence" would serve. "The conclusion has been reached that they are afraid of wounding the feelings of those who have written in the past by their papers—but we make them our bow and humbly ask them not to

> "View as with a Critic's eye
> But pass our imperfections by"
> As you'd scarce expect it at our age
> To speak in public on the stage.[22]

No essayist represented the Art Class in Bloomington that year.

The minutes of the tenth year chronicle no *annus mirabilis* of the Decatur Art Class, but they mark a subtle change in tone and spirit, much like that which occurred at women's colleges a decade later[23] as the hard-working, self-conscious student walking her solitary way to library or chapel gave way to groups of exuberant collegians linked by daisy chains. In both club and college there was an air of release, of creativity, a relaxation of rules, an awareness, perhaps, of coming of age. Among the year's activities of the Decatur women (a year which also saw the founding in New York of the General Federation of Women's Clubs), cause and effect remain inextricable. For the first time they embarked on the third consecutive year of study of one topic, English history. In December Mrs. Walston departed from the historical study to read her essay on "The English Woman." Later, Mrs. Hatch composed a Class song. In January the club for the first time devoted a whole meeting to the celebration of its anniversary. And in February Mrs. W. E. Nelson simply and quietly accepted the first-ballot nomination as Art Union essayist and delivered her paper, "Some Glimpses into the Picture Gallery of the Ages," at Jacksonville three months later as promised.[24]

In 1891 the Art Class again sponsored the Union gathering. This time, however, the election of essayist was perfunctory (Mrs. Millikin by unanimous vote) and secondary to the nomination by voice vote of one of their own (in membership and gender), Mrs. Walston, to deliver the welcoming address. Both matters were recorded in five brief and unadorned sentences before the business turned to logistical concerns. Two months of busy preparations had been completed when in mid-March the Art Class received a letter from the

Honorable J. S. Foley, president of the Art Union, requesting that the group consider postponement of the annual May meeting until October. The discussion was euphemistically "*warm* and enthusiastic," but the club acquiesced and sent an immediate reply to Judge Foley. After two weeks without communication from the judge, with "arrangements . . . in a state of confusion," the Class requested Mrs. Bering, in whose home the first telephone in Decatur had been installed ten years prior, "to communicate with Judge Foley by telephone in order that the class might know something of the time of the meeting . . . before adjournment." An October gathering was ascertained, arrangements were adjusted, but at the last meeting of the year the minutes note that "a general discussion regarding the Art Union was warm and wordy [no longer enthusiastic] but without serious results." A discussion topic two weeks after the convention was more to the point: "To decide whether or not the Art Class would remain connected with the organization known as the Central Illinois Art Union." The vote was affirmative, and although affiliation was questioned again the following year, Miss Jack (who earlier had not succumbed to threats or taffy) read her essay on "Women of Other Days and These" at the annual meeting in Champaign. In 1893 the Class duly elected its essayist (without either "warmth" or "enthusiasm"), but the annual convocation was postponed, this time indefinitely as the Art Union, without obituary, passively relinquished its existence.[25]

How much their thirteen-year experience with the Art Union contributed to the development of self-confidence and assertion of individuality among the Art Class members is impossible to determine from the records. At the least, Union proceedings exposed delegates to a larger world; at the most, they affirmed each essayist's intellectual worth. On the conscious level of these Decatur women, the Union may have registered, like the reflection from a storefront window, as a periodic reminder of their identity and, perhaps, of unfinished business.

The woman who had won by acclaim the honor of guiding the Decatur Art Class through its twentieth year was its founder, Anna B. Millikin, a paradigmatic leader of "strong personal character."[26] Born Anna Bernice Aston in 1832, Mrs. Millikin was a graduate of Washington (Pennsylvania) Female Seminary, where the sisters of James Millikin were in attendance. Accompanying her father from Pennsylvania in 1855 to his new pastorate in Mt. Zion, seven miles from Decatur, Anna Aston taught at the Mt. Zion Male and Female Academy until her marriage in 1857 to James Millikin, a dealer in livestock and land and soon-to-be prominent banker in Decatur.[27]

Like many study-club leaders, Mrs. Millikin was active during the Civil War in Decatur's Sick and Wounded Soldiers' Aid Society, part of the Sanitary Commission's efforts, serving as the local agency's president in 1864–65.[28] Childless, the prosperous Millikins after the war traveled extensively in the United States and abroad, developing their interest in art, which they expressed in the large Italianate home they built on six acres on North Pine Street in Decatur. In the Millikin Homestead today, which is listed in the National Register of Historic Places, may be seen the hand-painted name of the Decatur Art Class on the transom of the second-floor Snowball Room. The charming, airy white-woodworked room, named after the giant hydrangeas originally painted on its ceiling, is a delightfully playful element in an otherwise somber, solid, and conventionally Victorian structure, and it calls to mind immediately the guiding spirit of the club, who was "made in no common mold."[29]

To all outward appearances Anna Millikin properly filled the sober and supportive role of wife of a leading citizen. The comforts of husband and home were her first responsibilities, she rarely missed a service at the First Presbyterian Church, she sat on the board of the YWCA (James Millikin, on the YMCA), she prompted her husband's benevolence to orphans and elderly "genteel ladies" who lacked means of support, and, following her husband's death, she maintained his support of the fledgling Millikin University, which he had founded in 1903. To the community at large she was a quiet, serious, and dignified figurehead.[30] At her funeral services in 1913, the Rev. W. H. Penhallegon, a longtime family friend, hinted at another dimension:

> That we did not know Mrs. Millikin better is a testimony to her personality and individuality. She was made in no common mold. We were made of one mold and she of another. We did not all understand her but when she was understood she was deeply and fully appreciated. She did not take persons into her personal friendship but she took the whole community into her heart.[31]

Mrs. Millikin's reserve did not entirely desert her in the Art Class:

> The president [Mrs. Millikin] was near us
> And she could plainly hear us
> But we the same of her, could not relate.
> Her conversation meagre
> For which we all were eager
> Was given only when the need was great![32]

Although the organizing meeting in 1880 was held in her home and she presided as chairman, Mrs. Millikin declined to serve as an officer of the study club until the second year, when she accepted the post of secretary. In the minutes she rarely appears as a prime mover; weeks go by without mention of her name. Yet her joy and pride in this company of women sing when she is onstage. She is the first secretary to write the minutes in rhyme. It is she who first proposes special remembrance of the club's anniversary. On her trips south in the winter her presence is sustained through her letters and gifts of fruits and flowers—and by the spirit of playfulness, the sense of individuality, and the generosity of spirit that by her example she encouraged in her "sisters."

Stories of Anna Millikin still circulate among citizens in Decatur. They smile at the frugality (mentioned, too, in her funeral sermon) and distrust of this wealthy woman who covered her carpets with newspapers lest the sun fade them and who locked the door leading from the kitchen to the rest of the house while plumbers were installing a sink. They wink at the phone call Mrs. Millikin made one night to her husband who had not returned home at the appointed hour from a civic meeting at the home of a prominent Decatur benefactress.[33] "Anna B. Millikin Devoted Life to Husband's Dreams" reads the headline in a recent Decatur newspaper article. "She was not a 'liberated woman,'" the story continues, "and probably would never have desired that. Rather she chose to dedicate her life solely to the service of her husband James and the realization of his dreams."[34] The Art Class minutes reveal a much different woman, one more in keeping with the firsthand accounts of Eunice McKee, at ninety-two still a member of the Art Class. "I grew up next door to Mrs. Millikin's cousin. Aunt Anna had a team of black horses, Morning Star and Evening Star, and we were thrilled, of course, to be invited to ride in the carriage with her. Once when we were nine, we dressed up as ladies (I wore my grandmother's wedding dress) and went to pay a call on Aunt Anna. There was no answer to our knock at the front door, and when we went to the back, there was Aunt Anna in the kitchen with her apron on, canning with her maid. She stopped her work and gave us tea in the parlor. She wouldn't let us leave through the kitchen. 'Such dignified company,' she said, 'must depart by the front door.' "[35]

With that reminiscence, Mrs. Millikin's graceful but firm copper-plate entry in the Art Class minutes, written in lavender ink in March of 1881, comes as no surprise:

> Twas a miserable day, the last time we met,
> The streets were all muddy, the crossings were wet.
> It drizzled and rained, and the wind did blow,
> But before we came home, it had turned to snow.
> The beautiful snow, like a mantle of white,
> Hid all things ungainly completely from sight.
> Notwithstanding all this, I will say as I pass,
> Nine ladies were there, who belong to the class,
> With umbrellas and shawls, rubber cloaks, if you choose,
> But, who is afraid, when they have gum shoes.
> The lesson was Raphael, his wonderful skill
> Creating immortal pictures at will.
> Madonnas and frescoes, cartoon also came in,
> For tapestries such as are made at Gobelin.
> Mrs. Greene was our critic, quite perfect were we,
> Yet she noticed some errors—sans ceremonie—
> Few corrections were made on the proper names,
> This shows also improvement, if we only take pains.
> Six notes of excuse were handed in—
> Which releases the ladies from paying their tin.
> Adjourned to meet, as I see you all know.
> At Mrs. Walston's home, on N. Main row. [36]

Her playfulness and originality included depth as well as doggerel, as noted in the review of her Art Union essay "Some People and Art," delivered at age fifty-nine in 1891: "The paper was a witty satire on modern society. The writer ingeniously traced resemblances between the various geological strata and successive stages of society. The essay was characterized by much scientific information and bright application in an unusual direction."[37]

Anna Millikin's gentle, ironic humor was never gratuitous. With it she guided the Class, paradoxically, to further seriousness and with it she expressed the importance of the club in her life. "The Art Class met at the home of Mrs. Millikin. . . . We knew, since actions speak louder than words, that a true welcome was extended to us, as the clock had been set back in order to prolong our stay."[38]

While there is little doubt of the service of Mrs. James Millikin, "quiet in demeanor and unostentatious in manner of life,"[39] to her husband, it is equally clear that in the Art Class Anna Millikin came into her own. On a grand scale with an elegant seven-course luncheon for the group on its twentieth anniversary and in more intimate gestures, like the sprig of myrtle with its purple bloom (the Class color) presented to each member upon departure for a summer's recess, she openly expressed her creativity and affection just as in the minutes she zestfully and proudly displayed her ardent desire for and pride in learning and her fine, sparkling intelligence. Surviving her husband by four years, Anna Millikin left her entire estate in trust to be used for educational and charitable purposes as the trustees deemed most appropriate; her one stipulation was that her home, which had so often welcomed the Art Class, be bequeathed to the public as an art institute.[40]

The names of the officers who served with Anna Millikin in the club's twentieth year had long appeared on Art Class rolls. (Most names, in fact, had long appeared. Of the twenty founders, eleven were still active members in 1899–1900, three had moved from Decatur, and four had died.) The original Mrs. W. T. Wells, who died in 1892, had been a founder; the second Mrs. Wells, elected vice-president in 1899, was the former Elizabeth Jack, who had delivered the Art Union essay at its final convocation. The secretary, Mrs. E. A. Gastman, had held membership since 1881, and, like Mrs. Millikin, Mrs. J. F. Roach, the treasurer, had been a founder.

The components of the original nucleus of the Art Class were women who were not unfamiliar with the benefits of women's organizations. Mrs. W. H. Close had served with Mrs. Millikin in the Soldiers' Aid Society. The first Mrs. Wells, Mrs. A. T. Hill, Mrs. V. G. Hatch, and Mrs. A. J. Gallagher, daughter of Decatur pioneer E. O. Smith, had formed the Ladies' Library Association in 1867. Seven years later to counteract the growing attraction of saloons, a Reading Room Association was organized to augment the small rented space of the library. Although its officers were men, among

Study-club membership was predominantly white, middle-class, and middle-aged. Members of the Folio Club of Cleveland, Ohio, were at the turn of the century mature women "who have already entered upon the serious work of life."

Although urban club members often numbered in the hundreds and divided their work into "departments," most clubs, like the Bartlesville (Oklahoma) Tuesday Club, limited their membership in order to meet comfortably in each other's homes.

Elmer Chickering Co.

Club women took their study seriously, and even their light-hearted "off-days" had an educational design. In 1906 New England Women's Club members came to a Dickens Night dressed as their favorite character from the author's novels. Julia Ward Howe is seated center.

Students in early women's colleges often formed reading groups and later as graduates found in study clubs a similar circle of like-minded, inquiring minds. Pictured here is the Washburn House Reading Club of Smith College in 1886.

The Decatur Art Class often held its special celebrations at the Millikin residence on North Pine Street. The transom of the second-floor "Snowball Room," where the club gathered, still bears the hand-painted inscription of the club's name.

Anna B. Millikin, former teacher and founder of the Decatur (Illinois) Art Class in 1880, was described as "quiet in demeanor and unostentatious in manner of life." Club records reveal another side as she inspired the club with her witty rhymed minutes, searching curiosity, and exuberantly creative devices for making learning fun.

While members focused intently, under the watchful eye of "the critic," on Dante, Greek art, and Spencer's theory of music at biweekly club meetings, club anniversaries were celebrated lavishly with wine and song. Here the Decatur Art Class commemorates its twentieth year in 1900 in the Millikin dining room.

Asked to represent the Decatur Art Class with an essay delivered to a regional meeting of art clubs in 1881, Elizabeth M. Bering declined, "saying it would be impossible for her to read in public." Within three years she had found her public voice, and for her later interest in women's issues she was nicknamed in club minutes "our self-styled suffer-a-gist."

*Although discussion of politics, religion, and "the woman ques-
tion" was banned from most club agendas, a growing awareness of members' intellectual capabilities and resultant self-
confidence is captured in this 1895 photograph of three Decatur
Art Class members' departure, on their own, for Europe.*

CLUB NIGHT IN THE VALLEY.

Undaunted by the weather, study-club members by 1906 were a familiar sight to Syracuse, New York, cartoonist Ladendorf. These women appear to be on their way to an annual "Men's Night," the rare occasion where books and papers made no appearance.

Club mottoes, spelled out on seals and gold pins, expressed club purposes. The motto of the Decatur Art Class, inscribed around a portrait of helmeted Minerva, was Animi Cultus Humanitatus Cibus, *"Mental Culture Is the Food of Humanity."*

its directors were Mrs. Hill, Mrs. Gallagher, and Mrs. R. L. Walston.[41] Having served others, these women were now free in the Art Class to serve themselves.

Like college women of the time, members of the Art Class came from the rapidly expanding, economically and socially mobile middle class. A number were the wives of professional men—the superintendent of schools, a lawyer and former governor, two judges, and three physicians. Alice Roberts, a founder and one of the few unmarried women in the Art Class, was a schoolteacher, as had been Mrs. Millikin, Mrs. Ira Barnes, Mrs. Hill, and Mrs. Gastman. Later, Mrs. Nelson and Mrs. V. N. Hostetler continued to teach while married, the former a "much beloved" English teacher and the latter ending her long career as high school dean of girls. With the arrival of the railroad in Decatur in 1854, the town expanded rapidly, and business and industrial interests superseded family farming as economic mainstays. The husbands of two of the founding wives were partners in the Decatur Casket Company. Another was a manufacturer, and James Millikin was the banker for all these new enterprises. Three women were the wives of former mayors.[42]

On its fiftieth anniversary, early member Elizabeth Jack Wells spoke of the collective membership of the Art Class:

> It has been in no sense made up from a clique, or from a uniform measure of intelligence, or social position, or monetary importance, but has been made up of women who would seek culture and be steadfast in the pursuit of it. When once within the magic circle, they are assimilated and bound together by friendship and loyalty. Why, there are women in the class today whom I might not know when I meet them in Heaven had I not known them in the Art Class.[43]

While her comments about a democracy of intelligence and motivation undoubtedly apply, the membership in the first two decades belies any Whitmanesque catalogue of sisterhood. This was a tightly knit group. There were blood ties among the three Roberts members and between the two Jack sisters, daughters of the principal of Decatur High School. Mrs. Hill and Mrs. Ira Barnes were also sisters. In addition to being a sister-in-law to Mrs. Ira Barnes, Mrs. Will

Barnes was the sister of Mrs. Oglesby. Mrs. McReynolds was the aunt by marriage of Mrs. R. S. Bohon. The Roberts family, the Roaches, the Ewings, and the Clokeys were members of the First Methodist Church. Mrs. Hill, as well as Mrs. Millikin, attended the First Presbyterian Church. Four members were wives of business partners—Mrs. McReynolds and Mrs. Roach, Mrs. Greene and Mrs. T. T. Roberts. Mr. Millikin and Mr. Clokey were board members of the YMCA. Mrs. Quinlan, Mr. Gastman, and Dr. Will Barnes had been officers and directors of the Reading Room Association; Mrs. Quinlan, Mrs. Ira Barnes, and Mrs. McReynolds were on the board of the Carnegie-financed public library. Mrs. Millikin and Mrs. T. T. Roberts had long been close personal friends and served together on the board of the YWCA.[44] The exact relationships are not important; it is the hopelessly entangled skein configuration which indicates that this was no open-door society.

Population figures for Decatur from 1850 to 1890 suggest that the "magic circle," like other clubs and organizations of this period, was born in part as a reaction to the almost bewilderingly rapid social and economic changes occurring around it and of which it was a part. In 1850 Decatur had six hundred citizens. By 1860 the town had swelled to just short of four thousand. In 1880 it had more than doubled its 1860 population, and by 1890 there were almost seventeen thousand inhabitants.[45] While Macon County, of which Decatur is the seat, in 1890 had among the lowest percentage of foreign-born in the state,[46] as early as 1880 the railroads and industrial expansion had introduced enough "outsiders" so that those who were to become "ladies of the club" were no longer able to greet all their fellow citizens by name. In the Art Class they could. And they made sure it stayed that way. Despite the long waiting list for membership the first year, they firmly voted down a motion to enlarge their numbers to twenty-five,[47] and never in their hundred-year history have they deviated from the original maximum of twenty.

The minutes of the first twenty years seem to validate Mrs. Wells's observation about the unimportance of money or social position *within* the Art Class. Wealth and position seemed the cachet necessary, however, for entrance. "They were successful people," "the monied class," "the best families in town," according to long-time present-day members of the Class.[48] The *Decatur Herald* in

1914 reported that "the membership of the club has included a number of illustrious women."[49] What made them illustrious, the article implied, was the self-made wealth of their husbands. Unconsciously perhaps, the minutes hint at prosperity: "The class met at the elegant home of Mrs. Quinlan"; "The regular meeting of the class was held with Mrs. Alexander at her beautiful new home"; "Our vice president Miss Jack without requesting either the advice or consent of the class took her way with a companion to Pharoh's [sic] land, but when she returned and informed us that it was 'well' with her and 'well' with him, in fact that the two 'wells' made a plural, she was restored to the affection and confidence of the class."[50] These women played the roles expected of the wives of judges, lawyers, mayors, bankers, physicians, clergymen, educators, publishers, successful merchants, and manufacturers—the men who held the reins of the community. Like other study clubs, within their orderly, homogeneous, familiar circle, the Art Class could afford to be, and was, a model of high-minded and principled democracy.

October 14, 1899

The Topic Committee brought out the topics for 3 months all nicely printed in a booklet with a dress of our royal color and the golden seal in sight. This was a very happy surprise.[51]

The twentieth year was thus heralded by the Class's first printed program. The eight pages of topics and respondents, printed in lavender ink in a small and graceful serif typeface, had a cover of soft purple art paper, hand-bound with a gold metallic tasseled cord— all in striking resemblance to an elegant dance card. In the upper right-hand corner of the four-by-six-inch booklet was a gold notary stamp embossed with the Class seal, a profile of helmeted Minerva, encircled by the Latin *Animi Cultus Humanitatis Cibus,* "Mental Culture Is the Food of Humanity."

Like other study clubs, the Art Class had widened its founding purpose, "mutual improvement, especially in the direction of art," over time. The program announced the year's course of study to be English history; in fact, history got short shrift and art received a cursory glance, but Victorian literature was represented in lavish detail. The epigraph to the first volume of minutes had already suggested, however, the Class's sense of the impossibility of insulated learning:

> "A talent for any art is rare; but it is given to nearly every one to cultivate a taste for art; only it must be cultivated with earnestness. The more things thou learnest to know and to enjoy, the more complete and full will be for thee the delight of living." [52]

By its twentieth year the format of the Art Class meetings was down pat, and the work proceeded smoothly, but it had not always been so, as minutes from the fifth meeting, in February 1880, reveal:

> The usual interest manifested by all—however those who came last on the various topics showed signs of embarrassment to have to say what had already been said or say nothing after having spent no little time in preparing a lesson and feeling a desire for the promotion of the best interest of the Art Class—just to simply repeat information given and it was sufficient cause for dissatisfaction. Yet all seemed glad to be there. [53]

Through trial and error the Class refined its methods. The Topic Committee, elected annually instead of monthly as it had been in the beginning, with the aid of professionally written topical guides, assigned usually seven topics for each lesson. With everyone assigned a topic (it was an unwritten rule, according to the minutes, that each woman recite at each meeting) it is not clear how the initial frustrating overlap was eliminated. Quite likely the two or three presenters divided up the topic in conference outside of the Class, and there is also a suggestion that one of the group read directly from the work under consideration while the others gave background and explication.

With ten minutes allotted to a topic like "Turner's Paintings," the thought of repetition appears unlikely; yet it is well to keep in mind the paucity of reference books available in a prairie town where the library had no permanent quarters until 1903 and in 1876 contained little more than a thousand books. [54] Frequently the scarcity of books is noted in the minutes.

Some finding but little on the subject of [Assyrian] painting digressed a little.[55]

The class voted to authorize the Treasurer . . . to place the money then in the treasury in the hands of Mrs. Oglesby to be expended by her on books for the benefit of the class if she could do so during her stay in Boston, where she is to be for some three weeks.[56]

Miss Jillett met with us, also Mrs. Johns [from the Library Association] who urged the ladies to consider the expediency of contributing their funds to the Public Library, to be expended on such books, as the Class shall determine.[57] [The Class donated $12.50 in half-payment for Lübke's *Monuments of Art* but later had to add to it as the book cost $45 instead of $25 as originally quoted.]

The President stated that Mrs. Millikin had received from the state Library at Springfield through the courtesy of Mrs. Gov. Oglesby a copy of Hazlitt's early English literature. As the book was loaned for a limited time, the class decided by vote to listen to Mrs. Millikin's reading of portions of Ralph Royster Dirster [sic] in place of the regular lesson.[58]

The availability of books may also have been a direct cause of the expansion of the club's study beyond art. Novels and histories were more readily procured than volumes with expensive plates of reproductions. In their study in 1887 of ancient Greece, "the class was greatly assisted in their comprehension of the once magnificent temples and public edifices and works of art of the Athenians by a number of pictures kindly loaned them by Mrs. Ackerson."[59] And the following year for a lesson on English cathedrals, "wood engravings from Harper's Weekly and Bazaar for 1881–1882 aided greatly in impressing the appearance of these buildings on our minds."[60]

The year 1899–1900 was not the first time the Class had studied English history. Over the years the club returned to previous themes, especially Greek and English history and literature. In 1905–06 the Class studied Dante and acclaimed his work their all-time favorite.

If no other proof could be adduced for the increased interest felt in the study of Dante, the attendance this year would be sufficient to convince even the most skeptical of the fact. The members have been so faithful in meeting each week that they could not be accused of house-cleaning or having a seamstress, and yet we know they have had both—as appearances could not be so deceiving.[61]

Their delight clearly was the result of their patient, seasonal accretion of knowledge, which they earnestly pursued though they were perhaps unaware where it would lead. For two years between 1902 and 1904 the Class had studied Greek literature, "the interest in Greek writers proving greater as their dramas are more thoroughly understood."[62] It was not just *Antigone* they tackled; they read Homer, *Oedipus at Colonus*, *The Women of Trachis*, and *Philoctetes*. Their involvement, although lacking in intellectual sophistication, was spontaneous, genuine, whole-hearted—and endearing to any teacher, as is evident in this excerpt from the minutes:

> *Time*—First Year after the Olympiad or Leap Year, January 16th (B.S.L.E.) Before St. Louis Exposition.
> *Place*—Palace of Athene, 129 N. Pine Street, bounded in the West by Hall of Pericles, in the South by the Elysian fields, in the North by the arena set apart for Olympic games, and in the East by the temple of Delphi—Indiana.
> *Hostess*—Athene [Mrs. Millikin], goddess of wisdom, assisted by fifteen goddesses steeped in Grecian lore. . . .
> *The Motive*—Celebration of the twenty-fourth birthday of the twenty maidens in truly classic style!
> Athene, as would be expected from her position among the goddesses, having always taken the initiative in planning the annual meetings, "many a time and oft," had opened the spacious doors of her palace for this attic assembly, and not only during the "Olympiad" have feasting and gaming been held within, but at other times have these historic events been celebrated with such success that the gods have sulked in their tents for days at a time refusing to be comforted!
> On this special occasion of which I now speak Athene

was arrayed as if for conquest and justly so for soon her guests were lost in admiration of her clever arrangements. The feast preceded all else, for where is the goddess "that can live without dining," even if her husband does refuse to drink river water at hand while she is partaking of ambrosia. Athene had prepared a feast fitting the occasion (and that is saying volumes). This was quickly followed by toasts, story telling, conundrums and witticisms, the guests having gained inspiration from the example and wisdom of the hostess.[63]

Without guidance they found "relevance" in their study of the ancients: "Euripides' Alcestis won golden opinions from every side . . . and it seemed wonderful that Euripides with his domestic experience and his general reflections upon women should have created so beautiful a character."[64] They began to develop scope: "The afternoon was devoted to Euripides' Helen who was only a 'ghost of her former self' as presented by Euripides earlier."[65] And, finally, after a year of Roman literature, emphasizing the *Aeneid*, they began the *Inferno*—and made the connections, delighting in their contrasts of the underworld in Homer, Virgil, and Dante. Probably they didn't ask why. The minutes record few reflections on their learning, and those have little depth: "The main objects of interest being the granting of the Magna Charta and the establishment of the House of Commons. Showing that governmental reforms are a growth from increasing civilization and the result of the necessities arising from emergencies."[66] But they now carried around in their heads rather esoteric and erudite pieces of knowledge that they had earned and won for themselves, and they were no longer unexceptional women.

October 28, 1899

The lesson on English literature . . . was moving along finely when interrupted by Prof. Troop who called to talk University Extension lectures to the ladies. He occupied nearly a half hour of valuable time. But the lesson was finished and well finished with *Richard Carvel.*[67]

So much for Professor Troop, who had taken their "valuable time"! The Class later used his University of Chicago study outlines just as they had started out in 1880 using the "Topical Lessons"—"comprehensive enough to suit the gravest student and fascinating enough to charm the novice"[68]—of Professor Charles S. Farrar of Milwaukee College to guide their work.[69] It seems likely, even, that Mrs. Nelson enrolled in Troop's extension correspondence course in 1906 when the Class was studying *The Divine Comedy;* "Mrs. Hostetler . . . read a letter from Prof. Troop pertaining to the paper on the Purgatorio recently written by Mrs. Nelson. It was full of praise and appreciation of the excellent work done by our philosophic member . . . of whom we are all justly proud."[70]

It is not clear what motivated the Class's undoubtedly polite forbearance of Professor Troop. It hardly seems diffidence about their own work, which was "finished and well finished." Earlier, in 1891, there *had* been a moment of defensiveness. Professor Denton J. Snider of St. Louis had given a public lecture on Goethe's *Faust* to which the class went en masse. Because they were just beginning that work in their year's study of German literature, they invited him to attend their discussions. The secretary recorded, "The lesson was Act I, Part II of Faust with criticisms by Prof. Snider. It was of interest but suffered from interruptions." The next week the usual full page of happy self-congratulatory minutes (see Appendix 2) was reduced to a laconic three sentences: "Attendance good. Lesson Act II, Part II with the usual criticisms by Prof. Snider. Adjourned to meet with Mrs. Roberts."[71] Nor among these self-critical women can their impatience with Professor Troop be laid to arrogance. Their reaction might be that of any class, engaged, absorbed, heads bent over a purposeful task. Pleased and eager for her pupils to exceed themselves, the teacher interjects some information that she hopes will enable them to leap ahead, to make intuitive connections without tracing the tedious networks. They look up, listen impatiently, and return to their work untouched, knowing better than she at that moment the methodical steps a student must master.

And in their "class," these women were nothing more and nothing less than students. Although the founders may have chosen the name Art Class to avoid the connotation of *club,* significantly they did not choose *association* or *society;* in the minutes, most often the secretary refers to the group as "the class." For the first few years, attendance was recorded in the back of the secretary's book exactly

as a teacher's roll book is kept—*abs., ex.,* and so on. School imagery runs throughout: "preparing the lesson," "all study the subject," "new topics were assigned," "after the recitation of the lesson,"
"ladies who had been students for so many years." [72]

The Class paid tribute to education in a number of ways. Their
first honorary member was Mrs. Almira A. Powers, a graduate of
Emma Willard, one of Decatur's first teachers, and first president of
the Ladies' Library Association. [73] Although they rarely invited outside speakers, in 1893 Dr. Charles MacMurray, president of Teachers
College at DeKalb, lectured the Class on German universities and
the German system of education. [74] In their study of American colonial history, they held an extra discussion of "the earliest colleges
and their later developments, showing advances made." [75] Returning
home from Florida in the spring of 1904, Mrs. Millikin stopped at
"Tuskeegee College" and reported to the Class on its buildings and
curriculum. [76] While among the founders Mrs. Millikin probably
represented the highest degree of formal educational attainment,
these women were learners, it seems, through every pore. At their
first meeting in the fall of 1897, the members recounted their summer's activities. Mrs. Barnes reported on the Field Museum and the
Art Institute, which she had visited in Chicago; Mrs. Bohon "had
gone the world over for 6 weeks in her Century Dictionary of Questions." Mrs. Gastman read a poem she had composed; Mrs. Hill and
Mrs. Hostetler had studied Virgil; Mrs. Nelson had been to the
Nashville Exposition and read her comparison of the architecture
and grounds with those of the Acropolis and Parthenon. [77] Although
they probably had not heard Julia Ward Howe's advice to women to
extend their knowledge beyond the four corners of their homes,
members of the Class were relentless travelers. Eleven of the early
members had visited Europe by 1902. "They didn't feel completely
educated," recalls a now-retired Class member; "travel was how you
did it." "It was knowledge they cared about," another retired member confirms. "They were people who made it their choice to learn.
They couldn't go to school so they traveled." [78]

The Class took seriously the life of the mind. Upon the death of
the first Mrs. Wells, the Class prepared a memorial: "There is no
need to dwell upon the poise of her mind, the correctness of her
judgment, her good common sense in all practical matters, the

strength and firmness of her purpose, her quick perception of the fitness of things, her deep sincerity and her fine sense of justice."[79] It was her mind they mentioned first.

The twenty worked conscientiously and believed they had benefited from their efforts:

> The President called for remarks on subjects or topics assigned at the previous meeting. Judging from the close attention given each one—that the information given on the various topics was highly entertaining, each one seemed brighter and happier for having added something more to her stock of knowledge, thereby demonstrating the fact or belief that the source of genuine pleasure is from within.[80]

> We look upon the wonderful pictures of the old masters with a newer, deeper interest since we have learned something of their history. The interest of our members in the subject of Art has not been of transient duration, but has apparently increased as the months have rolled by.[81]

> The unanimous expression of the members as to the benefits accruing to them individually from the study of English history and literature was fully proven by their well prepared responses to the topics assigned.[82]

The lightheartedness that ripples through the minutes of the Art Class can be deceptive. It is, one suspects, more an expression of joy than of frivolity. The members took their work responsibly and seriously; it was not merely a diversion lightly dismissed. Dedication also required more than a commitment of the mind. The weather was a constant hindrance in their undrained, unpaved prairie town:

> During our session of five months we have assembled together twenty afternoons. The winter which is just making its adieus to us, will be recorded as among the coldest ever known—yet the beautiful snow has not fallen so rapidly, or covered the earth to such a depth, as to prevent a meeting—torrents of rain and gusts of wind have been powerless to prevent an assemblage of the Class,

and it has always met again whether in storm, in sunshine or in rain.[83]

Notwithstanding the very inclement weather, eleven
brave members of the Art Class assembled. Was there
ever an apple so meltingly delicious as the one slyly pil-
fered from the orchard? Was there ever a pleasure so perfectly fascinating as the one purchased by many incon-
veniences—so, was there ever a meeting so entirely
harmonious and interesting as this? The boisterous,
stormy elements without—the bright fire and cheerful
room within—each one was in her loveliest mood.[84]

Although the members took their work just as seriously as did
students at women's colleges, they were not deluded about its quality
or depth. They themselves had no pretensions to scholarship. "John
Milton was the main subject of the lesson. Four ladies gave the main
facts of his life. His deepest thought was not elucidated."[85] Returning to Milton seven years later, the Class at one meeting discussed
the first three books of *Paradise Lost* and regretted that the discussion "was necessarily so superficial."[86] Sometimes they grinned at
their scope: "The class proceeded to fight over again the battles of
the old Romans. After summarily disposing of five wars, taking a
glimpse of temples, public buildings, statues and other objects of
interest, the class tamely and peacefully continued the business before it."[87] Other times they scolded: "Mrs. Roach making a strong
appeal for thorough work, no matter what might be the course of
study."[88] Always they tried: "The lesson was a difficult one but the
ladies seemed determined to grasp the thought of Herbert Spencer
to a certain degree."[89]

January 20, 1900 (1880–1900)

Now in the fourth year of the reign of Hays [sic], there
were in the land of the Decaturites certain women who
came often together and they made a vow that they
would read much and search out mysteries and seek
knowledge all that it is meet for women to know.

Moreover they agreed that on every sixth day of the
week they would assemble themselves together and rehearse what they had learned. And the number of them
which took this vow was twenty.

And it came to pass as it drew nigh to twenty years
since they had thus consented to this pledge (though all
were not now with them as at the beginning, yet others
had taken their places) that they looked upon each other
and said, "The days of our years be nigh to a score. Is it
not meet that we make merry, rejoice and be glad."[90]
(For complete text, see Appendix 3.)

The elaborate celebration of the twentieth anniversary in 1900 of
the Art Class was a far cry from the first, which, in fact, went un-
marked. In 1882 when it did occur to the members to commemo-
rate the Club's founding, they merely changed the regular Saturday
meeting to a Wednesday so as to gather on the actual date, only to
discover that memory had played them false, and they had celebrated a day late.[91]

The twentieth anniversary was an official "play day," or "off day,"
one of those infrequent but regular occasions, such as the last meeting of the year, when "the lesson" was shortened or dispensed with
and the Class met to enjoy the "royal good fellowship of its members."[92] Their "work," however, was as usual incorporated into their
play. Each woman was required to wear or bring with her to the
luncheon at Mrs. Millikin's something to suggest the title of a book
the Class had studied: Mrs. Millikin, dressed in white, represented
The Woman in White; Mrs. Wells wore a tiny padlock serving as a
slipper buckle to signify Locke's "On Human Understanding"; Mrs.
Hostetler carried twenty-four sheets of paper in a parchment roll as
"The Choir Invisible"; and Mrs. Roach arrived "carrying and vigorously using two immense turkey wings," suggestive of "Wing and
Wing," a now lost allusion.[93]

In tribute to their own travel and to the foreign lands they had
studied, the theme of the day, carried out in table decoration and
menu, was Cuba, where Mrs. Millikin had spent a winter. They
celebrated with song and toasts (an activity usually reserved for men
in the public world) and were entertained afterward with harp selections. Several weeks later Mrs. Gastman presented each member
with a souvenir booklet containing the mock New Testament account of the anniversary. The handwritten text, with whimsical line
drawings of "devices" the members had used to suggest their books,

was mechanically reproduced, but each cover was an original water-color of considerable grace. It depicts in black and white with a small wash of purple background the strong profile of a youthful woman, reminiscent of a Degas figure in style and in her distinct character and vitality.

These women were ebullient about everything to do with their club. It was not only "off days" that produced high spirits:

> In a very modest way our presiding officer would call the class to order but modest calls were unheeded. She then resorted to a vigorous use of her umbrella which for a time was successful [this, after a discussion of the Columbian Exposition buildings].[94]

> There was too much hilarity which was only suppressed by sitting one of the delinquents near the President.[95]

> The warm weather caused much irregularity in the deportment of the younger members, but on account of their extreme youth and the approval of some of their elders, they were excused.[96]

There were some younger members, to be sure. In its fiftieth year, Mrs. Wells, who had joined in 1887 as Elizabeth Jack, served as Art Class president. Mrs. Ira Barnes, a founder, continued as a member, and Mrs. Nelson, Mrs. Hostetler, and Mrs. Roach were still alive. These, along with Mrs. Bohon, who gave birth to a child the year she joined the club in 1894, were certainly young women in the founding days. Anna Millikin, on the other hand, was forty-eight when she founded the Class, and the deaths of a number of members before hers in 1913 are indicative of age cohorts. The source of all "hilarity" cannot be laid at the feet of adolescents.

Yet throughout the minutes runs a sense of freshness, of innocent enthusiasm, of girlish imagination, of endless vitality and quest, and embodiment of "the energizing role of self-education [particularly] for women."[97]

> Byron was the theme and never has there been more enthusiasm in any topic. His life was well given and ex-

tracts from Don Juan, Prisoner of Chillon and some shorter poems. The ladies showed a reluctance to leave this poet and even proposed to meet on lawn or porch and discuss and recite at any happy time that the president sent them a reminder.[98]

Too "much learning doth make us mad" had a trial test—and still we are not satisfied, and today we call for more, and hope it may be expressed out to our complete satisfaction.[99]

Their desire for "more" was also expressed in their decision to hold weekly, rather than the more common biweekly, meetings. Like the Lowell mill girls, "their mental activity was overflowing at every possible outlet."[100] For two hours each week they abandoned themselves to learning. They threw themselves wholeheartedly into the effort; they turned everything to intellectual profit. In the midst of their study of colonial America, Mrs. Gastman held a party to which the Class was invited to come in Puritan garb, to eat pumpkin pie, and to take part in a program of early American song and dance. The minutes in rhyme of this gathering (see Appendix 4) are particularly illustrative of the Art Class spirit, incorporating what they had learned ("Dame Gastman") and their strong identification of themselves as "school girls." They lived what they learned; it became part of their vocabulary. In their colonial period, "In order to be consistent with the 'Blue Laws' of Connecticut, 16 members of the Art Class rigorously set aside Christmas shopping and attendance upon the 'Rummage Sale' to pay their respects to James Blair, William Byrd and John Lawson [i.e., to attend a Class session on colonial America] at the residence of Mrs. Bering."[102] After discussing the pros and cons of the old blue laws, the Class decided "in favor of abolishment since no man under that code of law was permitted to kiss his wife on Sunday."

They needed no controversial topics to spice up the proceedings. Even the most bland and ponderous topic seemed to generate partisanship and warm discussion.

The lesson [on English history] proceeded according to the topics laid out. The George's—1 and 2nd—were described and their merits, which were usually demerits—

were the theme of much comment even to the mystifying subject of heredity. [102]

On motion Mrs. McReynolds was put on record as a denouncer of Dickens in his aspersions of James the First. [103]

Discussion arose regarding the character of Napoleon. Some warmly supported him and others as earnestly condemned. [104]

Several interesting criticisms upon Carlyle's style and rank in literature were read, calling forth animated discussion in the class. [105]

Indeed, because True Women had been taught submission, bland and neutral topics may have been the perfect vehicle for teaching them the sound of their own voices. They could disagree with each other about Napoleon without real emotional involvement. Napoleon had no impact on their lives, there could be no "winner," and the club would move serenely on to another topic the next week.

They punned verbally and visually. During their study of English literature, even the weather was called into play: "The weather being such / One could not even touch / A Dry-den nor a Lamb." And later: "Time passed all too Swift-ly, and we did but Steele a glance at some of the characters. There was much from an interested Spectator." [106] Often on "off days" they played quotation-identification games or posed conundrums: "How do you make your shoes last?" "Put a Locke on your Understanding" was a superb try, but the answer was "With a rest cure for the sole." [107] On their twenty-first anniversary, their coming of age, one member surprised the Class by appearing as a society belle of days past, dressed for her "coming-out party." [108]

Although the minutes from the beginning are bright and animated and creative, they grow in high spirits over the years. Like college upperclasswomen, the members are comfortable with their knowledge, have fun showing it off, feel secure enough to play with it. Knowing that their intellectual efforts—serious endeavors or high jinks—will meet only with admiration and encouragement, they risk and reach and revel in their alchemical transformation, which has created a new element for them.

April 21, 1900

The gavel with a bunch of pinks attached to it was proffered the president. [109]

With that gesture of sorority, the Art Class welcomed the return of Mrs. Millikin from Florida, where she had been since just after the club's celebration of its twentieth anniversary. Their affection for her, expressed symbolically in the pinks, was returned in kind. While the Class chose to emphasize its intellectual purpose in the club motto, it endowed its color, "emblematic of the royal good fellowship of its members," [110] with the acknowledged importance of sorority. As it was for the first generations of college women, according to historian Barbara Solomon, "the most precious part of the experience became sharing discoveries and growing together." [111] Rarely explicit, the sense of sisterhood nevertheless shines through in countless ways. In the biblically inspired record of the twentieth anniversary, Queen Anna is pleased that the idea of commemoration "came into the hearts of the women"; their heads were not the prime source of inspiration on that important occasion. The wording of their rededication to their "vow that they would read much and search out mysteries" is perhaps an unconscious suggestion of the deep, religious sisterly bonding of the maidens in ancient Greece who guarded the secrets of the temple. On their tenth anniversary, the members extracted a pledge from a guest that she would not reveal what had transpired because "a special mystery and interest hangs about secret sessions." [112] In their memorial to the first Mrs. Roberts, their connection to each other was made more graphic: "Through that portal she has gone, and we . . . bring the tribute of our sisterly esteem and lay it like an offering of beautiful flowers on the altar of a dear memory. In her loss to our association we deplore this broken link in the chain by which in congenialities of taste and the love of the true, the pure, and the beautiful, our class was bound." [113]

As almost everything became grist for the mill in their intellectual endeavors, so too they turned the smallest detail to account in the establishment of their sodality. On their nineteenth anniversary, "the fruit of the vine was made to contribute of its sweetness for the benefit of the sisterhood." [114]

Distance did nothing to loosen the members' bonds; it may even have sharpened their awareness of the importance of their sister-hood. On her usual Florida vacation, Mrs. Millikin wrote to an Art Class friend on January 30, 1908:

> Dear Mrs. Haworth:
>
> I am hungry for another letter—and in no condition to *write* myself—but, in fine condition to *read* letters— "Grippe," has me in charge—after being so careful all winter. Missing the Art Class, and not allowed to step out on the piazza, here I am with this awful "Grippe." . . . I felt I could not miss a lesson of the Art Class, and missed nearly all—such are the disappointments in life. Regret not being with you on the 22nd [a special upcoming Class meeting]—will have to feel much better than I do now, if I can even send a greeting. . . .
>
> Everything lovely and green—vine on Woman's Club building up to roof; and a dense mass of blossoms when we first came down.. . . . Windows open, and white dresses—orange trees will soon bloom. Growing dark—
>
> Good bye—
> With love.
> A.B.M.[115]

In Florida on the twenty-sixth anniversary of the Class, Mrs. Millikin sent to the meeting a pink carnation for each member; "an expression of love accompanied the flowers." Arriving home from another winter's sojourn, in the middle of a Class meeting, Mrs. Millikin could not wait to reestablish her ties with a physical presence but telephoned the Class in session to confirm her spiritual union.[116] Mrs. Millikin was not the only one to remember the Class when far from Decatur. Mrs. Hill brought home to the Class from California a gavel of manzanita wood with silver mountings. While in Palm Beach, Mrs. Bering sent the Class a poem she had written for them; a box of cardboard birds from Mexico was her Easter remembrance to the group. At the opening fall meeting of 1898, the Class discovered that "Our Banker had gone (almost) to Canada, and had not left a statement of the Affairs of the Bank, but some beautiful 'blue fruits' a souvenir for each member of the class, made a balance in her favor." On its twentieth anniversary the Class received letters of congratulations and continued affection from eight former members who had moved as far away as Brooklyn, New York.[117]

Nor did the Class forget those nearby who were unable to meet with them because of serious illness. Upon hearing a particularly entertaining account of the fifteenth anniversary celebration written by Mrs. Hatch, the Class voted to send a copy to Mrs. Greene, whose infirmity had kept her confined at home for several months. In October 1902, when it became apparent that Mrs. Bering's illness was long-term, the Class sent a bouquet of flowers to her "every Saturday just before the time for the meeting so long as she can not be among our number"; their gesture of love continued until her death in January 1903. Paying homage to another venerable member, the Class suspended its tradition of meeting around at the homes of various members and held all meetings at the home of Mrs. Roberts during the last year of her life when she was unable to leave her house.[118]

To the members the Class had an entity and life of its own, one that would continue without them as would an alma mater. In recognition of the legacy of sisterhood, several years before her death Mrs. Walston presented to the Class her "collection of curios, neatly mounted and framed." Mrs. Walston was to remain custodian of the gift during her lifetime. Upon her death, the curios were to descend to the charter members in reverse alphabetical order.[119]

In a more substantial gesture of selfless and supportive sorority, in 1895 the Class sent three of its members—Mrs. Clokey, Mrs. Hill, and Mrs. Walston—on a summer trip to Europe. What prompted their generosity is not clear; the minutes record only their going-away party, the report on the travelers' return, and the consensus of the Class that they "felt well repaid for the deprivations and economies they had practiced in sending these brilliant ladies abroad."[120] In April "a letter of international importance" had been read to the Class. "It was written by a graduate of Oxford, a celebrated jurist, and contained a message to Queen Victoria which was to be conveyed across the ocean by one of the members of the Art Class this summer."[121] Cryptic in itself, that message cannot be tied to the members' tour, but it might suggest a rationale for sponsoring these three women who had no previous record in the minutes of having traveled abroad.

Linked in a common venture as were the early generations of college women, the Art Class gave expression to their sisterhood in ways similar to collegians'. They sang their Class song, enjoyed their "secret sessions," developed rituals and traditions, and adopted nicknames for each other: the Gad Fly, our Practical Member, the Three Prima Donnas, our Philosophic Member, our Jolly Member. Like college women, they also derived confidence from their aggregate. Although each was hesitant to display her written effort before even the limited audience of the Art Union, by unanimous vote in 1882 the Class sent its memorial for Mrs. Roberts to the *Decatur Daily Review*, requesting publication. By 1885 as a group they were not afraid to broach even the sensitive subject of money: dissatisfied with the amount assessed them for their share in the annual Art Union convention, the Class wrote a letter to the president demanding a more detailed accounting.[122]

Among the Art Class files is a large black and white photograph of Mrs. Clokey, Mrs. Hill, and Mrs. Walston on the eve of their Class-sponsored trip to Europe in 1895. Carrying valises, cloaks, and umbrellas, wearing long and voluminous leg-of-mutton sleeved traveling dresses and kid gloves, with tiny toques perched atop chignons and secured by ribbons under their chins, the three stand in a row with their backs to the camera, looking into the distance in attitudes of anticipation. The picture illustrates, as words cannot, the Art Class blend of True Woman and feminist. Their habiliments are every inch True Woman; their stance—three married women traveling without male accompaniment, turning their backs on home, facing out to a world they have not explored—is the emerging New Woman.

The dominant impression from the minutes, as it is from the photograph, is True Woman. In their memorial to Mrs. Roberts, the members announced to the world their "love of the true, the pure, and the beautiful." Mrs. Greene's essay for the Art Union in 1892 cited woman's mission: "to make home whatever is good and beautiful."[123] Homemakers they remained first of all: "fall duties as housekeepers" annually occasioned a low attendance.[124] The theme of chivalry which emerges in their fifteenth anniversary celebration underlines the members' acceptance of their submissive, domestic roles, but the postscript to the evening dinner meeting sounds a different note, not discordant, but softly suggestive of a new theme. After a review of the past year's study program,

> Mrs. Walston gave a tribute to "Our Husbands," made a little fun of them and told some good stories. Then Mrs.

Bering presented each member with a dainty little crystal glass—reading charming and witty little poems that fitted each member. After this came *the* surprise of the evening! Mr. Clokey arose as two gentlemen entered carrying a table on which were 20 cut glass bowls, one for each lady. Mr. Clokey made a happy little speech. Then followed the singing of the Class song written by Mrs. Hatch. [125]

Although in the minutes there is no sense of being upstaged at their own event, immediately after the celebration the Class began elaborate plans to make "some returns to the gentlemen for their thoughtfulness." Mrs. McReynolds headed a committee of "Grateful Dames to Generous Squires" to write some "resolutions" expressive of the "gratitude and beatitude" of the members. At a special evening gathering in late February, the Class presented to the "Knights of the Crystal Bowl" artistically decorated "diplomas" containing the resolutions, embossed with the Class seal, and tied with a purple ribbon. [126] Whether they intended it or not, the women had reclaimed the anniversary celebration as their own.

Certainly the members were sincerely appreciative of their husbands' generosity. On one occasion the Class even discussed conferring honorary membership "upon several gentlemen of the city," but the motion was tabled and not taken up again. [127] A number of entries in the minutes, however, chronicle a certain amused awareness of the changing status of women. In the autumn of 1890 Mrs. Gallagher invited the Class to a private parlor of the St. Nicholas Hotel to hear a talk on her recent travels through Europe. Her talk and the English tea and wafers "beguiled the ladies until the shades of night were falling fast, when all slipped out into the darkness and hurried home where the Ancient Householder sat upon his declining throne, musing sadly upon his belated dinner and the progressiveness of the age." [128] The subject of free will arose once during a study of Dante and "created much interest and amusement . . . and there was a disposition on the part of the members whose free wills had become weak from inaction to exercise them more in the future." [129]

At other times their awareness of their changing status had not the smallest hint of a smile. In her midyear report as secretary, Mrs.

Millikin wrote: "May the zeal of our ladies never grow less, and may the time soon arrive when it shall be said of a lady, not that she conducts a meeting as well as a man, but, she conducts a meeting better than a man—and, not that she knows as much as a man, but, that she knows more than a man."[130] Occasionally in conjunction with their studies, the Class devoted a topic to women's historical participation in society. In their discussion of Germany, there was a report on female German authors. A lesson on Queen Victoria included "a word upon American women who became subject to the Queen." Women reformers formed a part of their study of American history. And a reading of *Clarissa Harlowe,* that much wronged heroine, evoked indignation: "One feels like offering thanks that our foremothers left a country where this state of things was possible."[131]

Other reports focused on contemporary women: a paper on "The Work That Women Are Doing," another on the Woman's Building at the Columbian Exposition in Chicago, and a talk on the Rookwood Pottery, "giving many interesting facts relative to the work—it being distinctively woman's work and founded by a woman and still carried on by women." In 1894 in a program in honor of a former member, Mrs. Oglesby, "Miss Jack read a beautiful essay on woman."[132] Although infrequent, the references point to a heightened perception of the distinctiveness of woman, an increased identification with others of the gender, and a growing knowledge and appreciation of woman's achievements in the world outside her home.

In choosing to pattern the narrative of their twentieth anniversary on the advent of a new era, the Class invited parallels to the new age in which they were participating through their club, an age of higher education and suffrage for women. Only a month after the Art Class was founded, there appeared in the *Decatur Daily Review,* among a recipe for "a toothsome" lemon cake, instructions on cleaning kid gloves, an advertisement for Hop Hong's Laundry, and a summary of the latest temperance lecture, an address by Dr. Storrs on the fifth anniversary of Abbott Academy (for girls) in Andover, Massachusetts. Undoubtedly the article came as part of the "patent outsides" (the equivalent of today's wire service releases) that publishers often bought to supplement local news, and there can be no direct connection with the Art Class. But the appearance of the article at that time and in that place seems to invest the Class with a purpose more deep and more significant than its members realized. Dr. Storrs responded to the "foolish question of what is going to be the sphere of woman when she is so educated." There would be no special sphere for woman, he asserted; she would do just what she wanted. "If she wants suffrage she will get it, and woman suffrage will be the precious amethyst that drives drunkenness out of politics."[133] While remaining "precious amethysts," the members of the Art Class were determinedly engaged in educating themselves, a process that would eventually lead, beyond the lifetimes of most charter members, to women's suffrage.

Mention of suffrage in the minutes is scant but revealing. In 1891, the year in which the two main suffrage factions merged into the National American Woman Suffrage Association, the Class was read an invitation to attend the Woman's Suffrage Convention. The minutes record not a word more on the subject. A year later, however, there is a suggestion that perhaps Mrs. Bering attended the convention, for the Class was read a letter from her asking for the opinions of Class members "as to the advisability of female suffrage."

> It was found that a majority of the class held firmly to the opinion that enfranchisement of woman would tend to the righting of wrongs from which she suffers, would elevate the standards of morals and be productive of general good. A small minority were so conservative as to hold that woman's strongest influence for good, as it concerned her individually and the race generally would be exercised more effectively in and through the home rather than in the political arena. Good arguments were offered on each side and the discussion was dignified, earnest and thoughtful throughout.[134]

Suffrage involved profound questioning of each woman's identity; unlike debate on Napoleon, it could provoke intense emotional response, which study clubs tried to avoid. Perhaps for that reason, in recognition of the division already within the Class, there is no further mention of suffrage until 1895 when the club was requested to send a delegate to the convention of the Equal Suffrage Association. Mrs. Bering was elected, and a week later "our self-styled suffer a gist [sic] gave a most delightful and entertaining report of the speaker at . . . the convention."[135] It should be recalled that it was to Mrs. Bering, a much beloved "sister," that the members, in an unusual gesture, sent flowers at Class meeting time during the months of her final illness. One senses among the members a delight in Mrs. Bering for her vivacity and courage in confronting the outside world, for enabling them at a safe, "delightful" distance to be part of it. And surely they felt a symbolic pride in this particular member who grew from one who "found it impossible to read in public" to "our self-styled suffer a gist."

The minutes which conclude the twentieth year of the Decatur Art Class are atypically sober and subdued. They tally the number of meetings and the average number in attendance. They note without exclamation the club's twentieth anniversary, "which was celebrated in appropriate style."[136] The final quiet sentence seems unremarkable: "Some have bravely fought the infirmities of the body while cheerfully doing the duties of good members."[137] But there, in their unassuming way, they have illuminated not only the human condition but also the special spirit they brought to it. In the face of mortality, in a world which made few concessions to them and in which they went largely unrecognized, they cheerfully persisted in their duty—to education, to sisterhood, and to themselves.

Symbiosis

Study Clubs and Federation

*On receipt of a very courteous invitation from
the Decatur Woman's Club to be present at
their Club rooms and hear the reading of the
Report of the Federation of Woman's [sic]
Clubs held in Chicago, the Decatur Art Class
adjourned their own meeting to accept this invitation and heard with pleasure the delightful
Report so carefully prepared and well read by
Mrs. Ellen Philbrook. An interesting program
of musical numbers and the reading of papers
was rendered by the Ladies of the Club, and
our Art Class ladies acknowledge with pleasure
the afternoon's entertainment.* [1]

As a "delightful Report," part of an "afternoon's entertainment," the
General Federation of Women's Clubs made its way into the Art
Class minutes in 1892. Like Mrs. Bering with her suffrage connections, the Decatur Woman's Club, a charter member of the Federation, served as a window through which the Art Class could view at
a remove the national club movement, which was supplanting education for self with education for service.

The Decatur Woman's Club, a classic department club, was

founded in 1887 by Mrs. George Haworth, who was also a member of the Art Class. Born in New York City in 1845, Mary Haworth moved with her family to Chicago and then to Salem, Illinois, in the early 1860s. Before she married George Haworth, prosperous inventor of the check row planter, which enabled farmers to plant corn the same day they broke ground, she taught school in Decatur although her formal education had ended with secondary school.[2] Perhaps because of her urban roots, Mrs. Haworth's vision from the beginning was not so nearsighted as most others' in the Art Class. As early as 1886 she had suggested to the Class a "plan of fitting up a room for the use of the different literary societies in Decatur."[3] Receiving no encouragement from the Class, she set about achieving her goal another way: in the following year she organized and was elected president of the Woman's Club with a charter membership of 150. In three years the club had built its own spacious quarters, renting out its rooms for the special functions of "different literary societies."[4]

Although study was not absent from any of its six departments, the motto of the Woman's Club, "Truth, justice, and honor," signaled an emphasis quite different from that of the Art Class, *Animi Cultus Humanitatus Cibus* ("Mental Culture Is the Food of Humanity"). Its color, bright yellow, and its emblem, the four-leaf clover, also suggest a self-concept easily distinguishable from the Art Class's "royal" purple, often represented at its festivities by the pansy. The first of the Woman's Club's departments, Decatur Sorosis, met to discuss "topics of the day, parliamentary questions, national, State, and city government." The second section, Chautauqua, sponsored the Literary and Scientific Circle program of the parent society. Psalemas, meeting in the evening, was the section for working women; it devoted half of each session to nineteenth-century poets and the other half to "lively discussion of current topics." The fourth department studied Shakespeare and his contemporaries by means of papers and lecturers. The art and literature department took the magazine *The Arts* as its guide and discussed subjects introduced in its pages. The final section, music, studied composers and their works and organized a choral class.[5]

Gradually, as did others of the new wave of women's clubs after 1890, the Decatur club took a more active stance in the community. It brought about the election of a woman to the board of education, sponsored lectures and sewing classes for girls, engaged in charity work, urged the teaching of home economics in the schools, and established scholarships in art, music, and conservation for high school students.[6] The Decatur Woman's Club reported that it "is always found on the broad, advanced line of the thought of the day. Its circle of influence is wide, and through its range of interests, and the loyalty of its members, it is able to make itself felt in all matters of public importance."[7]

Mrs. Haworth did not relinquish her membership in the Art Class even though she presided over the Woman's Club, nor did she cease urging the Class's consideration of at least a statewide organization of clubs.

> A letter was read from Mrs. George Haworth which was an invitation to the class to visit the State Confederation of Clubs. This suggestion seemed to alarm some of the modest and conservative members, while others were ready to advance and glean from this broad field. The question was laid upon the table to be discussed in the future.[8]

The Class eventually consented to hear a representative from the State Federation talk about its work, and at the request of Mrs. Haworth it sent two delegates to the Woman's Club to discuss the advisability of organizing a confederation for the seventeenth congressional district,[9] but the Art Class remained unmoved in the assertion of its complete independence.

That the Decatur Art Class dug in its heels made not a whit of difference to the gathering momentum for change among women's clubs, a transformation perhaps foreshadowed by Anne Hutchinson's progression from explication of sermons to critique of the theocracy. In her inaugural address before the General Federation's convention in 1904, President Sarah P. Decker announced: "Ladies, you have chosen me as your leader. Well, I have an important piece of news to give you. Dante is dead. He has been dead for several centuries, and I think it is time that we dropped the study of his Inferno and turned our attention to our own."[10] "We prefer Doing to Dante, Being to Browning. . . . We've soaked in literary effort long enough," cries the heroine of *The President of Quex.*[11]

For some clubs, germination had begun early in the "soaking" period. "We begin to realize the want of a motive, apart from ourselves, to quicken us into permanent and useful activity," said Jane Croly in 1870 in her address as retiring president of Sorosis.[12] The Chicago Woman's Club was founded in 1876 by the younger contingent in Fortnightly who were dissatisfied with the narrow focus of the club on the life of the mind.[13] Desirous from the beginning to enter some "practical work," the offspring nevertheless acknowledged later that "it took time to educate the members up to the required degree of courage and experience."[14] Despite the club's departments on reform, home, and education as well as art and literature, Caroline M. Brown, first president, initially "feared that the Art and Literature committee would overshadow the club, as it was the only one that met for the purpose of pursuing its work in addition to attending the regular club meeting."[15] In 1883 the question "Should our club do practical work?" was voted on, and the various departments were "authorized to enter upon such work as they might select."[16] The following year the art and literature section dispensed with the reading of papers and offered music and recitation instead. It soon began to sponsor public recitals by local musicians, to arrange public exhibitions of the works of local artists, and to place "good art" in the public schools.[17]

By 1889 President Celia Woolley could state: "The Chicago Woman's Club is essentially a practical organization, made up of earnest intelligent women, banded together not in the mere pursuit of intellectual culture, but to promote the higher ends of a purer social state and the true enlightenment of mankind."[18] Among the club's early "practical" endeavors were the appointment of a night matron in the North Side Jail and women physicians in the Cook County Insane Asylum, the introduction of the kindergarten system into Chicago's public schools, and the direction of a "jail school" for boys imprisoned for minor offenses.[19] The Chicago path of evolution from an interest in the arts to a concern with their educational and social value, from "dead fact into quickened thought,"[20] was widespread and soon became a prescription for women's clubs:

> With a general knowledge of the history of art as a background, a club may arouse real enthusiasm by securing

pictures suitable for school buildings, and seeing that
they are well placed; by conducting a series of political
art lectures free, or nominally so, for the public; or by
starting a fund for the purchase and preservation of
works of art to become the property of the community.[21]

The principle motivating their progression from private to public
was nothing more than True Womanhood, club women averred:

> Woman's place is in the home. . . . Her task is home-
> making. . . . But Home is not contained within the four
> walls of an individual home. Home is the community.
> The city full of people is the Family. The public school
> is the real Nursery. And badly do the Home and the
> Family and the Nursery need their mother.[22]

Evolution was barely perceptible in some clubs. The Mothers'
and Daughters' Club of Plainfield, New Hampshire, still accompanied their literary discussions with the making of "rugs, curtains,
cover-lids and tablespreads such as our grandmothers fashioned," but
now these articles found "a ready market" which swelled club coffers
for philanthropic use.[23] Yet the term *revolution* more nearly described the process for other clubs, such as those which by 1912
could chalk up to their credit the saving of the Palisades along the
Hudson River and the establishment of the Mesa Verde National
Park.[24] Having spent twenty years educating themselves, it is not
surprising, however, that most clubs chose to make their public debut as "patrons and guardians of education."[25] In 1896, the Federation resolved: "That we recommend to the clubs a study of the science of education and educational conditions existing in their home
cities, to the end that the united influence of women's clubs be ex-
erted for the betterment of the state system of education, from the
kindergarten to the university."[26] While each club might shift its
view at its own rate and choose its own special focus, the Federation
urged "the club women who used to study Shakespeare's stage to
look around them upon life's stage."[27]

The change in the purpose of most women's clubs around the
turn of the century from study to service occurred for a variety of
reasons. At the Federation's convention in 1896, six years before her
death, Jane Croly announced the most obvious: "The eagerness

with which women's clubs all over the country have taken up history, literature, and art studies, striving to make up for the absence of opportunity and the absorption in household cares of their young womanhood, has in it something almost pathetic. But this ground will soon have been covered."[28] Formal institutions had helped women cover some of the ground. In 1870 of the 582 colleges and universities in existence, women were permitted entrance to only 239; by 1890 of the 1,082 institutions of higher education, women were eligible matriculants at 682, an increase in opportunity of twenty-two percent.[29] In 1870, 11,000 women were enrolled in colleges and universities; by 1890, 56,000 were enrolled. Though the numbers appear slight by today's standards, the 1890 figure represents nearly thirty-six percent of all enrolled college students.[30] The domino effect of the large increase in numbers of young women completing secondary schooling was making itself felt, career opportunities for women were increasing—between 1890 and 1920 the number of professional women rose 226 percent[31]—and through study clubs women had developed "the required degree of courage and experience" to envision for their daughters an education equal to men's.

In addition to expanded formal undergraduate opportunities for study, informal opportunities were growing rapidly through chautauquas, university extension, night schools, museums, and libraries. As the cost of printing decreased, books and magazines became everyday accouterments, no longer treasures to be passed from hand to hand and summarized in weekly club meetings. Knowledge had become much easier to acquire now that the American woman knew herself.

For many, that self-knowledge had come through their study clubs, by "working from within," as Sarah Hale had suggested. "Thought must precede action," a club member observed. "The clearer and more enlightened the one, the more effective the other."[32] Writing in 1925, Alice W. Ames, author of *The Business of Being a Club Woman,* looked back on days gone by: "The period of the old-fashioned culture club was one of incubation. Women had to turn in on themselves and learn to know each other before they dared or knew how to turn outward. . . . Human culture is a preparation of ourselves to become productive."[33]

The study club which had begun as an end unto itself soon became a means into a wider world.

> As a school for thought and training, every club is a national microcosm, a small republic in itself; it teaches, by means of a series of object-lessons, democratic methods and republican forms of government. The club was not originally designed for this purpose. No! We builded better than we knew; we organized with no ulterior plan, and many a club woman today, no doubt, would declare that, while she is willing and anxious to help govern a club, she has no desire to help govern her country, and is not training herself with any such idea in view. Be that as it may, if the time should ever arrive when the country's peril shall light the fires of patriotism within her breast, her club training will then stand her in good stead.[34]

The writer of that far-reaching prospectus was Ella Dietz Clymer, who in 1859 had become a charter member of Minerva in New Harmony, Indiana. "The club ought to be an evolution," said Jane Croly. "Once acquired, the knowledge of business ways, methods, and tactics can be put to better use than to aid or hinder the transaction of routine matters."[35] Another club member agreed: "Parliamentary practice gives women confidence in their ability to lead larger issues to a successful conclusion."[36] The movement to larger issues came naturally not only as women became more adept and confident in "methods and tactics" but also as a result of the change in the content of their studies, which reflected the movement in academe away from the humanities into the social sciences. The new intellectual inquiry looked on problems not as individual moral failings but as the effects of social conditions which could be changed. And at the same time that the focus of club members was shifting outward, there was a growing need for their social concern, especially in the cities as "pell-mell expansion destroyed the groups and neighborhoods that sustained social action."[37]

Despite pressure from the Federation and criticism that their studies were "the deadly work of the vampire tradition,"[38] Friends in Council, the Decatur Art Class, and countless other study clubs refused to alter their original purpose.

> When I hear the criticism that we are not public-spirited
> enough, or philanthropic enough, or social enough, it
> hurts me—hurts me as if some friend were maligned.
> Not any *one* thing can satisfy *all* the interests of life, but
> if earnestness of purpose, high ideals, and steadfast de-
> votion are worth anything, Friends in Council may be
> congratulated upon having found and possessed them.[39]

While other club women marched out to meet the world, study-
club women, like collegians within their ivied ivory towers, turned
their backs on it and maintained their sense of self as students.

Against a backdrop of rapid economic, political, and social
change in the outside world, innovations within the Decatur Art
Class occurred at a glacial rate. Most motions for change were
tabled indefinitely: "The motion to restore an honorary [usually
conferred upon those who moved from Decatur] to an active member was discussed but action was deferred until a future meeting"; "a
communication was read from the publisher of the 'Art Age' asking
the subscription of the class for the same. Mrs. Greene recommended the magazine as a desirable one on that subject but no action was taken."[40] Within its first twenty-five years, the club made
minute amendments to its constitution only three times. It remained a simple, clear, and direct document of eight articles and
three rules of order. Former members frequently attended Class
meetings when they visited Decatur and were undoubtedly relieved
as was Mrs. C. C. Clark, "who declared it was all just as it used
to be."[41]

The outside world seldom intruded upon Art Class gatherings.
Occasionally a weekly meeting was waived so that members could
attend Decoration Day celebrations, a Grand Army of the Republic
(GAR) or Christian Endeavor convention, the Decatur Corn Car-
nival, or a cooking school. At other times the Class listened to
guests describe their own societies, such as the Dante Club in Indianapolis and the Milwaukee Art Class. Only twice in its first
twenty-five years, however, aside from its single poll on suffrage, did
world events make their way, inexplicably, onto the Class program.
In 1886 the club planned to devote one meeting to a "discussion of
the Tariff question, Mrs. Millikin and Mrs. McReynolds to present
their views on the side of free trade and Mrs. Walston and Mrs.

Barnes on the side of protection and a general discussion to follow by the class."[42] Always a heated issue, the tariff may have aroused particularly strong sentiments in Decatur, with farmers resentful of a discriminating tax and Governor Oglesby, a native son, a proponent of it. Still it remains a puzzling inclusion, and even more intriguing is the absence of minutes (a highly unusual occurrence) for the scheduled date of the "discussion" (the Art Class seemed consciously to avoid the word *debate*) or any further reference to the topic. In 1892 another unexpected intrusion occurred as "a discussion of the Louisiana Lottery Question engaged the attention of the class for some time and the topics were not all discussed."[43] Otherwise, the workaday world was acknowledged only through its relation to the study at hand. During the Class study of German literature, each member was asked to describe a picture or statue which particularly interested her in the German exhibit at the Columbian Exhibition. Hull House, the Chicago settlement house founded by Jane Addams, was mentioned by Mrs. Gastman, but only in connection with an art exhibit she had viewed there. The Association for the Advancement of Woman was recognized only once, when the annual report of its art committee was read to the Class, "giving an idea of the interest in this branch of study all over the country." Twice "best-sellers" made their way into meetings alongside the classics, one member summarizing " 'Trilby' the late novel which is described in many reviews as a work of art," another giving "a deeply interesting synopsis of Mr. Jeckel and Dr. Hyde [sic]."[44] Beginning in 1883 once a month a member was appointed to report on "art news of the day." Although the art world was debating fiercely about styles of painting—realism, impressionism, and abstractionism—the minutes give not a hint of the controversy; instead the members heard descriptions of Japanese rice paper, "Trinity Cathedral in Boston over which Bishop Phillips Brooks presides," and the work of "a home artist now working in Chicago."[45]

While the Decatur Woman's Club attracted considerable attention as the first woman's stock company in Illinois, and the second in the nation, to build a club house and prided itself on its "wide circle of influence,"[46] the Art Class, amid the commercialism of the Gilded Age, disdained money matters. It allowed no club house to distract its attention or money-raising schemes to subvert its purpose. Once, in a weak moment, the club in 1895 discussed giving "a concert or something of that nature for pleasure, and charity as well, the proceeds to be given to the Library," but "the decision was left until the next meeting" and did not surface again.[47] At a time when the Decatur Woman's Club was encouraging art by offering scholarships to high school students, the Art Class was content to observe: "Mrs. Nelson had in hand some drawings from seventh grade pupils showing what is attempted in the Art line in our schools. The promise for the future artist seems great."[48] At one session the Class critic was asked to record during the week and report back to the members all the mispronunciations and grammatical errors she heard outside the club. No list was published, no corrections issued; the information was solely for the edification and instruction of Class members.[49] One local male observer, William Hardy, in an editorial occasioned by the fiftieth anniversary of the Art Class attributed the club's strength to its inwardness:

> In the half century in which the Art Class has lived a multitude of clubs and societies have come into existence, have flourished awhile and have winked out.
> Just as old people are asked their rules for longevity, so the Art Class may be asked how in the fierce competition of private and community interests it has managed to survive. We suspect that an absence of reforming zeal may have had something to do with it. Because the members were content to exhibit good taste in their own homes without urging it upon their neighbors there were none of those distressing clashes that are so disrupting. Nobody eagerly desired office. No ambitious community plans were launched. Peace was maintained. Unlike the University Club, a men's organization which loves highly controversial subjects, and cheers lance-breaking, the Art Class, woman-like, accepts the authority of the written word, and avoids argument. If this complacency would, in the opinion of many, leave something to be desired, it has satisfied the members and that is the main thing. A Class that has lived for 50 years can't be wrong.[50]

A successful organization must answer a need, Julia Ward Howe had observed in 1873. If we may judge by the clubs that women founded in the years immediately preceding and following Howe's call to association, the need was education. As with most needs, the process of fulfillment gave rise to others, and by the 1890s the small prairie town of Decatur, with its once endless flat acres of corn now abutting sharply rising new industrial plants and factories, offered two quite different clubs in response to the polyphonic chorus of women's voices.

While the Decatur Woman's Club assured women that change in their role was possible and, indeed, was in process, the Art Class reassured women that all was not flux, that they had lived rightly, and that there was a permanence to the values they cherished. While the Decatur Woman's Club acknowledged the multiplicity and complexity of the day and participated in it through its various purposes and goals, the Art Class championed simplicity. Its one committee, composed of the three women who structured the yearly program, needed no qualifiers; it was called simply "the Committee." The Class purpose remained single-minded: study through sorority. While the Decatur Woman's Club enmeshed itself interdependently in a network supporting large federations, the Art Class continued small, self-contained, and independent. Even while it maintained its uneasy alliance with the Art Union, it had drummed its own beat. At its fourth annual gathering, the president of the Art Union outlined a standard program which each member club was urged to adopt the following year: the study of modern French art; the inclusion of French music at each meeting; the regular discussion of current art topics; the presentation throughout the year of eight essays on general art topics; the sponsorship of an art loan exhibit; and the employment of an art teacher to conduct studio art classes.[51] Of the prescribed program, the Art Class engaged in none but the monthly discussion of current art topics, a practice already routine in its proceedings.

Like the age it represented, the Decatur Woman's Club, as its membership swelled, grew increasingly bureaucratic, impersonal, and dominated by key individuals at the top. In contrast, the Art Class divided labor and responsibilities equally among its members. Relationships were long and intimate. Although its members might disagree, as they did over suffrage, the Class, maternally, kept the peace and presented to the outside world a familial loyalty and unity. In an age that endorsed both tradition and transition in women's pursuits,[52] Decatur offered women a choice. In the Decatur

Woman's Club they could begin to shed female stereotypes and help carve out a new sphere for women. In the Art Class they could hold fast to their primary identification as True Women while further developing feelings of individual and collective self-worth and pride in women's special sphere. Finally, in symbolic symbiosis, the Decatur Woman's Club proved that women could act effectively in public, while the Art Class provided the private starting point of it all— education. "In social life," said Elizabeth Cady Stanton in 1873, "great facts maintain themselves before we take cognizance of their existence."[53] So it was with study clubs, which *were* education until women, through education, learned what education was.

In the heartland of America, which had witnessed the birth of study clubs, Decatur at the turn of the century mirrored the national club movement and the changing image of American women. Study clubs, once startling and suspect with their commitment to women's education for self, were now part of the tradition women took with them into the twentieth century. Out of that tradition and built of its strength (women thinking back through their mothers, to paraphrase Virginia Woolf),[54] service clubs continued to enlarge the definition of the American woman. Reflecting women's more complex role in a more complex society, department clubs gave their members opportunities to pursue their interests and to test their abilities beyond the literary. Like study clubs, service clubs are now themselves a part of American women's history. Though both groups persist, they do not sound (nor, in a narrative of change, should they) a dominant chord in the life of women today. But because both communities of women refused to be silenced, because they generated their own experiences, transformed their restraints, and wrote their own instructional texts, they have helped the American woman to know, educate, and speak, in her own voice, for herself.

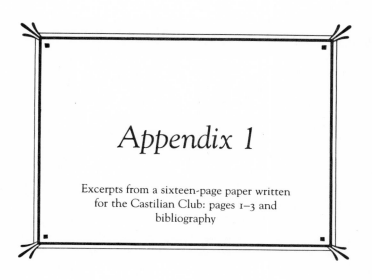

Appendix 1

Excerpts from a sixteen-page paper written
for the Castilian Club: pages 1–3 and
bibliography

Charles the Fifth as a Prince. Margaret of Austria

by Lorietta A. Eaton

Read before the Castilian Club 20 January 1895

In Ghent, that busy trade mart, in the old palace of the courts of
Flanders, where more than 600 years before, in the time of Saxon
England, Baldwin of the Iron Arm had brought his captured bride,
daughter of the king of France—in that same old palace Charles
the Fifth was born, February 24, 1500.

It chanced that the day was a holiday, celebrated in honor of St.
Matthias; and it can easily be imagined how greatly the merriment
was increased when the important news was known. Twelve days
later the young prince was baptized. The hour was late—but thousands of torches lighted the route from the palace to the grand
old church of St. Bavon. The place in the procession that it was
thought would confer the most honor, was given to two noted
women, walking side by side. They were the two god-mothers. On
the left was the elder—of middle age—Margaret of York, who carried the tiny heir of the richest inheritance of the century. The
other, clad in deepest mourning, was Margaret of Austria, his young
aunt, the widow of Prince John of Spain, from which country she

had just returned. The ceremony of naming this child was carried to the utmost limit of an imposing ritual. By his father he was given the title of Duke of Luxembourg. His name was bestowed in honor of Charles the Bold, through whom he had inherited the rich provinces of Burgundy and the Netherlands. The font used on the occasion is still preserved in the church and is shown to visitors.

Margaret of York, the godmother who presented him for baptism, was an English Princess, the widow of his grandfather, Charles the Bold, Duke of Burgundy. She was the sister of the cruel and self-indulgent Edward the Fourth. Born in the midst of the carnage of the Wars of the Roses, when only 14 years old she lost her father and a young brother in battle. Her marriage to the Duke of Burgundy was a political triumph over the French King. The Duke made this marriage an occasion of great splendor. For several months the looms of Bruges had been driven at their highest speed; shops had displayed their most beautiful goods; from all parts of the country had come decorators to renew the palace.

Margaret left her brother's court and "rode thurote London behynde the Erle of Warwick," that is, on the same horse with him; the usual way at the time. A fleet of sixteen ships carried her numerous suite of courtiers and ladies of waiting to the Flemish port of Sluys, where they remained a week. Thence by barges through canals they reached a small town near Bruges; there she was married on Sunday at five o'clock in the morning. Then came the entrance into Bruges, where a magnificent procession awaited Margaret. Her husband had withdrawn to the palace, leaving all the honor to be bestowed on her alone. Her litter was covered with cloth of gold, and was drawn by horses decorated with the same rich stuff. Her gown was of silver cloth. She wore a crown blazing with diamonds, but above it she had placed a simple wreath of roses given her by some nuns. Before her strode the English archers. On either side were the Knights of the Golden Fleece, in their most gorgeous attire. Behind her came the fair English women; the younger and unmarried riding on milkwhite horses; the matrons seated in carriages bearing the Arms of both England and Burgundy. From house-fronts were hung silk tapestries and sheets of cloth of gold. As Margaret passed beneath triumphal arches, white doves were uncaged. Some of them fluttering around settled upon the poles of her litter. At different points along the road were dramatic representations, jousts, and tilts. Fountains ran wine. The wedding feast was long continued. One appreciative participant wrote home to England that "Never Englishmen had so good cheer out of England, that I ever heard of." The same writer said of the Burgundian Court, "I never heard of none like it, save King Arthur's." Of the fine clothing he said they were "as rich beseem as cloth of gold and silk and silver and goldsmith work might make them." . . .

Margaret was much liked by the Burgundians, and seems to have taken kindly to the many minutiae of Court etiquette. She was ever zealous for the success of her family of York. She made peace between her brothers when they were at variance. She assisted them with money and induced her husband to favor them. After his death she wished to marry his only child, her much-sought step-daughter, Mary of Burgundy, to her favorite brother, Duke of Clarence. But Edward the Fourth, jealous of the power his brother would gain, would not consent. She so greatly troubled the English government during the reign of her brother's successor, that she was called Juno, because, to quote an old chronicle, "She being to that Prince as severe an enemy as that goddess was to Aeneas, moving Heaven and Earth against him."

This interesting woman lived only three years longer. But we have one more glimpse of her. At a meeting of the Golden Fleece she carried the young Prince Charles, then one year of age. The two were placed in a prominent spot in the midst of the assembly. At the request of the officers, Philip, the child's father, saluted him with the title of Sir Knight, and placed the collar of the Order around his neck.

Books Consulted

Altmeyer, J. J. "Marguerite d' Autriche. Sa Vie, sa Politique et sa Cour"

Conway, William M. "Early Flemish Artists"

Coxe, William. "History of the House of Austria"

Fenn, John, compiler. "Original Letters of the Reigns of Henry VI, Edward IV, and Richard III"

Juste, Theodore. "Charles Quint et Marguerite d'Autriche"

Kirk, John F. "History of Charles the Bold, Duke of Burgundy"

Littenhove, Baron Kervyn de. "Commentaires de Charles Quint"

Motley, John L. "The Rise of the Dutch Republic"

Robertson, William. "History of the Reign of the Emperor Charles the Fifth"

Vera, Antonio de. "La Vida y Hechos del Invicto Emperador Carlos Quinto"

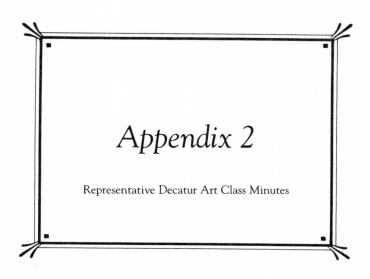

Appendix 2

Representative Decatur Art Class Minutes

November 2, 1889

Class convened at the residence of the Pres. Mrs. Wells. Called to order with nine members present—7 excused—1 absent—2 in Chicago—1 in Paris, France. With pride be it stated that notwithstanding the pending problem of "Free Trade versus protection," one worthy member, to keep pace with old world sights, needs new world shoes.

The Sec. being absent, Mrs. Hatch was, unfortunately, named for the day. The lesson proceeded according to the Topics laid out. The George's—1 and 2nd—were described and their merits, which were usually demerits—were the theme of much comment even to the mystifying subject of heredity. Mrs. Nelson, in her usually clear style, gave an interesting talk on the English Church. As a confection, after the heavy draughts of substantials—one guest, Mrs. Carson of Madison, Wis. gave us some of her experiences among the artists [sic] studios and pictures of the Paris Exposition. It was a treat—the enjoyment of which, we regretted, was lost to so many of the ladies. On motion, a vote of thanks was tendered Mrs. Carson for her kind courtesy, and many expressions of pleasure were added to the yeas of all present.

The critic failed to criticise, and, on motion, Class adjourned to meet with Mrs. Hill November 19, 1889.

Mrs. Wells, Pres.

Mrs. Hatch
Sec.
[Decatur Art Class, Minutes (1889), 2:249–50.]

March 1, 1890

At the home of Mrs. Millikin.

In the absence of the Pres. the Vice Pres. occupied the chair. Members dropped in, one by one, until the number reached twelve. Class called to order and minutes of previous meeting read and approved. By order of the Pres. class proceeded to the lesson—commencing with George Crabb, born in 1754—followed by George Wolcott—(Peter Pindar)—Robert Burns—David Garrick—Richard Brinsley Sheridan—Queen Anne architecture—and closing this part of our lesson with Sir Walter Scott who died at Abbottsford, Scotland in 1832—ever in our minds as the author of—

"Burned Marmion's swarthy cheek like fire,
And shook his very frame with ire."

It was impossible to condense a lesson so full of interest within the limits of our time, with any degree of justice—but the ladies made a brave and commendable effort. Interest in the lesson so great that the report of the Critic was almost "non est"—else, perhaps, the class was unusually perfect. The Topic committee asked for an expression on the lessons given—responded to by a number of members present, and all well pleased. Excuses received from several of the members. On motion Class adjourned to meet with Mrs. Roach, Saturday, March 8th, 1890.

Mrs. Wells Pres.

Mrs. James Milliken,
Sec.
[Decatur Art Class, Minutes (1890), 2:273.]

November 24, 1906

The Art Class enjoyed a very pleasant meeting at the home of Mrs. Ira Barnes. Mrs. Milliken presiding. Twelve members were present to continue the discussion of "Paradise Lost" and to finish that beautiful allegory. Chapters ten, eleven and twelve comprised the lesson and the best points in each were brought out during the recitations. There was a difference of opinion in regard to the two closing lines of the poem. Some of the members would have preferred a less sad ending while others agreed with Milton. The Art topic "Van Dyke and his Contemporaries" came last in the program and was given by Mrs. Ira Barnes who had prepared an interesting account of the artist Van Dyke. Mrs. Galleway was critic. Excuses were read from Mrs. Hostetler, Mrs. Wells, Mrs. Roberts, and Mrs. Andersen. Mrs. Haworth being excused by a vote of the Class since her health did not permit her attendance. A motion was carried that the Class meet with Mrs. Andersen on Saturday, December 1st at two o'clock [the usual meeting time was two-thirty] in order that Mrs. Nelson might not be limited in time while reading her "Paradiso" [a paper apparently written for an extension course through the University of Chicago]. Adjourned at the usual hour.

Jeannete Rogers
Sec.
[Decatur Art Class, Minutes (1906), 4:177.]

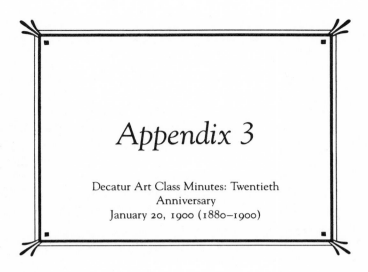

Appendix 3

Decatur Art Class Minutes: Twentieth
Anniversary
January 20, 1900 (1880–1900)

Chapter I

In the fourth year of the reign of Rutherford whose name was also Hays [sic] there were in the land of the Decaturites certain women who came often together and they made a vow that they would read much and search out mysteries and seek all knowledge that it is meet for women to know.

Moreover they agreed that on every sixth day of the week they would assemble themselves together and rehearse what they had learned. And the number was twenty who took this vow.

Now it came to pass as it drew nigh to twenty years since they had thus consented to this pledge (though all were not with them as at the beginning, yet others had taken their places) that they looked upon each other and said, "The days of our years be nigh to a score, is it not meet that we make merry, rejoice and be glad."

Now when the Queen heard this she was pleased that this thing came into the hearts of the women, and she made request that the chief counselor, the scribe and she who carried the purse, should come to her for a season, and reason about the matter.

Therefore Mary, Elizabeth and Caroline made a journey to the palace of the Queen; there they communed together and assented to all the desires of the Queen.

Chapter II

Now it was so that on the sixth day of the first month they were with one accord at the house of Mary whose husband was a physician and they talked much and took counsel together, and the Queen even Anna put forth her hand and she spake on this wise.

Come ye all to my house, to the palace of James the money changer on the thirteenth day of the first month at the hour of one called also the seventh hour; and ye would do well to fast before ye come, saying meat shall be set before you in this palace. And they said in their hearts, long live the Queen; while they yet hungered and talked of the good things prepared for them, behold, the chariot of the Queen came and bore her away.

Now when the Queen was departed there was the rejoicing of such as were bidden to a feast.

And one said our Queen is a discreet woman and keepeth counsel with none, let us do a pleasant and a secret thing. As we make ready and go up to the feast let us each bear a symbol or token that we have read much and are acquainted with the learning of the kingdoms of the earth.

This saying pleased the women and they said we will think on these things.

When the full time was come for which the banquet was set, even the thirteenth day of the first month it being now twenty years since the women had first banded together they came with haste to the palace at the hour of one.

And they bore indeed strange devices, some banners, necklaces, precious stones and many others, some carried in their hands boxes, candlesticks, spoons, wings of birds, lilies of the field, and parchment with manuscripts.

Now were all filled with wonder and great confusion as to what these things meant. Nevertheless in the fullness of time the mysteries were revealed to them and they were filled with mirth till the Queen came and said my feast is prepared, behold, all things are now ready.

Chapter III

Now as they sat at meat the Queen sat with her chief counselor over against her and the honorable women on her right hand and on her left round about, eight upon this side and eight upon that.

The table was spread with fine linen, embroidery, lordly dishes, glasses, silver and flowers, such things as are found in kings' houses.

And the hand maidens of the Queen brought in the products of other lands, fruits, wines and pleasant viands and set before the women, seven times did they bring forth things well pleasing to the taste.

After the feast was ended the women were asked to speak forth words of mirth and wisdom, and Queen Anna was first to speak, for she said to herself is it not written, "A word spoken in due season how good it is."

So she stood before them and uttered words of sweetness and hospitality.

The chief counselor also spoke of things past and things present, and thus did they all even to the last.

They were words fitly spoken, which indeed are like apples of gold in pictures of silver.

Now there had been messages sent from women in a far country to the rulers of the feast and a message also from one William whose sirname was Nelson (a wise man, his wife also being a member of the band) and the scribe read the parchment in the presence of the women, and it contained amiable words acceptable to their ears.

Now when all the epistles had been read they left the banquet hall and assembled in the hall which is by the east court and here a damsel played upon a harp and the women sang one of the songs of their forefathers.

And as the day was now far spent they departed to their homes. And the rest of the acts of these women behold they are written in the pages of the fourth book of Chronicles of the Art Class.

C. S. Gastman
Sec.
[Decatur Art Class, Minutes (1900), 4:35–38.]

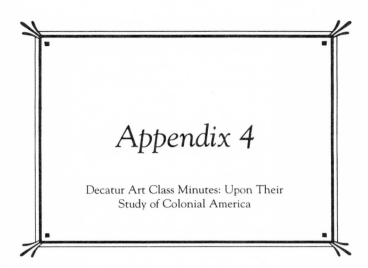

Appendix 4

Decatur Art Class Minutes: Upon Their
Study of Colonial America

December 29, 1900

T'was [sic] Saturday a week from now
That maidens young with classic brow
All hurried forth in costumes rare
Lest they should cause a smile or stare
While on the road to school they trod
In stockings white and slippers shod!

Dame Gastman had in kindness sent
For all the girls on study bent
And many friends of Art Class fame
Obeyed her call at two P.M.
Some wore the garb and had the way
That puritans had in former day!

One maid was French, at least her gown
Was certainly from out of town,
But who can give in language clear
The "toute ensemble" that did appear
When our dear friend and teacher wise
Came in full view of all our eyes?

No words can paint the cap and gown
The apron white, and none can drown
The melody of that refrain
When Captain Kidd was sung again!
All realized, I have no doubt,
What sweetness was when long drawn out,

So well did all the voices three
Combine in reaching upper G!
For even yet most notes appear
Harmonious to every ear!
The spinning wheel, the spinning song,
The recitations all belong

To that program, so quaint and old!
Friendly too, the gossip told
About the girls assembled there
And all their vanities laid bare
Before the dame, who looked agrieved
To think those maids had her deceived!

But soon the pie, of pumpkin gold
The pound cake rich, of ample mould,
And cup of tea were served "au fait"
And every one forgot dismay!
Another ditty then did ring
From A.A.A. whose voice did bring

While skipping round, both mirth and cheer
When carolling, the trumpeteer!
And 'twas quite late when school adjourned
And all the maidens homeward turned
Each one in retrospective bent
And in each heart a glad content

That good dame Gastman should have planned
A treat so rare as to command
The gratitude and praises loud
Of every school girl in the crowd!

Jeannette Rogers
Sec.
[Decatur Art Class, Minutes (1900), 4:58–59.]

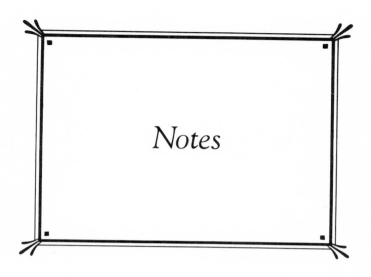

Notes

Preface

1. George F. Kennan, "History, Literature and the Road to Peterhof," *New York Times Book Review,* 29 June 1986.

Introduction

1. Elizabeth C. Agassiz, quoted in Sally Schwager, "'Harvard Women': A History of the Founding of Radcliffe College" (Ed.D. thesis, Harvard Graduate School of Education, 1982), 113.

2. Muriel Beadle, *The Fortnightly of Chicago* (Chicago: Henry Regnery, 1973), 47.

3. Karen Blair, *The Clubwoman as Feminist* (New York: Holmes & Meier, 1980); Anne F. Scott, *Making the Invisible Woman Visible* (Urbana: University of Illinois Press, 1984); and Anne F. Scott, "On Seeing and Not Seeing: A Case of Historical Invisibility," *The Journal of American History* 71, no. 1 (1984): 7–21.

4. Thomas Woody, *A History of Women's Education in the United States* (New York: Science Press, 1929), 2:243; L. Clark Seelye, *The Early History of Smith College* (Boston: Houghton Mifflin, 1923), 36.

5. Anne F. Scott, "The 'New Woman' in the South," in Jean E. Friedman and William G. Shade, eds., *Our American Sisters: Women in American Life and Thought,* 3d ed. (Boston: Allyn & Bacon, 1973), 190.

6. Margaret G. Wilson, *The American Woman in Transition: The Urban Influence, 1870–1920* (Westport, CT: Greenwood Press, 1979), 100–101.

7. Mrs. Percy V. Pennybacker, "The Eighth Biennial of the General Federation of Women's Clubs," *The Annals of the American Academy of Political and Social Science* 28, no. 2 (1906): 81–82.

8. Jane C. Croly, *The History of the Woman's Club Movement in America* (New York: Henry G. Allen, 1898), vii.

Chapter 1

The chapter title is taken from the minutes of the Decatur (Illinois) Art Class (1894), 3:88.

1. Helen M. Winslow, "The Modern Club Woman," *The Delineator* 80, no. 6 (1912): 473.

2. Jane C. Croly, *The History of the Woman's Club Movement in America* (New York: Henry G. Allen, 1898), 2.

3. Mildred W. Wells, *Unity in Diversity* (Washington, DC: General Federation of Women's Clubs, 1953), 10.

4. Anne F. Scott, *Making the Invisible Woman Visible* (Urbana: University of Illinois Press, 1984), 262.

5. John Winthrop, quoted in Wellington Newcomb, "Anne Hutchinson versus Massachusetts," *American Heritage* 25, no. 4 (1974): 12.

6. Gerda Lerner, *The Woman in American History* (Menlo Park, CA: Addison-Wesley, 1971), 71.

7. Ibid.

8. Croly, *History*, 8.

9. Mid-nineteenth-century woman was idealized in the phrase *True Woman*. Historian Barbara Welter identifies her attributes as piety, purity, submissiveness, and domesticity in "The Cult of True Womanhood: 1820–1860," *American Quarterly* 18, no. 2 (1966): 153.

10. Mary I. Wood, *The History of the General Federation of Women's Clubs* (Norwood, MA: General Federation of Women's Clubs, 1912), 30–31.

11. Louise H. Tharp, *The Peabody Sisters of Salem* (Boston: Little, Brown, 1950), 87–88.

12. Ibid., 88.

13. Scott, *Invisible Woman*, 56.

14. Helen M. Winslow, "The Story of the Woman's Club Movement," *New England Magazine* 38 (July 1908): 552.

15. Inez H. Irwin, *Angels and Amazons* (Garden City, NY: Doubleday, Doran, 1934), 64.

16. Charles T. Davis, Introduction to Lucy Larcom, *A New England Girlhood* (Gloucester, MA: Peter Smith, 1973), viii.

17. Daniel D. Addison, *Lucy Larcom: Life, Letters, and Diary* (Boston: Houghton Mifflin, 1895), 6–7.

18. Larcom, *Girlhood*, 222–23.

19. Ibid., 223.

20. Ibid., 241–42.

21. Ibid., 209–11.

22. Quoted in Ann Douglas, *The Feminization of American Culture* (New York: Avon Books, 1977), 83.

23. Henry Baldwin, "An Old-time Sorosis," *Atlantic Monthly* 74, no. 447 (1894): 749; Mary S. Cunningham, *The Woman's Club of El Paso* (El Paso: Texas Western Press, 1978), viii.

24. Quoted in Grace G. Courtney, *History: Indiana Federation of Clubs* (Fort Wayne, IN: Fort Wayne Printing Company, 1939), 1.

25. Edgeworthalean Society, Minutes, quoted in Courtney, *Indiana*, 7.

26. Ibid., 8.

27. Ibid., 6–7.

28. Ibid., 7.

29. Ibid., 8.

30. Quoted in Courtney, *Indiana*, 13.

31. Wells, *Unity*, 15.

32. Courtney, *Indiana*, 15–16.

33. Winslow, "Woman's Club Movement," 550.

34. Quoted in Croly, *History*, 1106.

Chapter 2

1. Julia W. Howe, "How Can Women Best Associate?" in Association for the Advancement of Woman, *Papers and Letters Presented at the First Woman's Congress of the Association for the Advancement of Woman, 1873* (New York, 1874), 8.

2. Vida D. Scudder, *On Journey* (New York: E. P. Dutton, 1937), 110.

3. Mary I. Wood, "The Woman's Club Movement," *The Chautauquan* 59, no. 1 (1910): 14.

4. Arthur M. Schlesinger, *Paths to the Present* (New York: Macmillan, 1949), 28.

5. Jane C. Croly, *The History of the Woman's Club Movement in America* (New York: Henry G. Allen, 1898), 12.

6. Karen J. Blair, *The Clubwoman as Feminist* (New York: Holmes & Meier, 1980), 13; Anne F. Scott, "On Seeing and Not Seeing: A Case of Historical Invisibility," *The Journal of American History* 71, no. 1 (1984): 12.

7. Quoted in Lewis Mumford, *The Brown Decades* (New York: Harcourt, Brace, 1931), 13.

8. *The Education of Henry Adams* (New York: Random House, 1931), 236.

9. Ibid., 239.

10. Ibid., 239–40.

11. Robert H. Wiebe, *The Search for Order* (New York: Hill & Wang, 1967), xiv.

12. Ibid., 58.

13. Croly, *History*, 456–57.

14. Carroll Smith-Rosenberg, *Disorderly Conduct: Visions of Gender in Victorian America* (New York: Knopf, 1985), 138.

15. Shirley Ardener, quoted in Sara Delamont and Lorna Duffin, eds., *The Nineteenth-Century Woman: Her Cultural and Physical World* (New York: Barnes & Noble Books, 1978), 11–12.

16. Delamont and Duffin, *Nineteenth-Century*, 11–12.

17. Allan Nevins and Henry S. Commager, *America: The Story of a Free People* (Boston: Little, Brown, 1942), 282.

18. Sheila M. Rothman, *Woman's Proper Place* (New York: Basic Books, 1978), 14–15.

19. Daniel S. Smith, "Family Limitation, Sexual Control, and Domestic Feminism in Victorian America," in Nancy F. Cott and Elizabeth M. Pleck, eds., *A Heritage of Her Own: Toward a New Social History of American Women* (New York: Simon & Schuster, 1979), 226.

20. Ibid., 223.

21. Anne F. Scott, *The Southern Lady* (Chicago: University of Chicago Press, 1970), 106.

22. Ellen C. DuBois, *Feminism and Suffrage* (Ithaca, NY: Cornell University Press, 1978), 128.

23. Viola Klein, *The Feminine Character: History of an Ideology* (Urbana: University of Illinois Press, 1972), 10; Catherine Clinton, *The Other Civil War* (New York: Hill & Wang, 1984), 18–19.

24. Margaret G. Wilson, *The American Woman in Transition: The Urban Influence, 1870–1920* (Westport, CT: Greenwood Press, 1979), 17.

25. Quoted in Barbara Welter, "The Cult of True Womanhood: 1820–1860," *American Quarterly* 18, no. 2 (1966): 173.

26. Willystine Goodsell, *The Education of Women: Its Social Background and Its Problems* (New York: Macmillan, 1923), 4.

27. Gerda Lerner, "The Lady and the Mill Girl," in Cott and Pleck, *Heritage*, 192.

28. Quoted in Aileen S. Kraditor, *Up from the Pedestal* (Chicago: Quadrangle Books, 1968), 192.

29. Glenda G. Riley, "The Subtle Subversion: Changes in the Traditional Image of the American Woman," *The Historian* 33, no. 2 (1970): 214; Welter, "True Womanhood," 171–72.

30. William D. Howells, *The Rise of Silas Lapham* (1885; reprint, New York: New American Library, 1980), 47.

31. Ibid., 45.

32. Ibid., 10.

33. Wilson, *Transition*, 19.

34. Welter, "True Womanhood," 152.

35. William R. Taylor and Christopher Lasch, "Two 'Kindred Spirits': Sorority and Family in New England, 1839–1846," *The New England Quarterly* 36, no. 1 (1963): 35.

36. Riley, "Subtle Subversion," 214.

37. Rothman, *Proper Place*, 63.

38. Le Baron R. Briggs, *To College Girls and Other Essays* (Boston: Houghton Mifflin, 1911), 55.

39. Robert Grant, *Unleavened Bread* (New York: Charles Scribner's Sons, 1915), 49.

40. Briggs, *To College Girls,* 79.

41. Ibid., 52.

42. Welter, "True Womanhood," 159.

43. Quoted in Merle Curti, *The Social Ideas of American Educators* (New York: Charles Scribner's Sons, 1935), 189.

44. Quoted in Rothman, *Proper Place,* 22.

45. Nancy F. Cott, *The Bonds of Motherhood* (New Haven: Yale University Press, 1977), 105.

46. Mary I. Wood, *The History of the General Federation of Women's Clubs* (Norwood, MA: General Federation of Women's Clubs, 1912), 6.

47. Welter, "True Womanhood," 153.

48. Quoted in Welter, "True Womanhood," 160–61.

49. Smith-Rosenberg, *Disorderly Conduct,* 200.

50. Quoted in Jean Strouse, *Alice James* (Boston: Houghton Mifflin, 1980), 45.

51. Quoted in Marjorie H. Dobkin, ed., *The Making of a Feminist: Early Journals and Letters of M. Carey Thomas* (Kent, OH: Kent State University Press, 1979), 50.

52. Helen M. Winslow, *The President of Quex* (Boston: Lothrop, Lee & Shepard, 1906), 53.

53. Christopher Lasch, "Divorce and the Family in America," *Atlantic* 218, no. 5 (1966): 59.

54. Quoted in Jessie Bernard, *The Future of Motherhood* (New York: Penguin Books, 1974), 7.

55. Quoted in Sally Schwager, "'Harvard Women': A History of the Founding of Radcliffe College" (Ed.D. thesis, Harvard Graduate School of Education, 1982), 18.

56. United States Commissioner of Education, *Report* (Washington, DC, 1907), 1:336.

57. Quoted in Welter, "True Womanhood," 168.

58. Quoted in Strouse, *Alice James,* 43–44.

59. Welter, "True Womanhood," 166.

60. Catharine E. Beecher, "On Endowments for Woman's Colleges," in Association for the Advancement of Woman, *Papers and Letters Presented at the First Woman's Congress of the Association for the Advancement of Woman, 1873* (New York, 1874), 157.

61. Ibid., 155–57.

62. Lucy Larcom, *A New England Girlhood* (Gloucester, MA: Peter Smith, 1973), 157.

63. Quoted in Laura E. Richards and Maud H. Elliott, *Julia Ward Howe, 1819–1910* (Boston: Houghton Mifflin, 1916), 1:122.

64. Riley, "Subtle Subversion," 224.

65. Ann Douglas, *The Feminization of American Culture* (New York: Avon Books, 1977), 89.

66. Jane Addams, *Twenty Years at Hull House* (New York: Macmillan, 1914), 93.

67. Winslow, *Quex*, 74–76.

68. Rosalind Rosenberg, *Beyond Separate Spheres: The Intellectual Roots of Modern Feminism* (New Haven: Yale University Press, 1982), 14.

69. Ladies Literary Club of Grand Rapids, Michigan (1892), unpaged yearbook, by courtesy of the Trustees of the Boston Public Library.

70. Smith-Rosenberg, *Disorderly Conduct*, 60.

71. Ibid., 67.

72. Constance Smith and Anne Freedman, *Voluntary Associations: Perspectives on the Literature* (Cambridge: Harvard University Press, 1972), 14, 20.

73. Ibid., 3.

Chapter 3

The chapter title is taken from the motto of the Woman's Literary Club of Portsmouth, Ohio, quoted in Jane C. Croly, *The History of the Woman's Club Movement in America* (New York: Henry G. Allen, 1898), 1006.

1. Croly, *History*, 456.

2. Ralph W. Emerson, "Education," in *Selected Prose and Poetry*, ed. Reginald L. Cook (New York: Rinehart, 1954), 208.

3. Hamlin Garland, *A Son of the Middle Border* (1917; reprint, New York: Macmillan, 1962), 89.

4. Quoted in Eleanor W. Thompson, *Education for Ladies 1830–1860* (New York: King's Crown Press, 1947), 40.

5. Louise H. Tharp, *The Peabody Sisters of Salem* (Boston: Little, Brown, 1950), 10.

6. Quoted in Carl Bode, *The American Lyceum* (New York: Oxford University Press, 1956), 68.

7. Quoted in Bode, *Lyceum*, 7.

8. Herbert B. Adams, *Report of the Commissioner of Education for the Year 1899–1900* (Washington, DC: Government Printing Office, 1901), 290.

9. Bode, *Lyceum*, 135–36.

10. Ibid., 30.

11. Anne F. Scott, *Making the Invisible Woman Visible* (Urbana: University of Illinois Press, 1984), 39.

12. Helen H. Santmyer, *". . . And Ladies of the Club"* (New York: G. P. Putnam's Sons, 1982), 25.

13. Viola Klein, *The Feminine Character: History of an Ideology* (Urbana: University of Illinois Press, 1972), 23.

14. Quoted in Arthur M. Schlesinger, *Paths to the Present* (New York: Macmillan, 1949), 9.

15. Mabel Newcomer, *A Century of Education for American Women* (New York: Harper & Brothers, 1959), 16.

16. Glenda G. Riley, "The Subtle Subversion: Changes in the Traditional Image of the American Woman," *The Historian* 33, no. 2 (1970): 211.

17. Andrew Sinclair, *The Better Half: The Emancipation of the American Woman* (1965; reprint, Westport, CT: Greenwood Press, 1981), 319.

18. Julia W. Howe, "How Can Women Best Associate?" in Association for the Advancement of Woman, *Papers and Letters Presented at the First Woman's Congress of the Association for the Advancement of Woman, 1873* (New York, 1874), 6.

19. Karen J. Blair, *The Clubwoman as Feminist* (New York: Holmes & Meier, 1980), 27.

20. Quoted in Marjorie H. Dobkin, ed., *The Making of a Feminist: Early Journals and Letters of M. Carey Thomas* (Kent, OH: Kent State University Press, 1979), 99.

21. Quoted in Schlesinger, *Paths*, 45.

22. General Federation of Women's Clubs, *Third Biennial* (Louisville: Flexner Brothers, 1896), 368.

23. Ibid., 368–69.

24. Croly, *History*, 11.

25. Sara Delamont and Lorna Duffin, eds., *The Nineteenth-Century Woman: Her Cultural and Physical World* (New York: Barnes & Noble Books, 1978), 147.

26. Mary I. Wood, *The History of the General Federation of Women's Clubs* (Norwood, MA: General Federation of Women's Clubs, 1912), 310.

27. Ina B. Roberts, ed., *Club Women of New York, 1910–1911* (New York: Club Women of New York Company, 1910), 65.

28. Mary S. Cunningham, *The Woman's Club of El Paso* (El Paso: Texas Western Press, 1978), 19; Muriel Beadle, *The Fortnightly of Chicago* (Chicago: Henry Regnery, 1973), 22; Olive T. Miller, *The Woman's Club* (New York: United States Book Company, 1891), 50; Judith B. Ranlett, "Sorority and Community: Women's Answer to a Changing Massachusetts, 1865–1895" (Ph.D. diss., Brandeis University, 1974), 124.

29. Croly, *History*, 16.

30. Quoted in Croly, *History*, 556, 600, 612.

31. Quoted in Beadle, *Fortnightly*, 47.

32. Quoted in Roberts, *New York*, 72.

33. Quoted in Croly, *History*, 366.

34. Quoted in Croly, *History*, 367, 406, 433, 440, 446, 456, 467, 739.

35. Quoted in Ranlett, "Sorority and Community," 100.

36. Alma A. Rogers, "The Woman's Club Movement: Its Origin, Significance and Present Results," *The Arena* 34, no. 191 (1905): 350.

37. Glenda G. Riley, "Origins of the Argument for Improved Female Education," *History of Education Quarterly* 9, no. 4 (1969): 464.

38. Lucy Larcom, *A New England Girlhood* (Gloucester, MA: Peter Smith, 1973), 256.

39. Quoted in Anne F. Scott, *The Southern Lady* (Chicago: University of Chicago Press, 1970), 68.

40. Thomas Woody, *A History of Women's Education in the United States* (New York: Science Press, 1929), 1:397.

41. Ibid., 418.

42. Anna H. Knipp and Thaddeus P. Thomas, *The History of Goucher College* (Baltimore: Goucher College, 1938), 3.

43. Woody, *History*, 1:396.

44. Ibid., 392–95.

45. Richard G. Boone, *Education in the United States* (New York: D. Appleton, 1889), 366.

46. U.S. Department of Commerce, *Historical Statistics of the United States, Colonial Times to 1970* (Washington, DC: U.S. Bureau of the Census, 1975), 15.

47. Ibid., 379.

48. Boone, *Education*, 370.

49. Willystine Goodsell, *The Education of Women: Its Social Background and Its Problems* (New York: Macmillan, 1923), 24.

50. Jill K. Conway, "Perspectives on the History of Women's Education in the United States," *History of Education Quarterly* 14, no. 4 (1974): 6.

51. Mary L. Ely and Eve Chappell, *Women in Two Worlds* (New York: American Association for Adult Education, 1938), 20–21.

52. Goodsell, *Education*, 25.

53. Newcomer, *Century*, 19.

54. Woody, *History*, 2:171–72.

55. Newcomer, *Century*, 12.

56. Woody, *History*, 2:174.

57. Martha C. Thomas, *The College Women of the Present and Future* (n.p.: McClure's Syndicate, 1901), 1.

58. Beadle, *Fortnightly*, 10.

59. The College Club, *Bi-annual Directory* (Boston: Samuel Usher, 1916), 4.

60. Newcomer, *Century*, 19; U.S. Department of Commerce, *Historical Statistics*, 15.

61. Newcomer, *Century*, 24–25.

62. Quoted in Elaine Kendall, *"Peculiar Institutions": An Informal History of the Seven Sister Colleges* (New York: G.P. Putnam's Sons, 1975), 85.

63. Quoted in Grace E. Hawk, *Pembroke College in Brown University* (Providence: Brown University Press, 1968), 20.

64. Quoted in L. Clark Seelye, *The Early History of Smith College* (Boston: Houghton Mifflin, 1923), 47.

65. Carroll Smith-Rosenberg, *Disorderly Conduct: Visions of Gender in Victorian America* (New York: Knopf, 1985), 44.

66. Wood, *General Federation*, 28.

67. Winnifred H. Cooley, "The Future of the Woman's Club," *The Arena* 27, no. 4 (1902): 373.

68. Ella D. Clymer, "The National Value of Women's Clubs," in Rachel F. Avery, ed., *Transactions of the National Council of Women of the United States, Assembled in Washington, D.C., February 22 to 25, 1891* (Philadelphia: National Council of Women of the United States, 1891), 297.

69. Croly, *History*, xi.

70. "Women's Clubs—A Symposium," *The Arena* 6, no. 33 (1892): 378–79.

71. Quoted in Croly, *History*, 452.

72. Quoted in Croly, *History*, 454.

73. Scott, *Invisible Woman*, 264.

74. William L. O'Neill, *Everyone Was Brave: The Rise and Fall of Feminism in America* (Chicago: Quadrangle Books, 1969), 78–79.

75. Quoted in Woman's Press Club of New York, *Memories of Jane Cunningham Croly* (New York: G.P. Putnam's Sons, 1904), 81.

Chapter 4

The chapter title is taken from Lucy Larcom, *A New England Girlhood* (Gloucester, MA: Peter Smith, 1973), 12.

1. Jane C. Croly, *The History of the Woman's Club Movement in America* (New York: Henry G. Allen, 1898), 15.

2. Ibid., 16.

3. Jane C. Croly, *Sorosis* (New York: J. J. Little, 1886), 35.

4. Croly, *History*, 20.

5. Croly, *Sorosis*, 10.

6. Croly, *History*, 16, 24.

7. Sorosis constitution, quoted in Croly, *Sorosis*, 8.

8. Ibid., 9.

9. Croly, *Sorosis*, 7.

10. Croly, *History*, 25.

11. Croly, *Sorosis*, 19.

12. Croly, *History*, 23.

13. Sorosis Executive Committee Report, 1869, quoted in Croly, *History*, 25.

14. Croly, *History*, 24.

15. Address by Jane C. Croly, Sorosis May Festival, 1875, quoted in Croly, *Sorosis*, 35.

16. Croly, *Sorosis*, 37.

17. Quoted in Croly, *Sorosis*, 23.

18. Quoted in Croly, *History*, 21.

19. Alice Cary, quoted in Croly, *History*, 21.

20. Croly, *Sorosis*, 24.

21. Ibid., 40.

22. Ibid., 15.

23. Quoted in Croly, *Sorosis*, 14.

24. Croly, *History*, 29.

25. Address by Jane C. Croly, Sorosis May Festival, 1875, quoted in Croly, *Sorosis*, 35.

26. Croly, *History*, 26.

27. Quoted in Karen J. Blair, *The Clubwoman as Feminist* (New York: Holmes & Meier, 1980), 24.

28. Croly, *History*, 26.

29. Ibid., 21.

30. Quoted in Croly, *History*, 23.

31. Croly, *History*, 25.

32. Blair, *Feminist*, 37.

33. Sorosis "Call to a Woman's Congress," 1873, quoted in Croly, *Sorosis*, 31.

34. Association for the Advancement of Woman, *Papers and Letters Presented at the First Woman's Congress of the Association for the Advancement of Woman*, 1873 (New York, 1874), 31–33.

35. Croly, *Sorosis*, 36.

36. Mary I. Wood, "The Woman's Club Movement," *The Chautauquan* 59, no. 1 (1910): 34–35.

37. Quoted in Croly, *History*, 90.

38. Ellen C. DuBois, *Feminism and Suffrage* (Ithaca, NY: Cornell University Press, 1978), 150.

39. Edward T. James, ed., *Notable American Women* (Cambridge: Belknap Press of Harvard University Press, 1971), 1:459–60.

40. Ibid., 1:630–31; 3:312–13.

41. Ibid., 1:295–97.

42. Ibid., 2:543–45.

43. Ibid., 2:126–27.

44. Ibid., 3:24–25.

45. Ibid., 1:441–42.

46. Ibid., 2:440–42.

47. Ibid., 1:212–13.

48. Croly, *History*, 16.

49. Ibid.

50. James, *Notable Women*, 1:409–11.

51. Jane C. Croly, quoted in Helen M. Winslow, "Among Women's Clubs," *Boston Evening Transcript*, 12 Jan. 1896.

52. Jane C. Croly, quoted in James, *Notable Women*, 1:410.

53. Quoted in Woman's Press Club of New York, *Memories of Jane Cunningham Croly* (New York: G. P. Putnam's Sons, 1904), 3.

54. Haryot H. Dey, quoted in Woman's Press Club of New York, *Croly*, 83.

55. Quoted in Woman's Press Club of New York, *Croly*, 149.

56. Patricia A. Palmieri, "In Adamless Eden: A Social Portrait of the Academic Community at Wellesley College 1875–1920" (Ed.D. thesis, Harvard Graduate School of Education, 1981); Helen L. Horowitz, *Alma Mater* (New

York: Knopf, 1984); Barbara M. Solomon, *In the Company of Educated Women* (New Haven: Yale University Press, 1985).

57. Palmieri, "Adamless Eden," 72.

58. Quoted in Woman's Press Club of New York, *Croly,* 156.

59. Croly, *History,* 873.

60. Quoted in Croly, *History,* 54.

61. Croly, *History,* 554.

62. Ibid., 661.

63. Ibid., 461.

64. Ibid., 464.

65. Ibid., 249.

66. Ibid., 389.

67. Ibid., 365.

68. Ibid., 546.

69. Ibid., 565.

70. Ibid., 1105.

71. Ibid., 572.

72. Blair, *Feminist,* 37.

73. Croly, *History,* 639.

74. Saturday Morning Club, Papers, B-28, series I, vol. 4a, The Arthur and Elizabeth Schlesinger Library on the History of Women in America, Radcliffe College.

75. Croly, *History,* 444.

76. Decatur Art Class, Minutes (1884), 2:31.

77. The Cristobal Woman's Club, *Twenty-Five Years of Club Work on the Isthmus of Panama, 1907–1932* (Panama: The Star and Herald Company, 1932), 5–13.

78. Saturday Morning Club, Papers, series II, vol. 3.

79. Quoted in Margaret G. Wilson, *The American Woman in Transition: The Urban Influence, 1870–1920* (Westport, CT: Greenwood Press, 1979), 96.

80. The New Hampshire Federation of Women's Clubs, *A History of the New Hampshire Federation of Women's Clubs* (Bristol, NH: Musgrove Printing House, 1941).

81. Act of Incorporation, New England Women's Club, quoted in Julia A. Sprague, *History of the New England Women's Club from 1868–1893* (Boston: Lee & Shepard, 1894), 55.

82. Sprague, *New England Women's Club,* 10–11, 31–32.

83. Quoted in Grace G. Courtney, *History: Indiana Federation of Clubs* (Fort Wayne, IN: Fort Wayne Printing Company, 1939), 28.

84. Quoted in Croly, *History,* 393.

85. Quoted in Croly, *History,* 646.

86. Croly, *History,* 466.

87. Ibid., preface.

88. Quoted in Croly, *History,* 533.

89. Croly, *History,* 560.

90. Inez H. Irwin, *Angels and Amazons* (Garden City, NY: Doubleday, Doran, 1934), 223.

91. Croly, *History*, 602.

92. Quoted in Croly, *History*, 394.

93. Ibid., 395.

94. Quoted in Croly, *History*, 558.

95. Croly, *History*, 554.

96. Ibid., 555.

97. Ibid., 454.

98. Quoted in *The Mayflower Club, 1893–1931* (Cambridge, MA: privately printed, 1933), 15–16.

99. Croly, *History*, 1077.

100. Muriel Beadle, *The Fortnightly of Chicago* (Chicago: Henry Regnery, 1973), 12.

101. Blair, *Feminist*, 34.

102. Croly, *History*, 575.

103. Mary L. Ely and Eve Chappell, *Women in Two Worlds* (New York: American Association for Adult Education, 1938), 139.

104. Wood, "Woman's Club Movement," 13.

105. Croly, *History*, 555.

106. Ibid., 363, 264, 564.

107. Ibid., 567.

108. Ibid., 446.

109. Ibid., 567.

110. Ibid., 396, 431.

111. Quoted in Croly, *History*, 433.

112. Croly, *History*, 540.

113. Forthian Club of Somerville, Papers, acc. 79-M308, vol. 19, Schlesinger Library, Radcliffe College.

114. Ina B. Roberts, ed., *Club Women of New York, 1910–1911* (New York: Club Women of New York Company, 1910), 117.

115. Croly, *History*, 809.

116. Julia W. Howe, "How Can Women Best Associate?" in Association for the Advancement of Woman, *Papers and Letters Presented at the First Woman's Congress of the Association for the Advancement of Woman, 1873* (New York, 1874), 7–8.

117. Croly, *History*, 624.

118. Howe, "How Can Women Associate?", 7–8.

119. Croly, *History*, 256.

120. Ibid., 870.

121. Mary S. Cunningham, *The Woman's Club of El Paso* (El Paso: Texas Western Press, 1978), 3–20.

122. Forthian Club of Somerville, Papers, vol. 20.

123. Croly, *History*, 60.

124. Ibid., 403.

125. Ibid., 385.

126. Ibid., 252.

127. Quoted in Croly, *History*, 414.

128. Croly, *History*, 403, 381.

129. Ibid., 1062.

130. Ibid., 247.

131. Quoted in Croly, *History*, 404.

132. Croly, *History*, 241.

133. Harriet J. Robinson, Papers, A-80, vol. 7, Schlesinger Library, Radcliffe College.

134. Cunningham, *El Paso*, 19.

135. Quoted in Laura E. Richards and Maud H. Elliott, *Julia Ward Howe 1819–1910* (Boston: Houghton Mifflin, 1916), 1:295–96.

136. DuBois, *Feminism*, 29.

137. Irwin, *Angels and Amazons*, 123.

138. Quoted in Sally Schwager, "'Harvard Women': A History of the Founding of Radcliffe College" (Ed.D. thesis, Harvard Graduate School of Education, 1982), 113.

139. Judith B. Ranlett, "Sorority and Community: Women's Answer to a Changing Massachusetts, 1865–1895" (Ph.D. diss., Brandeis University, 1974), 285–86.

140. Henriette G. Frank and Amalie H. Jerome, *Annals of the Chicago Woman's Club* (Chicago: Chicago Woman's Club, 1916), 64.

141. Mrs. Percy V. Pennybacker, "The Eighth Biennial Convention of the General Federation of Women's Clubs," *The Annals of the American Academy of Political and Social Science* 28, no. 2 (1906): 79.

142. Mary I. Wood, *The History of the General Federation of Women's Clubs* (Norwood, MA: General Federation of Women's Clubs, 1912), 25.

143. Quoted in Ranlett, "Sorority and Community," 90.

144. Glenda Riley, *Inventing the American Woman* (Arlington Heights, IL: Harlan Davidson, 1986), 2:28.

145. Maria Mitchell, "The Higher Education of Woman," in Association for the Advancement of Woman, *Papers and Letters Presented at the First Woman's Congress of the Association for the Advancement of Woman, 1873* (New York, 1874), 93.

146. Irwin, *Angels and Amazons*, 215.

147. Helen M. Winslow, "The Story of the Woman's Club Movement," *New England Magazine* 38 (July 1908): 549–50.

148. Croly, *History*, 244.

149. Quoted in Frank and Jerome, *Chicago Woman's Club*, 145.

150. Riley, *Inventing the American Woman*, 2:45.

151. Ranlett, "Sorority and Community," 113.

152. Beadle, *Fortnightly*, 9–13.

153. Wilson, *Transition*, 101.

154. Croly, *History*, 560.

155. Massachusetts State Federation of Women's Clubs, *Progress and*

Achievement: A History of the Massachusetts State Federation of Women's Clubs, 1893–1962 (Lexington, MA: Lexington Press, 1962), 5.

156. DuBois, *Feminism*, 27.

157. Wood, *General Federation*, 26.

158. Quoted in Croly, *History*, 670.

159. "Women's Clubs—A Symposium," *The Arena* 6, no. 33 (1892): 371.

160. Croly, *History*, 547.

161. Ibid., 624, 555, 613.

162. Saturday Morning Club, Papers, series I, vol. 6.

163. Ibid., series I, vol. 3.

164. *Saturday Morning Club of Boston, Massachusetts, 1871–1931* (privately printed, 1932), 1.

165. Saturday Morning Club, Papers, series I, vol. 4a.

166. Ibid., series I, vols. 5, 3.

167. Ibid., series II, vol. 1.

168. Ibid., series I, vol. 3.

169. Ibid., series I, vols. 4a, 3, 5; series II, vol. 2.

170. Ibid., series I, vols. 4, 5.

171. Quoted in *Saturday Morning Club*, 46.

172. Saturday Morning Club, Papers, series I, vols. 4a, 8.

173. Ibid., series I, vol. 4a.

174. Ibid., series I, vols. 4a, 5.

175. Ibid., series II, vol. 2.

176. Ibid., series I, vol. 4a.

177. Ibid., series I, vols. 4, 4a.

178. Ibid., series I, vol. 8.

179. Wood, "Woman's Club Movement," 15.

180. Harriet J. Robinson, Papers, vol. 9.

181. Ibid., vol. 10.

182. "Women's Clubs—A Symposium," 378.

183. Wood, *General Federation*, 374.

184. "Women's Clubs—A Symposium," 371.

185. Courtney, *Indiana*, 9.

186. Croly, *History*, 540.

187. Ibid., 612.

188. Quoted in Alice Schlenker, "The Literary Clubs," unpublished paper, Bloomington, IL (1983), 12.

189. Quoted in Richards and Elliott, *Howe*, 1:292.

190. Croly, *History*, 432.

191. Quoted in Croly, *History*, 432.

192. Croly, *History*, 251.

193. Ibid., 245.

194. Ibid., 561.

195. Ibid., 1057.

196. Ibid.

197. Ibid., 1058.

198. Annie N. Meyer, "A New Phase of Woman's Education in America," in Rachel F. Avery, ed., *Transactions of the National Council of Women of the United States, Assembled in Washington, D.C., February 22 to 25, 1891* (Philadelphia: National Council of Women of the United States, 1891), 185.

199. Croly, *History*, 447.

200. Ibid., 540.

201. Lois Vosburgh, "The Coterie Toasts 100 Years of Study," (Syracuse) *Post Standard*, 23 Mar. 1985.

202. Courtney, *Indiana*, 50–102.

203. "Women's Clubs—A Symposium," 371.

204. May A. Ward, "The Influence of Women's Clubs in New England and in the Middle-Eastern States," *The Annals of the American Academy of Political and Social Science* 28, no. 2 (1906): 19.

Chapter 5

The chapter title is taken from a poem written by a member of the Monday Club, Mount Vernon, Ohio, quoted in Jane C. Croly, *The History of the Woman's Club Movement in America* (New York: Henry G. Allen, 1898), 995–96.

1. Quoted ibid.

2. "Women's Clubs—A Symposium," *The Arena* 6, no. 33 (1892): 380.

3. Croly, *History*, 12.

4. Ibid., 296.

5. Ibid., 555.

6. Anne F. Scott, *The Southern Lady* (Chicago: University of Chicago Press, 1970), 75.

7. Quoted in Eleanor W. Thompson, *Education for Ladies 1830–1860* (New York: King's Crown Press, 1947), 55.

8. Judith B. Ranlett, "Sorority and Community: Women's Answer to a Changing Massachusetts, 1865–1895" (Ph.D. diss., Brandeis University, 1974), 125.

9. Theodore Morrison, *Chautauqua* (Chicago: University of Chicago Press, 1974), 63.

10. Croly, *History*, 548.

11. Helen M. Winslow, *The President of Quex* (Boston: Lothrop, Lee & Shepard, 1906), 16.

12. Le Baron R. Briggs, *To College Girls and Other Essays* (Boston: Houghton Mifflin, 1911), 80.

13. Rose L. Brown, *Cavewoman to Clubwoman* (Philadelphia: Dorrance, 1938), 47.

14. Mary S. Cunningham, *The Woman's Club of El Paso* (El Paso: Texas Western Press, 1978), 19.

15. Forthian Club of Somerville, Papers, acc. 79-M308, vol. 20, Schlesinger Library, Radcliffe College.

16. Robert Grant, *Unleavened Bread* (New York: Charles Scribner's Sons, 1915), 61.

17. Alma Rogers, "The Woman's Club Movement: Its Origin, Significance and Present Results," *The Arena* 34, no. 191 (1905): 348.

18. Carolyn Heilbrun, review of *Virginia Woolf: A Writer's Life,* by Lyndall Gordon, *New York Times Book Review,* 10 Feb. 1985.

19. Cunningham, *El Paso,* 55; Croly, *History,* 447; Caroline F. Benton, *The Complete Club Book for Women* (Boston: Page, 1915), 241.

20. Olive T. Miller, *The Woman's Club* (New York: United States Book Company, 1891), 52.

21. Croly, *History,* 54–57.

22. Vassar College, *Eleventh Annual Catalogue of the Officers and Students of Vassar College* (Poughkeepsie, NY, 1875–76), 19.

23. Lucy Larcom, *A New England Girlhood* (Gloucester, MA: Peter Smith, 1973), 266.

24. Croly, *History,* 57.

25. Quoted in Croly, *History,* 57–59.

26. Croly, *History,* 60.

27. Muriel Beadle, *The Fortnightly of Chicago* (Chicago: Henry Regnery, 1973), 22.

28. Miller, *Woman's Club,* 57.

29. Henriette G. Frank and Amalie H. Jerome, *Annals of the Chicago Woman's Club* (Chicago: Chicago Woman's Club, 1916), 147, 168, 237.

30. Croly, *History,* 541.

31. Miller, *Woman's Club,* 56–57.

32. Jane C. Croly, *Sorosis* (New York: J. J. Little, 1886), 43.

33. Croly, *History,* 665.

34. Frank and Jerome, *Chicago Woman's Club,* 34.

35. Gertrude S. Eiler, "The Social Art Club of Syracuse, New York," unpublished paper, Syracuse (1984), 12.

36. Benton, *Complete Club Book,* 118.

37. Caroline F. Benton, *Work and Programs for Women's Clubs* (Boston: Dana Estes, 1913), 19–20.

38. Eiler, "Social Art Club," 21.

39. Christopher Jencks and David Riesman, *The Academic Revolution* (Chicago: University of Chicago Press, 1968), 303.

40. Vassar College, *Catalogue,* 19.

41. Quoted in Barbara M. Cross, *The Educated Woman in America: Selected Writings of Catharine Beecher, Margaret Fuller and M. Carey Thomas* (New York: Teachers College, 1965), 115–16.

42. Vassar College, *Catalogue,* 19.

43. Croly, *History,* 734.

44. Ibid., 562.

45. Ibid., 658.

46. Quoted in Alice Schlenker, "The Literary Clubs," unpublished paper, Bloomington, IL (1983), 4.

47. Miller, *The Woman's Club,* 49.

48. Quoted in Ranlett, "Sorority and Community," 85.

49. Croly, *History,* 665.

50. Julia A. Sprague, *History of the New England Women's Club from 1868–1893* (Boston: Lee & Shepard, 1894), 24.

51. Croly, *History,* 601.

52. Croly, *History,* 600.

53. General Federation of Women's Clubs, *Third Biennial* (Louisville: Flexner Brothers, 1896), 42.

54. Mary L. Ely and Eve Chappell, *Women in Two Worlds* (New York: American Association for Adult Education, 1938), 152.

55. Benton, *Work and Programs,* 21.

56. Croly, *History,* 542.

57. Ibid., 251.

58. *Saturday Morning Club of Boston, Massachusetts 1871–1931* (privately printed, 1932), 27.

59. Croly, *History,* 549.

60. Ibid., 551.

61. Ibid., 543.

62. Ibid.

63. Ibid., 654.

64. Cunningham, *El Paso,* 19.

65. Croly, *History,* 438.

66. Quoted in Cross, *Educated Woman,* 117.

67. Croly, *Sorosis,* 16.

68. Larcom, *Girlhood,* 266.

69. Croly, *History,* 1060.

70. Miller, *Woman's Club,* 50.

71. Scott, *Southern Lady,* 152.

72. "Women's Clubs—A Symposium," 379.

73. General Federation of Women's Clubs, *Third Biennial,* 369.

74. Miller, *Woman's Club,* 36–37.

75. Beadle, *Fortnightly,* 46.

76. Augusta H. Leypoldt and George Iles, eds., *List of Books for Girls and Women and Their Clubs* (Boston: Library Bureau, 1895), 20, 89.

77. Sinclair Lewis, *Main Street* (New York: Harcourt, Brace & World, 1920), 125–26.

78. Croly, *History,* 664.

79. Beadle, *Fortnightly,* 50.

80. Croly, *History,* 899–900.

81. Frank and Jerome, *Chicago Woman's Club,* 196.

82. Laura E. Richards and Maud H. Elliott, *Julia Ward Howe, 1819–1910* (Boston: Houghton Mifflin, 1916), 1:292.

83. "Women's Clubs—A Symposium," 387.

84. Croly, *History,* 363.

85. Quoted in Croly, *History,* 243–44.

86. Ibid., 72.

87. Ina B. Roberts, ed., *Club Women of New York, 1910–1911* (New York: Club Women of New York Company, 1910), 49.

88. Croly, *History*, 244.

89. Quoted in Croly, *History*, 66.

90. Ibid., 1099.

91. Ibid.

92. Frank and Jerome, *Chicago Woman's Club*, 10.

93. Ibid., 35.

94. Julia A. Sprague, quoted in Croly, *History*, 47.

95. Ibid.

96. Julia A. Sprague, *New England*, 22.

97. Croly, *History*, 49–50.

98. Frank and Jerome, *Chicago Woman's Club*, 186.

99. Kathleen Rockhill, *Academic Excellence and Public Service* (New Brunswick, NJ: Transaction Books, 1983), 41.

100. Croly, *History*, 61.

101. L. Clark Seelye, *The Early History of Smith College* (Boston: Houghton Mifflin, 1923), 181.

102. General Federation of Women's Clubs, *Third Biennial*, 369.

103. Quoted in Richards and Elliott, *Howe*, 1:292.

104. Croly, *History*, 248.

105. Ibid., 251.

106. Ibid., 455.

107. Quoted in Croly, *History*, 255.

108. Ibid., 248.

109. Ibid., 241.

110. Ibid., 566, 893.

111. Ibid., 446, 444.

112. Ibid., 246.

113. Ibid., 442.

114. Quoted in Croly, *History*, 554.

115. Croly, *History*, 563.

116. Ibid., 908.

117. Ibid., 70.

118. Winslow, *Quex*, 180.

119. Karen J. Blair, *The Clubwoman as Feminist* (New York: Holmes & Meier, 1980), 69.

120. Helen H. Santmyer, ". . . And Ladies of the Club" (New York: G. P. Putnam's Sons, 1982), 494.

121. Croly, *History*, 449.

122. Ibid., 894.

123. Ibid., 567.

124. Ibid., 545.

125. Beadle, *Fortnightly*, 47.

126. Vassar College, *Catalogue*, 13–15.

127. Larcom, *Girlhood*, 268.

128. Vassar College, *Catalogue*, 18.

129. Anna H. Knipp and Thaddeus P. Thomas, *The History of Goucher College* (Baltimore: Goucher College, 1938), 28.

130. Louise Stockton, quoted in General Federation of Women's Clubs, *Third Biennial*, 372.

131. Southern Association of College Women, *Proceedings*, Bulletin II (1912), 50–51.

132. Knipp and Thomas, *Goucher*, 27.

133. Jane Addams, *Twenty Years at Hull House* (New York: Macmillan, 1914), 51.

134. Vida D. Scudder, *On Journey* (New York: E. P. Dutton, 1937), 65–66.

135. Seelye, *Smith College*, 36–37.

136. Knipp and Thomas, *Goucher*, 27.

137. Seelye, *Smith College*, 35.

Chapter 6

The chapter title is taken from a speech by Hester M. Poole, quoted in Rachel F. Avery, ed., *Transactions of the National Council of Women of the United States, Assembled in Washington, D.C., February 22 to 25, 1891* (Philadelphia: National Council of Women of the United States, 1891), 301.

1. Louise D. Bowen, quoted in Muriel Beadle, *The Fortnightly of Chicago* (Chicago: Henry Regnery, 1973), 18.

2. Rosalind Rosenberg, *Beyond Separate Spheres: The Intellectual Roots of Modern Feminism* (New Haven: Yale University Press, 1982), 3.

3. Quoted in Karen J. Blair, *The Clubwoman as Feminist* (New York: Holmes & Meier, 1980), 34.

4. Quoted in Christopher Lasch, "Woman as Alien," in Jean E. Friedman and William G. Shade, eds., *Our American Sisters: Women in American Life and Thought*, 1st ed. (Boston: Allyn & Bacon, 1973), 172.

5. Mary I. Wood, "The Woman's Club Movement," *The Chautauquan* 59, no. 1 (1910): 63.

6. Mrs. Percy V. Pennybacker, "The Eighth Biennial Convention of the General Federation of Women's Clubs," *The Annals of the American Academy of Political and Social Science* 28, no. 2 (1906): 80.

7. Quoted in Mary S. Cunningham, *The Woman's Club of El Paso* (El Paso: Texas Western Press, 1978), 29.

8. "Men's Views of Women's Clubs," *The Annals of the American Academy of Political and Social Science* 28, no. 2 (1906): 87; Grover Cleveland, "Woman's Mission and Woman's Clubs," *Ladies' Home Journal* 22 (May 1905): 3–4.

9. Quoted in Grace G. Courtney, *History: Indiana Federation of Clubs* (Fort Wayne, IN: Fort Wayne Printing Company, 1939), 27.

10. Quoted in Blair, *Feminist*, 70.

11. Quoted in Courtney, *Indiana*, 29.

12. Jean E. Friedman, *The Enclosed Garden* (Chapel Hill: University of North Carolina Press, 1985), xii, 9.

13. "Women's Clubs—A Symposium," *The Arena* 6, no. 33 (1892): 347.

14. Jane C. Croly, *The History of the Woman's Club Movement in America* (New York: Henry G. Allen, 1898), 18.

15. Thomas H. Macbride, *Culture and Women's Clubs* (Iowa City: State University of Iowa, 1916), 10.

16. Ibid., 11.

17. Quoted in Elaine Kendell, *"Peculiar Institutions": An Informal History of the Seven Sister Colleges* (New York: G. P. Putnam's Sons, 1975), 80.

18. "Women's Clubs—A Symposium," 371.

19. Helen M. Winslow, *The President of Quex* (Boston: Lothrop, Lee & Shepard, 1906), 77.

20. A. O. Granger, "The Effect of Club Work in the South," *The Annals of the American Academy of Political and Social Science* 28, no. 2 (1906): 57.

21. "Women's Clubs—A Symposium," 365.

22. "Men's Views of Women's Clubs," 90.

23. Rosenberg, *Separate Spheres*, 9.

24. Quoted in Anne F. Scott, *The Southern Lady* (Chicago: University of Chicago Press, 1970), 137.

25. Olive T. Miller, *The Woman's Club* (New York: United States Book Company, 1891), 14.

26. Ibid., 82.

27. "Women's Clubs—A Symposium," 375.

28. Quoted in Julia A. Sprague, *History of the New England Women's Club from 1868–1893* (Boston: Lee & Shepard, 1894), 6.

29. Caroline M. Severance, "The Genesis of the Club Idea," *The Woman's Journal* 33, no. 22 (1902): 174.

30. Harriet J. Robinson, Papers, A-80, vol. 19, Schlesinger Library, Radcliffe College.

31. Le Baron R. Briggs, *To College Girls and Other Essays* (Boston: Houghton Mifflin, 1911), 81.

32. Croly, *History*, 597.

33. Quoted in Viola Klein, *The Feminine Character: History of an Ideology* (Urbana: University of Illinois Press, 1972), 37.

34. Edith Wharton, *"Xingu" and Other Stories* (New York: Charles Scribner's Sons, 1916), 3.

35. Inez H. Irwin, *Angels and Amazons* (Garden City, NY: Doubleday, Doran, 1934), 211.

36. Sinclair Lewis, *Main Street* (New York: Harcourt, Brace & World, 1920), 124.

37. Quoted in William L. O'Neill, *Everyone Was Brave: The Rise and Fall of Feminism in America* (Chicago: Quadrangle Books, 1969), 85.

38. Miller, *Woman's Club*, 79–80.

39. Wood, "Club Movement," 29.

40. Mary I. Wood, *The History of the General Federation of Women's Clubs* (Norwood, MA: General Federation of Women's Clubs, 1912), 29.

41. Winslow, *Quex*, 281–82.

42. Wharton, *"Xingu"*, 8.

43. Lucy Larcom, *A New England Girlhood* (Gloucester, MA: Peter Smith, 1973), 269.

44. John H. Newman, *The Idea of a University* (London: Longmans, Green, 1889), 178.

45. Klein, *Feminine Character*, 9.

46. Helen L. Horowitz, *Alma Mater* (New York: Knopf, 1984), 189.

47. Quoted in Poole, "Difficulties and Delights," 302.

48. Miller, *Woman's Club*, 20.

49. Croly, *History*, 16.

50. Quoted in Mabel Newcomer, *A Century of Education for American Women* (New York: Harper & Brothers, 1959), 61.

51. Martha E. White, "The Work of the Woman's Club," *Atlantic Monthly* 93, no. 559 (1903): 620.

52. Gertrude Atherton, *Can Women Be Gentlemen?* (Boston: Houghton Mifflin, 1938), 40.

53. Julia W. Howe, "How Can Women Best Associate?" in Association for the Advancement of Woman, *Papers and Letters Presented at the First Woman's Congress of the Association for the Advancement of Woman, 1873* (New York, 1874), 6.

54. Winnifred H. Cooley, "The Future of the Woman's Club," *The Arena* 27, no. 4 (1902): 376.

55. Madam Blanc, *The Condition of Women in the United States: A Traveller's Notes* (Boston: Roberts Brothers, 1895), 44.

56. Winslow, *Quex*, 46.

57. Laura E. Richards and Maud H. Elliott, *Julia Ward Howe, 1819–1910* (Boston: Houghton Mifflin, 1916), 1:294.

58. "Women's Clubs—A Symposium," 365.

59. L. Clark Seelye, *The Early History of Smith College* (Boston: Houghton Mifflin, 1923), 205.

60. Croly, *History*, 901.

61. Ibid., 459.

62. Ibid., 256.

63. "Women's Clubs—A Symposium," 365.

64. Alma A. Rogers, "The Woman's Club Movement: Its Origin, Significance and Present Results," *The Arena* 34, no. 191 (1905): 349.

65. Mary B. Sherman, "The Women's Clubs in the Middle Western States," *The Annals of the American Academy of Political and Social Science* 28, no. 2 (1906): 33.

66. Virginia Woolf, *A Room of One's Own* (New York: Harcourt, Brace & World, 1929), 88.

67. Croly, *History*, 546.

68. Quoted in Richards and Elliott, *Howe*, 1:295.

69. Helen H. Santmyer, ". . . *And Ladies of the Club*" (New York: G. P. Putnam's Sons, 1982), 37.

70. Sherman, "Middle Western," 32.

71. "Women's Clubs—A Symposium," 379.

72. Jane C. Croly, quoted in Woman's Press Club of New York, *Memories of Jane Cunningham Croly* (New York: G. P. Putnam's Sons, 1904), 117.

73. Howe, "How Can Women Best Associate?" 7.

74. Blythe M. Clinchy et al., "Connected Education for Women," *Journal of Education* 167, no. 3 (1985): 24–44.

75. Augusta H. Leypoldt and George Iles, eds. *List of Books for Girls and Women and Their Clubs* (Boston: Library Bureau, 1895), 130.

76. "Women's Clubs—A Symposium," 381.

77. Quoted in Wood, *General Federation*, 51.

78. Judith B. Ranlett, "Sorority and Community: Women's Answer to a Changing Massachusetts, 1865–1895" (Ph.D. diss., Brandeis University, 1974), 171.

79. Miller, *Woman's Club*, 22.

80. Quoted in Croly, *History*, 449.

81. Quoted in Croly, *History*, 27.

82. Henriette G. Frank and Amalie H. Jerome, *Annals of the Chicago Woman's Club* (Chicago: Chicago Woman's Club, 1916), 13.

83. Anne F. Scott, "On Seeing and Not Seeing: A Case of Historical Invisibility," *The Journal of American History* 71, no. 1 (1984): 19.

84. Celia Burleigh, quoted in Croly, *History*, 27.

85. Charlotte E. Brown, "The Moral Influence of Women's Associations," in Avery, *Transactions*, 307.

86. Carroll Smith-Rosenberg, *Disorderly Conduct: Visions of Gender in Victorian America* (New York: Knopf, 1985), 64.

87. Quoted in Croly, *History*, 70.

88. Ellen C. DuBois, *Feminism and Suffrage* (Ithaca, NY: Cornell University Press, 1978), 18.

89. Croly, *History*, 436.

90. Ibid.

91. Quoted in Wood, *General Federation*, 51.

92. Daniel S. Smith, "Family Limitation, Sexual Control, and Domestic Feminism in Victorian America," in Nancy F. Cott and Elizabeth H. Pleck, eds., *A Heritage of Her Own: Toward a New Social History of American Women* (New York: Simon & Schuster, 1979), 232.

93. Quoted in Gerda Lerner, *The Woman in American History* (Menlo Park, CA: Addison-Wesley, 1971), 72.

94. Quoted in DuBois, *Feminism*, 22.

95. Quoted in Croly, *History*, 467.

Chapter 7

The chapter title is taken from remarks by Elizabeth J. Wells, member of the Decatur (Illinois) Art Class, quoted in Vivian Barnes, "History of the Decatur Art Class," unpublished paper, Decatur, IL (1976), 13.

1. Decatur Art Class, Minutes (1899), 4:29.
2. Ibid. (1880), 1:7–8.
3. Ibid. (1890), 2:259.
4. Ibid. (1898), 4:5–6.
5. Ibid. (1880), 1:13–14.
6. Ibid. (1905), 4:142.
7. Ibid. (1880), 1:23.
8. Ibid. (1880), 1:23–24.
9. Ibid. (1880), 1:29.
10. Ibid. (1881), 1:129.
11. Ibid. (1883), 1:216.
12. Ibid. (1884), 2:27–28.
13. Ibid. (1886), 2:128.
14. Ibid. (1890), 2:270.
15. Ibid. (1904), 4:150.
16. Ibid. (1905), 4:150; (1903), 4:96; (1894), 3:91.
17. *Proceedings of the Art Union,* 1883, 14, Decatur Art Class Files.
18. Decatur Art Class, Minutes (1881), 1:115.
19. Ibid. (1884), 2:18–34.
20. Ibid. (1885), 2:63–85.
21. Ibid. (1888), 2:188–94.
22. Ibid. (1889), 2:225–35.
23. Helen L. Horowitz, *Alma Mater* (New York: Knopf, 1984), 147–78.
24. Decatur Art Class, Minutes (1888–1890), 2:242–85.
25. Ibid. (1892–1894), 3:40–101.
26. Albert Taylor, *The Life Story of James Millikin* (Decatur: Millikin University, 1926), 68.
27. Ibid., 64–66.
28. Mabel E. Richmond, *Centennial History of Decatur and Macon County* (Decatur: Decatur Review, 1930), 250.
29. *Decatur Review,* 1 Aug. 1913.
30. Taylor, *James Millikin,* 63–81.
31. *Decatur Review,* 1 Aug. 1913.
32. Decatur Art Class, Minutes (1904), 4:118.
33. O. T. Banton, interview with author, Decatur, IL, 9 Jan. 1985.
34. *Decatur Herald and Review,* 4 Jan. 1976.
35. Eunice McKee, interview with author, Decatur, IL, 12 Jan. 1985.
36. Decatur Art Class, Minutes (1881), 1:105.
37. *Proceedings of the Twelfth Annual Meeting of the Art Union of Central Illinois,* 1891, unpaged, Decatur Art Class Files.
38. Decatur Art Class, Minutes (1904), 4:127.

39. *The James Millikin University Bulletin* 11 (1913): 1.

40. *Decatur Herald,* 21 Oct. 1913.

41. Richmond, *Decatur,* 248, 280.

42. Biographical Files, Decatur Public Library; Decatur Art Class, Minutes (1880–1907); Richmond, *Decatur.*

43. Quoted in Barnes, "History of the Decatur Art Class," 13.

44. Biographical Files, Decatur Public Library; Richmond, *Decatur.*

45. Richmond, *Decatur,* 208, 290, 327.

46. Ernest L. Bogart and Charles C. Thompson, *The Industrial State, 1870–1893* (Springfield, IL: Illinois Centennial Commission, 1920), 52.

47. Decatur Art Class, Minutes (1880), 1:19.

48. Glea Simshauser, interview with author, Decatur, IL, 7 Jan. 1985; Carolyn Banton, interview with author, Decatur, IL, 9 Jan. 1985.

49. *Decatur Herald,* 1 Feb. 1914.

50. Decatur Art Class, Minutes (1889), 2:222; (1894), 3:105; (1896), 3:190.

51. Ibid. (1899), 4:29.

52. Ibid. (1880), 1: flyleaf.

53. Ibid. (1880), 1:17.

54. Richmond, *Decatur,* 282–83.

55. Decatur Art Class, Minutes (1880), 1:11.

56. Ibid. (1881), 1:83.

57. Ibid. (1882), 1:155.

58. Ibid. (1888), 2:191.

59. Ibid. (1887), 2:142.

60. Ibid. (1888), 2:183.

61. Ibid. (1905), 4:155.

62. Ibid. (1903), 4:115.

63. Ibid. (1904), 4:119–20.

64. Ibid. (1904), 4:121.

65. Ibid. (1904), 4:123.

66. Ibid. (1887), 2:175.

67. Ibid. (1899), 4:30.

68. *Proceedings of the Art Union,* 1886, 13, Decatur Art Class Files.

69. *Decatur Review,* 1 Feb. 1914.

70. Decatur Art Class, Minutes (1906), 4:165.

71. Ibid. (1891), 2:318–19.

72. Ibid. (1880), 1:17, 19; (1884), 2:54, 255.

73. Ibid. (1880), 1:15; Richmond, *Decatur,* 112–14.

74. Decatur Art Class, Minutes (1894), 3:93.

75. Ibid. (1900), 4:57.

76. Ibid. (1904), 4:126.

77. Ibid. (1897), 3:unpaged insert.

78. Vivian Barnes, interview with author, Decatur, IL, 8 Jan. 1985; Glea Simshauser, interview with author, Decatur, IL, 7 Jan. 1985.

79. Decatur Art Class, Minutes (1892), 3:50–51.

80. Ibid. (1880), 1:18.

81. Ibid. (1881), 1:109.

82. Ibid. (1887), 2:170.

83. Ibid. (1881), 1:109.

84. Ibid. (1881), 1:93.

85. Ibid. (1899), 4:17.

86. Ibid. (1906), 4:175.

87. Ibid. (1884), 2:51.

88. Ibid. (1903), 4:107.

89. Ibid. (1900), 4:41.

90. Ibid. (1900), 4:35–38.

91. Ibid. (1882), 1:149.

92. Ibid. (1895), 3:150.

93. Decatur Art Class File, Decatur Public Library.

94. Decatur Art Class, Minutes (1893), 3:76.

95. Ibid. (1897), 3:200.

96. Ibid. (1896), 3:175.

97. Lawrence A. Cremin, *Traditions of American Education* (New York: Basic Books, 1977), 29.

98. Decatur Art Class, Minutes (1899), 4:27.

99. Ibid. (1889), 2:214.

100. Lucy Larcom, *A New England Girlhood* (Gloucester, MA: Peter Smith, 1973), 223.

101. Decatur Art Class, Minutes (1900), 4:57.

102. Ibid. (1889), 2:249.

103. Ibid. (1889), 2:219.

104. Ibid. (1894), 3:90.

105. Ibid. (1898), 3:235.

106. Ibid. (1899), 4:18–19.

107. Ibid. (1905), 4:138.

108. Ibid. (1901), 4:57.

109. Ibid. (1900), 4:43.

110. Ibid. (1895), 3:150.

111. Barbara M. Solomon, *In the Company of Educated Women* (New Haven: Yale University Press, 1985), 96.

112. Decatur Art Class, Minutes (1890), 2:261.

113. Ibid. (1882), 1:188.

114. Ibid. (1899) 4:15.

115. Anna B. Millikin, Biographical File, Millikin University Library Archives.

116. Decatur Art Class, Minutes (1906), 4:160; (1889), 2:157.

117. Ibid. (1899), 4:23–24; (1906), 4:167; (1898), 4:5; Decatur Art Class File, Decatur Public Library.

118. Decatur Art Class, Minutes (1895), 3:118; (1902), 4:92; (1902), 4:98; O. T. Banton, interview.

119. Decatur Art Class, Minutes (1895), 3:60.

120. Ibid. (1895), 3:148.
121. Ibid. (1895), 3:138.
122. Ibid. (1885), 2:82.
123. Decatur Art Class Files.
124. Decatur Art Class, Minutes (1887), 2:167.
125. Decatur Art Class Files, unsigned account.
126. Decatur Art Class, Minutes (1895), 3:119; (1895), 3:127.
127. Ibid. (1884), 2:15.
128. Ibid. (1890), 2:294.
129. Ibid. (1906), 4:163.
130. Ibid. (1881), 1:111.
131. Ibid. (1892), 3:26; (1900), 4:43; (1910), 4:68; (1899), 4:21.
132. Ibid. (1882), 1:165; (1893), 3:78; (1893), 3:70–71; (1894), 3:88.
133. *Decatur Daily Review,* 6 Feb. 1880.
134. Decatur Art Class, Minutes (1892), 3:36.
135. Ibid. (1895), 3:137.
136. Ibid. (1900), 4:47.
137. Ibid.
138. Ibid.

Chapter 8

1. Decatur Art Class, Minutes (1892), 3:38–39.
2. Biographical Files, Decatur Public Library.
3. Decatur Art Class, Minutes (1886), 2:129.
4. Mabel E. Richmond, *Centennial History of Decatur and Macon County* (Decatur: The Decatur Review, 1930), 237.
5. Jane C. Croly, *The History of the Woman's Club Movement in America* (New York: Henry G. Allen, 1898), 384.
6. Richmond, *Decatur,* 238; O. T. Banton, *History of Macon County* (Decatur: Macon County Historical Society, 1976), 362.
7. Croly, *History,* 385.
8. Decatur Art Class, Minutes (1893), 3:unpaged insert.
9. Ibid. (1898), 3:236.
10. Quoted in Rheta C. Dorr, *A Woman of Fifty* (New York: Funk & Wagnalls, 1924), 119.
11. Helen M. Winslow, *The President of Quex* (Boston: Lothrop, Lee & Shepard, 1906), 186.
12. Quoted in Jane Croly, *Sorosis* (New York: J. J. Little, 1886), 27.
13. Olive T. Miller, *The Woman's Club* (New York: United States Book Company, 1891), 36.
14. Croly, *History,* 63.
15. Quoted in Inez H. Irwin, *Angels and Amazons* (Garden City, NY: Doubleday, Doran, 1934), 215.
16. Croly, *History,* 63.

17. Henriette G. Frank and Amalie H. Jerome, *Annals of the Chicago Woman's Club* (Chicago: Chicago Woman's Club, 1916), 45, 157.

18. Quoted in Frank and Jerome, *Chicago Woman's Club,* 69.

19. Frank and Jerome, *Chicago Woman's Club,* 42; Croly, *History,* 66–69.

20. Mary I. Wood, *The History of the General Federation of Women's Clubs* (Norwood, MA: General Federation of Women's Clubs, 1912), 213.

21. Alice H. Cass, *Practical Programs for Women's Clubs* (Chicago: A. C. McClurg, 1915), 62.

22. Rheta C. Dorr, *What Eight Million Women Want* (Boston: Small, Maynard, 1910), 237.

23. Mary I. Wood, "The Woman's Club Movement," *The Chautauquan* 59, no. 1 (1910): 61.

24. Wood, *General Federation,* 296.

25. Mary L. Ely and Eve Chappell, *Women in Two Worlds* (New York: American Association for Adult Education, 1938), 130.

26. Quoted in Ely and Chappell, *Two Worlds,* 130.

27. A. O. Granger, "The Effect of Club Work in the South," *The Annals of the American Academy of Political and Social Science* 28, no. 2 (1906): 55.

28. Quoted in Croly, *History,* 112.

29. Mabel Newcomer, *A Century of Higher Education for American Women* (New York: Harper & Brothers, 1959), 37.

30. Ibid., 46.

31. Mary P. Ryan, *Womanhood in America: From Colonial Times to the Present* (New York: New Viewpoint, 1975), 232.

32. "Women's Clubs—A Symposium," *The Arena* 6, no. 33 (1892): 381.

33. Quoted in Karen J. Blair, *The Clubwoman as Feminist* (New York: Holmes & Meier, 1980), 98–99.

34. Ella D. Clymer, "The National Value of Women's Clubs," in Rachel F. Avery, ed., *Transactions of the National Council of Women of the United States, Assembled in Washington, D.C., February 22 to 25, 1891* (Philadelphia: National Council of Women of the United States, 1891), 297–98.

35. Quoted in Woman's Press Club of New York, *Memories of Jane Cunningham Croly* (New York: G. P. Putnam's Sons, 1904), 119.

36. Martha E. White, "The Work of the Woman's Club," *Atlantic Monthly* 93, no. 559 (1903): 614.

37. Robert H. Wiebe, *The Search for Order* (New York: Hill & Wang, 1967), 13.

38. Quoted in Mary S. Cunningham, *The Woman's Club of El Paso* (El Paso: Texas Western Press, 1978), x.

39. Anna B. McMahan, quoted in Croly, *History,* 59.

40. Decatur Art Class, Minutes (1887), 2:168; (1888), 2:197.

41. Ibid. (1893), 3:83.

42. Ibid. (1886), 2:127.

43. Ibid. (1892), 3:35.

44. Ibid. (1893), 3:82; (1902), 4:85; (1888), 2:202; (1894), 3:104; (1887), 2:151.

45. Ibid. (1889), 2:245; (1904), 4:123; (1900), 4:42.

46. Croly, *History*, 384–85.

47. Decatur Art Class, Minutes (1895), 3:141.

48. Ibid. (1899), 4:26.

49. Ibid. (1888), 2:205.

50. Quoted in Vivian Barnes, "History of the Decatur Art Class," unpublished paper, Decatur, IL (1976), 13; Decatur Art Class File, Decatur Public Library.

51. Alice Schlenker, "The Literary Clubs," unpublished paper, Bloomington, IL (1983), 6–7.

52. Barbara M. Solomon, *In the Company of Educated Women* (New Haven, Yale University Press, 1985), 41.

53. Elizabeth C. Stanton, "The Co-education of the Sexes," in Association for the Advancement of Woman, *Papers and Letters Presented at the First Woman's Congress of the Association for the Advancement of Woman, 1873* (New York, 1874), 39.

54. Virginia Woolf, *A Room of One's Own* (New York: Harcourt, Brace and World, 1929), 101.

Appendix 1

Text of Appendix 1 from the Castilian Club, Papers, by courtesy of the Trustees of the Boston Public Library.

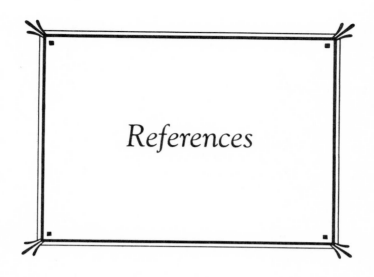

References

Adams, Henry. *The Education of Henry Adams.* New York: Random House, 1931.

Adams, Herbert B. *Report of the Commissioner of Education for the Year 1899–1900.* Washington, DC: Government Printing Office, 1901.

Adams, James T. *Frontiers of American Culture.* New York: Charles Scribner's Sons, 1944.

Addams, Jane. *Twenty Years at Hull House.* New York: Macmillan, 1914.

Addison, Daniel D. *Lucy Larcom: Life, Letters, and Diary.* Boston: Houghton Mifflin, 1895.

Allmendinger, David F., Jr. "History and the Usefulness of Women's Education." *History of Education Quarterly* 18, no. 1 (1979): 117–23.

———. "Mount Holyoke Students Encounter the Need for Life-Planning, 1837–1850." *History of Education Quarterly* 18, no. 1 (1979): 27–46.

The Annals of the American Academy of Political and Social Science 28, no. 2 (1906): 1–93.

Association for the Advancement of Woman. *Papers and Letters Presented at the First Woman's Congress of the Association for the Advancement of Woman, 1873.* New York, 1874.

Atherton, Gertrude. *Can Women Be Gentlemen?* Boston: Houghton Mifflin, 1938.

Avery, Helen M., and Frank W. Nye. *The Clubwoman's Book.* New York: Henry Holt, 1954.

Avery, Rachel F., ed. *Transactions of the National Council of Women of the United States, Assembled in Washington, D.C., February 22 to 25, 1891.* Philadelphia: National Council of Women of the United States, 1891.

Baker, Liva. *I'm Radcliffe! Fly Me!: The Seven Sisters and the Failure of Women's Education*. New York: Macmillan, 1976.

Baldwin, Henry. "An Old-time Sorosis." *Atlantic Monthly* 74, no. 447 (1894): 748–52.

Banton, Carolyn. Interview with author. Decatur, IL, 9 Jan. 1985.

Banton, O. T. *Growing Up on a Farm*. Decatur, IL, privately printed, 1983.

———, ed. *History of Macon County*. Decatur, IL: Macon Country Historical Society, 1976.

———. Interview with author. Decatur, IL, 9 Jan. 1985.

Barnes, Ira. Interview with author. Decatur, IL, 8 Jan. 1985.

Barnes, Vivian. "History of the Decatur Art Class." Unpublished paper. Decatur, IL, 1976.

———. Interview with author. Decatur, IL, 8 Jan. 1985.

Beadle, Muriel. *The Fortnightly of Chicago*. Chicago: Henry Regnery, 1973.

Beard, Charles A., and Mary R. Beard. *The Rise of American Civilization*. New York: Macmillan, 1930.

Beard, Mary R. *Woman as a Force in History*. New York: Macmillan, 1946.

Beecher, Catharine E. "How to Redeem Woman's Profession from Dishonor." *Harper's New Monthly Magazine* (Nov. 1865): 710.

———. "On Endowments for Woman's Colleges." In Association for the Advancement of Woman, *Papers and Letters Presented at the First Woman's Congress of the Association for the Advancement of Woman, 1873*. New York, 1874.

———. *Woman Suffrage and Woman's Profession*. Hartford, 1891.

Benton, Caroline F. *The Complete Club Book for Women*. Boston: Page, 1915.

———. *Work and Programs for Women's Clubs*. Boston: Dana Estes, 1913.

Bernard, Jessie. *The Future of Motherhood*. New York: Penguin Books, 1974.

Beston, Arthur E. *Chautauqua Publications*. Chautauqua, NY: Chautauqua Press, 1934.

Bing, Jennifer. "Harvard Women: The Early Years." *Second Century/Radcliffe News* 5, no. 3 (1984): 14.

Blair, Karen J. *The Clubwoman as Feminist*. New York: Holmes and Meier, 1980.

Blanc, Madam. *The Condition of Women in the United States: A Traveller's Notes*. Boston: Roberts Brothers, 1895.

Bode, Carl. *The American Lyceum*. New York: Oxford University Press, 1956.

Bogart, Ernest L., and Charles C. Thompson. *The Industrial State, 1870–1893*. Springfield, IL: Illinois Centennial Commission, 1920.

Bond, Marjorie N., and Richard P. Bond. "Adventures in Reading, Fourth Series, Current Books, 1930–1931." *University of North Carolina Extension Bulletin* 11, no. 1 (1931).

Boone, Richard G. *Education in the United States*. New York: D. Appleton, 1889.

Bourjaily, Vance. Review of ". . . And Ladies of the Club," by Helen H. Santmyer. *New York Times Book Review*, 24 June 1984.

Breckinridge, Sophonisba P. *Women in the Twentieth Century.* New York: McGraw-Hill, 1933.

Brickley, Lynne T. "'Female Academies Are Every Where Establishing': The Beginnings of Secondary Education for Women in the United States 1790–1830." Ed.D. qualifying paper, Harvard Graduate School of Education, 1982.

Briggs, Le Baron R. *To College Girls and Other Essays.* Boston: Houghton Mifflin, 1911.

Brockway, Edith. *The Antebellum Days of Decatur and Macon County, 1816–1860.* Decatur, IL: The Heritage Committee, 1968.

Brown, Charlotte E. "The Moral Influence of Women's Associations." In *Transactions of the National Council of Women of the United States, Assembled in Washington, D.C., February 22 to 25, 1891,* edited by Rachel F. Avery. Philadelphia: National Council of Women of the United States, 1891.

Brown, Rose L. *Cavewoman to Clubwoman.* Philadelphia: Dorrance, 1938.

Bunkle, Phillida. "Sentimental Womanhood and Domestic Education." *History of Education Quarterly* 14, no. 4 (1974): 13–30.

Burstyn, Joan N. *Victorian Education and the Ideal of Womanhood.* Totowa, NJ: Barnes & Noble Books, 1980.

Campbell, Barbara K. *The "Liberated" Woman of 1914.* N.p.: UMI Research Press, 1979.

Cass, Alice H. *Practical Programs for Women's Clubs.* Chicago: A. C. McClurg, 1915.

The Castilian Club. Papers. By courtesy of the Trustees of the Boston Public Library.

City Directory of Decatur Illinois, 1871–1872. Springfield: Illinois State Register and Job Print, 1871.

Clarke, Edward. *Sex in Education; or, A Fair Chance for the Girls.* Boston: Osgood, 1873.

Cleveland, Grover. "Woman's Mission and Woman's Clubs." *Ladies' Home Journal* 22, no. 6 (1905): 3–4.

Clinchy, Blythe, Mary Belenky, Nancy Goldberger, and Jill Tarule. "Connected Education for Women." *Journal of Education* 167, no. 3 (1985): 28–45.

Clinton, Catherine. *The Other Civil War: American Women in the Nineteenth Century.* New York: Hill & Wang, 1984.

Clymer, Ella D. "The National Value of Women's Clubs." In *Transactions of the National Council of Women of the United States, Assembled in Washington, D.C., February 22 to 25, 1891,* edited by Rachel F. Avery. Philadelphia: National Council of Women of the United States, 1891.

Cohen, Elizabeth S. "On Doing the History of Women's Education." *History of Education Quarterly* 18, no. 1 (1979): 151–55.

Cole, Arthur C. *A Hundred Years of Mount Holyoke.* New Haven: Yale University Press, 1940.

The College Club. *Bi-annual Directory.* Boston: Samuel Usher, 1916.

Conable, Charlotte W. *Women at Cornell: The Myth of Equal Education.* Ithaca, NY: Cornell University Press, 1977.

Converse, Florence. *Wellesley College: A Chronicle of the Years 1875–1938.* Wellesley, MA: Hathaway House Bookshop, 1939.

Conway, Jill K. *The Female Experience in Eighteenth- and Nineteenth-Century America.* New York: Garland, 1982.

———. "Perspectives on the History of Women's Education in the United States." *History of Education Quarterly* 14, no. 4 (1974): 1–12.

———. "Women Reformers and American Culture, 1870–1930." In *Our American Sisters: Women in American Life and Thought.* 3d ed. Edited by Jean E. Friedman and William G. Shade. Lexington, MA: D. C. Heath, 1982.

Cooley, Winnifred H. "The Future of the Woman's Club." *The Arena* 27, no. 4 (1902): 373–80.

Cott, Nancy F. *The Bonds of Womanhood: "Woman's Sphere" in New England, 1780–1835.* New Haven: Yale University Press, 1977.

Cott, Nancy F., and Elizabeth H. Pleck, eds. *A Heritage of Her Own: Toward a New Social History of American Women.* New York: Simon & Schuster, 1979.

Courtney, Grace G. *History: Indiana Federation of Clubs.* Fort Wayne, IN: Fort Wayne Printing Company, 1939.

Cremin, Lawrence A. *Traditions of American Education.* New York: Basic Books, 1977.

The Cristobal Woman's Club. *Twenty-Five Years of Club Work on the Isthmus of Panama, 1907–1932.* Panama: The Star and Herald Company, 1932.

Croly, Jane C. *The History of the Woman's Club Movement in America.* New York: Henry G. Allen, 1898.

———. *Sorosis.* New York: J. J. Little, 1886.

Cross, Barbara M. *The Educated Woman in America: Selected Writings of Catharine Beecher, Margaret Fuller and M. Carey Thomas.* New York: Teachers College Press, 1965.

Cunningham, Mary S. *The Woman's Club of El Paso.* El Paso: Texas Western Press, 1978.

Curti, Merle. *The Social Ideas of American Educators.* New York: Charles Scribner's Sons, 1935.

Davis, Angela Y. *Women, Race, and Class.* New York: Random House, 1981.

Decatur Art Class. Minutes, Papers, and Files. 1880–1910.

Decatur Art Class File and Biographical Files. Decatur Herald and Review. Decatur, IL.

Decatur Art Class File and Biographical Files. Decatur Public Library. Decatur, IL.

Decatur Illinois Women's Club Reports. 1887–1888. By courtesy of the Trustees of the Boston Public Library.

Decatur Public Library, the Decatur Herald and Review, and the Decatur Association of Commerce, eds. *Calendar of Historic Events: Decatur, Macon County, Illinois, 1960.*

Decker, Sarah P. "The Meaning of the Woman's Club Movement." *The Annals of the American Academy of Political and Social Science* 28, no. 2 (1906): 1–6.

Delamont, Sara, and Lorna Duffin, eds. *The Nineteenth-Century Woman: Her Cultural and Physical World.* New York: Barnes & Noble Books, 1978.

de Tocqueville, Alexis. *Democracy in America.* New York: Knopf, 1944.

———. "Education of Women in the United States, 1835." *Improving College and University Teaching* 20, no. 1 (1972): 9–10.

Dobkin, Marjorie H., ed. *The Making of a Feminist: Early Journals and Letters of M. Carey Thomas.* Kent, OH: Kent State University Press, 1979.

Dorr, Rheta C. *A Woman of Fifty.* New York: Funk & Wagnalls, 1924.

———. *What Eight Million Women Want.* Boston: Small, Maynard, 1910.

Douglas, Ann. *The Feminization of American Culture.* New York: Avon Books, 1977.

DuBois, Ellen C. *Feminism and Suffrage: The Emergence of an Independent Women's Movement in America, 1848–1869.* Ithaca, NY: Cornell University Press, 1978.

"Editor's Table." *Godey's Lady's Book* 24 (1842): 342–43.

Eiler, Gertrude S. "The Social Art Club of Syracuse, New York." Unpublished paper. Syracuse, 1984.

Ely, Mary L., and Eve Chappell. *Women in Two Worlds.* New York: American Association for Adult Education, 1938.

Emerson, Ralph W. *Selected Prose and Poetry.* Edited by Reginald L. Cook. New York: Rinehart, 1954.

Evans, Anne M. "Women's Rural Organizations and Their Activities." U.S. Department of Agriculture Bulletin No. 719. 29 Aug. 1918.

Extension Division of the University of Oklahoma. *Education for Every Oklahoman.* Norman: University of Oklahoma Press, 1931.

Federal Writers' Project of the Work Projects Administration for the State of Illinois. *Illinois: A Description and Historical Guide.* Chicago: A. C. McClurg, 1939.

First Annual Catalogue of the Officers and Students of the Ladies Collegiate Institute in Worcester, Massachusetts for the Academic Year Ending July, 1857. Boston, 1857.

Forthian Club of Somerville. Papers. Acc. 79-M308. Schlesinger Library, Radcliffe College.

Frank, Henriette G., and Amalie H. Jerome. *Annals of the Chicago Woman's Club.* Chicago: Chicago Woman's Club, 1916.

Friedman, Jean E. *The Enclosed Garden: Women and Community in the Evangelical South.* Chapel Hill: University of North Carolina Press, 1985.

Friedman, Jean E., and William G. Shade, eds. *Our American Sisters: Women in American Life and Thought.* 1st ed. Boston: Allyn & Bacon, 1973.

———. *Our American Sisters: Women in American Life and Thought.* 3d ed. Lexington, MA: D. C. Heath, 1982.

Garland, Hamlin. *A Son of the Middle Border.* 1917. Reprint. New York: Macmillan, 1962.

Garnett, Lucy M. "The Fallacy of the Equality of Woman." In *The Woman's World*, edited by Oscar Wilde. London: Caswell & Company, 1888.

Garraty, John A. *The New Commonwealth, 1877–1890*. New York: Harper & Row, 1968.

General Federation of Women's Clubs. *Third Biennial*. Louisville: Flexner Brothers, 1896.

Gilligan, Carol. *In a Different Voice: Psychological Theory and Women's Development*. Cambridge: Harvard University Press, 1982.

Glasscock, Jean. *Wellesley College 1875–1975: A Century of Women*. Wellesley, MA: Wellesley College, 1975.

Goodsell, Willystine. *The Education of Women: Its Social Background and Its Problems*. New York: Macmillan, 1923.

Graham, Patricia A. "The Cult of True Womanhood: Past and Present." In *All of Us Are Present*, edited by Eleanor M. Bender, Bobbie Burk, and Nancy Walker. Columbia, MO: James Madison Woods Research Institute, 1984.

———. "Expansion and Exclusion: A History of Women in American Higher Education." *Signs* 3 (1978): 759–73.

Granger, A. O. "The Effect of Club Work in the South." *The Annals of the American Academy of Political and Social Science* 28, no. 2 (1906): 51–58.

Grant, Robert. *Unleavened Bread*. New York: Charles Scribner's Sons, 1915.

Green, Harvey. *The Light of the Home: An Intimate View of the Lives of Women in Victorian America*. New York: Pantheon Books, 1983.

Hall, G. Stanley. *Adolescence*. Vol. 2. New York: D. Appleton, 1904.

Hartman, Mary S., and Lois Ganner, eds. *Clio's Consciousness Raised: A New Perspective on the History of Women*. New York: Farrar, Straus & Giroux, 1976.

Hawk, Grace E. *Pembroke College in Brown University*. Providence: Brown University Press, 1968.

Hazard, Caroline. *Some Ideals in the Education of Women*. New York: Thomas Y. Crowell, 1900.

Heilbrun, Carolyn. Review of *Virginia Woolf: A Writer's Life*, by Lyndall Gordon. *New York Times Book Review*, 10 Feb. 1985.

Henry, Elizabeth G. *Helps for Club Program Makers*. Chicago: American Library Association, 1935.

Hilliard, Caroline E. "Smith College—An Historical Sketch." *Education* 8, no. 1 (1887): 13–18.

Hinding, Andrea. *Women's History Sources*. New York: R. R. Bowker, 1979.

Hofstadter, Richard. *The Age of Reform: From Bryan to F.D.R.* New York: Knopf, 1955.

Horowitz, Helen L. *Alma Mater: Design and Experience in the Women's Colleges from Their Nineteenth-Century Beginnings to the 1930s*. New York: Knopf, 1984.

Howe, Julia W. "How Can Women Best Associate?" In Association for the Advancement of Woman, *Papers and Letters Presented at the First Woman's Congress of the Association for the Advancement of Woman, 1873*. New York, 1874.

————. *Reminiscences, 1819–1899.* Boston: Houghton Mifflin, 1900.

Howells, William D. *The Rise of Silas Lapham.* 1885. Reprint. New York: New American Library, 1980.

Irwin, Inez H. *Angels and Amazons: A Hundred Years of American Women.* Garden City, NY: Doubleday, Doran, 1934.

James, Edward T., ed. *Notable American Women.* Vols. 1–3. Cambridge: Belknap Press of Harvard University Press, 1971.

The James Millikin University Bulletin, 1913, 11 (2).

Jencks, Christopher, and David Riesman. *The Academic Revolution.* Chicago: University of Chicago Press, 1968.

Johns, Jane M. *Personal Recollections.* Decatur, IL: Decatur Chapter, Daughters of the American Revolution, 1912.

Kendall, Elaine. "Beyond Mother's Knee." *American Heritage* 24, no. 4 (1973): 13–16, 73–78.

————. *"Peculiar Institutions": An Informal History of the Seven Sister Colleges.* New York: G. P. Putnam's Sons, 1975.

Kennan, George F. "History and Literature and the Road to Peterof." *New York Times Book Review,* 29 June 1986.

Kerber, Linda K. "Daughters of Columbia: Educating Women for the Republic, 1787–1805." In *Our American Sisters: Women in American Life and Thought.* 3d ed. Edited by Jean E. Friedman and William G. Shade. Lexington, MA: D. C. Heath, 1982.

Kerber, Linda K., and Jane D. Mathews, eds. *Women's America.* New York: Oxford University Press, 1982.

"The Kind of Girl They Want to Marry." *Ladies' Home Journal* 21, no. 3 (1904): 4.

Klein, Viola. *The Feminine Character: History of an Ideology.* Urbana: University of Illinois Press, 1972.

Knipp, Anna H., and Thaddeus P. Thomas. *The History of Goucher College.* Baltimore: Goucher College, 1938.

Knowles, Malcolm. *A History of the Adult Education Movement in the United States.* Huntington, NY: Robert E. Krieger, 1977.

Koos, L. V., and C. Crawford. "College Aims, Past and Present." *School and Society* 14, no. 362 (1921): 499–509.

Kraditor, Aileen S. *Up from the Pedestal: Selected Writings in the History of American Feminism.* Chicago: Quadrangle Books, 1968.

Ladies Literary Club of Grand Rapids, Michigan. Yearbook, 1892. By courtesy of the Trustees of the Boston Public Library.

Lagemann, Ellen C. *A Generation of Women: Education in the Lives of Progressive Reformers.* Cambridge: Harvard University Press, 1979.

Larcom, Lucy. *A New England Girlhood.* Introduction by Charles T. Davis. Gloucester, MA: Peter Smith, 1973.

Lasch, Christopher. "Divorce and the Family in America." *Atlantic* 218, no. 5 (1966): 57–61.

————. "Woman as Alien." In *Our American Sisters: Women in American Life and Thought.* 1st ed. Edited by Jean E. Friedman and William G. Shade. Boston: Allyn & Bacon, 1973.

Lerner, Gerda. *The Female Experience: An American Documentary.* Indianapolis: Bobbs-Merrill, 1977.

———. *The Woman in American History.* Menlo Park, CA: Addison-Wesley, 1971.

Levy, Amy. "Women and Club Life." In *The Woman's World,* edited by Oscar Wilde. London: Caswell & Company, 1888.

Lewis, Sinclair. *Main Street.* New York: Harcourt, Brace & World, 1920.

Leypoldt, Augusta, and George Iles, eds. *List of Books for Girls and Women and Their Clubs.* Boston: Library Bureau, 1895.

Lynn, Naomi, Ann Matasar, and Marie Rosenberg. *Research Guide in Women's Studies.* Morristown, NJ: General Learning Press, 1974.

Macbride, Thomas H. *Culture and Women's Clubs.* Iowa City: State University of Iowa, 1916.

Marx, Leo. *The Machine in the Garden.* London: Oxford University Press, 1964.

Massachusetts State Federation of Women's Clubs. *Progress and Achievement: A History of the Massachusetts State Federation of Women's Clubs, 1893–1962.* Lexington, MA: Lexington Press, 1962.

The Mayflower Club, 1893–1931. Cambridge, MA: privately printed, 1933.

McKee, Eunice. Interview with author. Decatur, IL, 12 Jan. 1985.

"Men's Views of Women's Clubs." *The Annals of the American Academy of Political and Social Science* 28, no. 2 (1906): 85–93.

Meyer, Annie N. *Barnard Beginnings.* Boston: Houghton Mifflin, 1935.

———. "A New Phase of Woman's Education in America." In *Transactions of the National Council of Women of the United States, Assembled in Washington, D.C., February 22 to 25, 1891,* edited by Rachel F. Avery. Philadelphia: National Council of Women of the United States, 1891.

Miller, Jean B. *Toward a New Psychology of Women.* Boston: Beacon Press, 1976.

Miller, Olive T. *The Woman's Club.* New York: United States Book Company, 1891.

Millikin, Anna B. Biographical File. James Millikin University Library Archives. Decatur, IL.

Mitchell, Maria. "The Higher Education of Woman." In Association for the Advancement of Woman, *Papers and Letters Presented at the First Woman's Congress of the Association for the Advancement of Woman, 1873.* New York, 1874.

Montgomery County Federation of Women's Clubs. *Guidebook for Clubwomen.* State College, PA: Pennsylvania State College Central Extension Services, 1947.

Moore, Dorothea. "The Work of the Women's Clubs in California." *The Annals of the American Academy of Political and Social Science* 28, no. 2 (1906): 59–62.

Moore, Mrs. Philip N. "Woman's Clubs Training Women for the Larger Citizenship." In *The Woman's Citizen Library*. Vol. 12. Edited by Shailer Mathews. Chicago: Civic Society, 1914.

Morgan, Wayne H. "The Gilded Age." *American Heritage* 35, no. 5 (1984): 42–48.

Morrison, Theodore. *Chautauqua*. Chicago: University of Chicago Press, 1974.

Mount Holyoke Female Seminary. *Thirty-ninth Annual Catalogue of the Mount Holyoke Female Seminary 1875–76*. Northampton, MA.

Muirhead, Evelina and Glen. Interview with author, Decatur, IL, 7 Jan. 1985.

Mumford, Lewis. *The Brown Decades: A Study of the Arts in America, 1865–1895*. Harcourt, Brace, 1931.

Nelson, Narka. *The Western College for Women*. Oxford, OH: Western College, 1954.

Nelson, William, ed. *City of Decatur and Macon County Illinois*. Chicago: Pioneer Publishing Company, 1910.

Nevins, Allan, and Henry S. Commager. *America: The Story of a Free People*. Boston: Little, Brown, 1942.

New Century Club History as Told at the Coming-of-Age Celebration 1877–98. Philadelphia, 1899. By courtesy of the Trustees of the Boston Public Library.

Newcomb, Wellington. "Anne Hutchinson versus Massachusetts." *American Heritage* 25, no. 4 (1974): 12–15, 78–81.

Newcomer, Mabel. *A Century of Higher Education for American Women*. New York: Harper & Brothers, 1959.

New Hampshire Federation of Women's Clubs. *A History of the New Hampshire Federation of Women's Clubs*. Bristol, NH: Musgrove Printing House, 1941.

Newman, John H. *The Idea of a University*. London: Longmans, Green, 1889.

North, Douglass C. *The Economic Growth of the United States 1790–1860*. New York: W. W. Norton, 1966.

O'Neill, William L. *Everyone Was Brave: The Rise and Fall of Feminism in America*. Chicago: Quadrangle Books, 1969.

———. "Feminism as a Radical Ideology." In *Our American Sisters: Women in American Life and Thought*. 1st ed. Edited by Jean E. Friedman and William G. Shade. Boston: Allyn & Bacon, 1973.

Palmer, Alice F. "A Review of Higher Education." In *Woman and the Higher Education*, edited by Anna C. Brackett. New York: Harper & Brothers, 1893.

Palmieri, Patricia A. "In Adamless Eden: A Social Portrait of the Academic Community at Wellesley College 1875–1920." Ed.D. thesis, Harvard Graduate School of Education, 1981.

Parsons, Katherine B. *History of Fifty Years of the Ladies' Literary Club of Salt Lake City, Utah 1877–1927*. Salt Lake City: Arrow Press, 1927.

Past and Present of the City of Decatur and Macon County Illinois. Chicago: S. J. Clarke, 1903.

Pederson, Joyce C. "The Reform of Women's Secondary and Higher Education:

Institutional Change and Social Values in Mid and Late Victorian England." *History of Education Quarterly* 18, no. 1 (1979): 61–92.

Peffer, Nathaniel. "A Recantation." *Journal of Adult Education* 7, no. 2 (1935): 125–29.

Pennybacker, Mrs. Percy V. "The Eighth Biennial Convention of the General Federation of Women's Clubs." *The Annals of the American Academy of Political and Social Science* 28, no. 2 (1906): 79–84.

Poole, Hester M. "Difficulties and Delights of Women's Clubs." In *Transactions of the National Council of Women of the United States, Assembled in Washington, D.C., February 22 to 25, 1891,* edited by Rachel F. Avery. Philadelphia: National Council of Women of the United States, 1891.

Ranlett, Judith B. "Sorority and Community: Women's Answer to a Changing Massachusetts, 1865–1895." Ph.D. diss., Brandeis University, 1974.

Raymond, John H. "The Demand of the Age for a Liberal Education of Women and How It Should Be Met." In *The Liberal Education of Women,* edited by James Orton. New York: A. S. Barnes, 1873.

———. *Vassar College: Its Foundation Aims, Resources and Course of Study.* Poughkeepsie, NY, 1873.

The Reading Circle. *A Post-Graduate Course of Reading Enjoyed by a Group of Friends Composed Mostly of Grandmothers, 1917–1937.* N.p.: privately printed.

Rich, Adrienne. *On Lies, Secrets, and Silence: Selected Prose 1966–1978.* New York: W. W. Norton, 1979.

Richards, Laura E., and Maud H. Elliott. *Julia Ward Howe, 1819–1910.* 2 vols. Boston: Houghton Mifflin, 1916.

Richmond, Mabel E. *Centennial History of Decatur and Macon County.* Decatur, IL: Decatur Review, 1930.

Riley, Glenda. *Inventing the American Woman.* 2 vols. Arlington Heights, IL: Harlan Davidson, 1986.

Riley, Glenda G. "Origins of the Argument for Improved Female Education." *History of Education Quarterly* 9, no. 4 (1969): 455–76.

———. "The Subtle Subversion: Changes in the Traditional Image of the American Woman." *The Historian* 33, no. 2 (1970): 210–27.

Robbins, Mary L. *Alabama Women in Literature.* Selma: Selma Printing Company, 1895.

Roberts, Ina B., ed. *Club Women of New York, 1910–1911.* New York: Club Women of New York Company, 1910.

Robinson, Harriet J. Papers. A-80. Schlesinger Library, Radcliffe College.

Rockhill, Kathleen. *Academic Excellence and Public Service: A History of University Extension in California.* New Brunswick, NJ: Transaction Books, 1983.

Rogers, Alma A. "The Woman's Club Movement: Its Origin, Significance and Present Results." *The Arena* 34, no. 191 (1905): 347–50.

Rosenberg, Rosalind. *Beyond Separate Spheres: The Intellectual Roots of Modern Feminism.* New Haven: Yale University Press, 1982.

Rothman, Sheila M. *Woman's Proper Place: A History of Changing Ideals and Practices, 1870 to the Present.* New York: Basic Books, 1978.

Rudolph, Frederick. *The American College and University.* New York: Knopf, 1965.

Ryan, Mary P. *Womanhood in America: From Colonial Times to the Present.* New York: New Viewpoint, 1975.

Santmyer, Helen H. *". . . And Ladies of the Club."* New York: G. P. Putnam's Sons, 1982.

Saturday Morning Club. Papers. B-28. Schlesinger Library, Radcliffe College.

Saturday Morning Club of Boston, Massachusetts 1871–1931. Boston: privately printed, 1932.

Scherer, Helen. Interview with author, Decatur, IL, 7 Jan. 1985.

Schlenker, Alice. "The Literary Clubs." Unpublished paper. Bloomington, IL, 1983.

Schlesinger, Arthur M. *Paths to the Present.* New York: Macmillan, 1949.

Schwager, Sally. "'Harvard Women': A History of the Founding of Radcliffe College." Ed.D. thesis, Harvard Graduate School of Education, 1982.

Scott, Anne F., ed. *The American Woman: Who Was She?* Englewood Cliffs, NJ: Prentice-Hall, 1971.

———. *Making the Invisible Woman Visible.* Urbana: University of Illinois Press, 1984.

———. "The 'New Woman' in the South." In *Our American Sisters: Women in American Life and Thought.* 1st ed. Edited by Jean E. Friedman and William G. Shade. Boston: Allyn & Bacon, 1973.

———. "On Seeing and Not Seeing: A Case of Historical Invisibility." *The Journal of American History* 71, no. 1 (1984): 7–21.

———. *The Southern Lady.* Chicago: University of Chicago Press, 1970.

Scudder, Vida D. *On Journey.* New York: E. P. Dutton, 1937.

Seelye, L. Clark. *The Early History of Smith College.* Boston: Houghton Mifflin, 1923.

Severance, Caroline M. "The Genesis of the Club Idea." *The Woman's Journal* 33, no. 22 (1902): 174.

Sewall, May W. "The General Federation of Women's Clubs." *The Arena* 6 (1892): 367.

Sheehy, Gail. *Spirit of Survival.* New York: William Morrow, 1986.

Sherman, Mary B. "The Women's Clubs in the Middle Western States." *The Annals of the American Academy of Political and Social Science* 28, no. 2 (1906): 29–49.

Showalter, Elaine, ed. *Feminist Criticism: Essays on Women, Literature and Theory.* New York: Pantheon, 1985.

Sicherman, Barbara, and Carol H. Green, eds. *Notable American Women: The Modern Period.* Cambridge: The Belknap Press of Harvard University Press, 1980.

Simshauser, Glea. Interview with author. Decatur, IL, 7 Jan. 1985.

Sinclair, Andrew. *The Better Half: The Emancipation of the American Woman.* 1965. Reprint. Westport, CT: Greenwood Press, 1981.

Sloan, Douglas. "Harmony, Chaos, and Consensus: The American College Curriculum." *Teachers College Record* 73, no. 2 (1971): 221–51.

Smith College. *Official Circular*, no. 3, 1876. Northampton, MA.

Smith, Constance, and Anne Freedman. *Voluntary Associations: Perspectives on the Literature*. Cambridge: Harvard University Press, 1972.

Smith, Daniel S. "Family Limitation, Sexual Control, and Domestic Feminism in Victorian America." In *A Heritage of Her Own: Toward a New Social History of American Women*, edited by Nancy F. Cott and Elizabeth H. Pleck. New York: Simon & Schuster, 1979.

Smith, John W. *History of Macon County, Illinois*. Springfield: Rokker's Printing House, 1876.

Smith-Rosenberg, Carroll. *Disorderly Conduct: Visions of Gender in Victorian America*. New York: Knopf, 1985.

Solomon, Barbara M. *In the Company of Educated Women*. New Haven: Yale University Press, 1985.

Southern Association of College Women. *Proceedings*, Bulletin II (1912).

Sprague, Julia A. *History of the New England Women's Club from 1868–1893*. Boston: Lee & Shepard, 1894.

Strouse, Jean. *Alice James: A Biography*. Boston: Houghton Mifflin, 1980.

Stanton, Elizabeth C. "The Co-education of the Sexes." In Association for the Advancement of Woman, *Papers and Letters Presented at the First Woman's Congress of the Association for the Advancement of Woman, 1873*. New York, 1874.

Taylor, Albert R. *The Life Story of James Millikin*. Decatur: Millikin University, 1926.

Taylor, William, and Christopher Lasch. "Two 'Kindred Spirits': Sorority and Family in New England, 1839–1846." *The New England Quarterly* 36, no. 1 (1963): 23–41.

Tharp, Louise H. *The Peabody Sisters of Salem*. Boston: Little, Brown, 1950.

Thomas, Martha C. *The College Women of the Present and Future*. N.p.: McClure's Syndicate, 1901.

———. "Present Tendencies in Women's Education." *Educational Review* 35, no. 1 (1908): 64–85.

Thompson, Eleanor W. *Education for Ladies 1830–1860*. New York: King's Crown Press, 1947.

Thwing, Charles F. *A History of Education in the United States Since the Civil War*. Boston: Houghton Mifflin, 1910.

U.S. Commissioner of Education. *Report*. Washington, DC, 1907.

U.S. Department of Commerce. *Historical Statistics of the United States, Colonial Times to 1970*. Washington, DC: U.S. Bureau of the Census, 1975.

Vassar College. *Eleventh Annual Catalogue of the Officers and Students of Vassar College*. Poughkeepsie, NY, 1875–76.

Veysey, Laurence. *The Emergence of the American University*. Chicago: University of Chicago Press, 1965.

Ward, May A. "The Influence of Women's Clubs in New England and in the

Middle-Eastern States." *The Annals of the American Academy of Political and Social Science* 28, no. 2 (1906): 7–28.

Webster, Helen L. "Woman's Progress in Higher Education." In *Transactions of the National Council of Women of the United States, Assembled in Washington, D.C., February 22 to 25, 1891,* edited by Rachel F. Avery. Philadelphia: National Council of Women of the United States, 1891.

Wein, Roberta. "Women's Colleges and Domesticity." *History of Education Quarterly* 14, no. 4 (1974): 31–47.

Wells, Mildred W. *Unity in Diversity.* Washington, DC: General Federation of Women's Clubs, 1953.

Welter, Barbara. "The Cult of True Womanhood: 1820–1860." *American Quarterly* 18, no. 2 (1966): 151–74.

Westervelt, Esther M., and Deborah A. Fixter. *Women's Higher and Continuing Education: An Annotated Bibliography with Selected References in Related Aspects of Women's Lives.* New York: College Entrance Examination Board, 1971.

Wharton, Edith. *"Xingu" and Other Stories.* New York: Charles Scribner's Sons, 1916.

White, Martha E. "The Work of the Woman's Club." *Atlantic Monthly* 93, no. 559 (1903): 614–23.

Wiebe, Robert H. *The Search for Order, 1877–1920.* New York: Hill & Wang, 1967.

Wilkins, Kay S. *Women's Education in the United States: A Guide to Information Sources.* Detroit: Gale Research Company, 1979.

Wilson, Margaret G. *The American Woman in Transition: The Urban Influence, 1870–1920.* Westport, CT: Greenwood Press, 1979.

Winslow, Helen M. "The Modern Club Woman." *The Delineator* 80, no. 6 (1912): 473–74.

———. *The President of Quex.* Boston: Lothrop, Lee & Shepard, 1906.

———. "The Story of the Woman's Club Movement." *New England Magazine* 38 (July 1908): 543–57.

Woman's Press Club of New York. *Memories of Jane Cunningham Croly.* New York: G. P. Putnam's Sons, 1904.

"Women's Clubs—A Symposium." *The Arena* 6, no. 33 (1893): 362–88.

Wood, Mary I. *The History of the General Federation of Women's Clubs.* Norwood, MA: General Federation of Women's Clubs, 1912.

———. "The Woman's Club Movement." *The Chautauquan* 59, no. 1 (1910): 13–64.

Woody, Thomas. *A History of Women's Education in the United States.* 2 vols. New York: Science Press, 1929.

Woolf, Virginia. *A Room of One's Own.* New York: Harcourt, Brace & World, 1929.

Photograph
Acknowledgments

Lucy Larcom, Margaret Fuller, Julia Ward Howe, New England Women's Club, courtesy of the Boston Athenaeum; Elizabeth P. Peabody, courtesy of the Massachusetts Historical Society, Boston, Massachusetts; Fauntleroy Home, courtesy of New Harmony Workingmen's Institute, New Harmony, Indiana; The Bee, 1863, 1890, 1900, courtesy of the Cambridge Historical Society, Cambridge, Massachusetts; Saturday Morning Club, courtesy of the Schlesinger Library, Radcliffe College, Cambridge, Massachusetts; The Folio Club, courtesy of the Western Reserve Historical Society, Cleveland, Ohio; Bartlesville Tuesday Club, courtesy of Bartlesville Area History Museum and Archives, Bartlesville Public Library, Bartlesville, Oklahoma; Washburn House Reading Club, courtesy of Smith College Archives, Northampton, Massachusetts; Millikin Homestead, courtesy of Altrusa Club, Decatur, Illinois; Anna B. Millikin, Elizabeth M. Bering, Three Members Departing for Europe, Decatur Art Class Seal, courtesy of Decatur Art Class, Decatur, Illinois; Decatur Art Class Twentieth Anniversary, courtesy of the *Decatur Herald and Review*; Club Night in the Valley, pen and ink drawing, courtesy of Jeannette H. Dixson, Syracuse, New York.

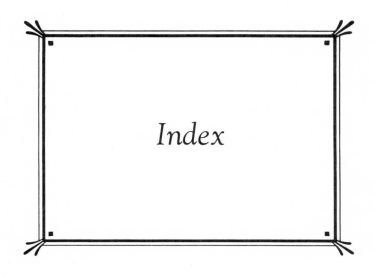

Index

Entries for individual clubs are listed under the name of the club rather than under the city or state in which the club is located.

This book was set in Goudy Old Style by Graphic Composition, Inc.
The text and jacket were designed by Christine Leonard
Raquepaw. The text was printed on acid-free Sebago
Antique Cream paper; the illustrations were
printed on Lustro Dull Cream paper.
The book was printed and
bound by the Maple
Press.